AMERICAN INDIAN SCULPTURE
A STUDY OF THE NORTHWEST COAST

PAUL S. WINGERT

AMERICAN INDIAN SCULPTURE

A STUDY OF THE NORTHWEST COAST

HACKER ART BOOKS
New York
1976

First Published, New York, 1949.
Reissued 1976 by
Hacker Art Books, New York.

Library of Congress Catalogue Card Number 75-11063
ISBN 0-87817-168-1

Printed in the United States of America.

ACKNOWLEDGEMENTS

WITHOUT the generous cooperation of many persons and institutions the writing of this book would not have been possible. For invaluable council, constant encouragement and wise editing of the manuscript very special thanks are given to Dr. Marian W. Smith of the Department of Anthropology of Columbia University. The author is also indebted to Dr. Ralph Linton of the Department of Anthropology of Yale University for his initial sponsorship of the subject and for his advice and suggestions in its development. Valuable aid was also rendered by Dr. Meyer Schapiro and Dr. Emerson H. Swift of the Department of Fine Arts and Archaeology of Columbia University in the organization and presentation of the material; while the author wishes to express his appreciation to the following persons for their interest and assistance in bringing this book to completion: Dr. William B. Dinsmoor, Dr. W. Duncan Strong, and Dr. Julian H. Steward of Columbia University and Mr. René d'Harnoncourt of the Museum of Modern Art, New York City.

The following institutions very generously placed their facilities at the author's disposal, or, where it was not possible for him to visit them, kindly sent the necessary information: the American Museum of Natural History and the Museum of the American Indian, Heye Foundation, in New York City; the Chicago Natural History Museum; the National Museum of Canada in Ottawa; the Provincial Museum in Victoria, B. C.; the University Museum of the University of Pennsylvania in Philadelphia; the University Museum of the University of Washington in Seattle; the Milwaukee Public Museum; the Royal Ontario Museum of Archaeology in Toronto; the City Museum in Vancouver, B. C.; the Museum of Fine Arts in Denver; the Washington State Historical Society in Tacoma; the Peabody Museum of Salem, Mass.; and the Peabody Museum of Harvard University.

Special acknowledgements are also made to the following persons: Miss Bella Weitzner of the American Museum of Natural History; Dr. Paul S. Martin of the Chicago Natural History Museum; Dr. Diamond Jenness and Dr. Douglas Leechman of the National Museum of Canada; Dr. W. C. McKern of the Milwaukee Public Museum; Dr. G. Clifford Carl and Mr. A. E. Pickford of the Provincial Museum in Victoria; Dr. J. Alden Mason of the University Museum in Philadelphia; Dr. E. K. Burnett and Mr. Kenneth C. Miller of the Museum of the American Indian, Heye Foundation; Dr. Erna Gunther, Dr. Melville Jacobs, Dr. Verne F. Ray and Mr. H. Frank Barnett of the University of Washington; Dr. T. P. O. Menzies of the City Museum in Vancouver; Dr. T. C. McIlwraith of the Royal Ontario Museum of Archaeology; Mr. W. A. Newcombe of Victoria, B. C.; Dr. H. G. Barnett of the University of Oregon; Mr. W. P. Bonney of the Washington State Historical Society; Dr. Ernest S. Dodge of the Peabody Museum of Selem; Dr. Donald Scott of the Peabody Museum of Harvard University; and Miss Elizabeth Colson.

The author also wishes to express his thanks to The American Ethnological Society Inc. for undertaking this publication and to J. J. Augustin for the publication of it. Credit for illustrations, unless otherwise indicated, is due the museum in whose collection the object belongs. The maps and drawings in the text are the work of Miss Alexandra Rienzi.

Columbia University   Paul S. Wingert
February, 1947

Contents

List of Illustrations

ix

MAPS AND FIGURES IN TEXT

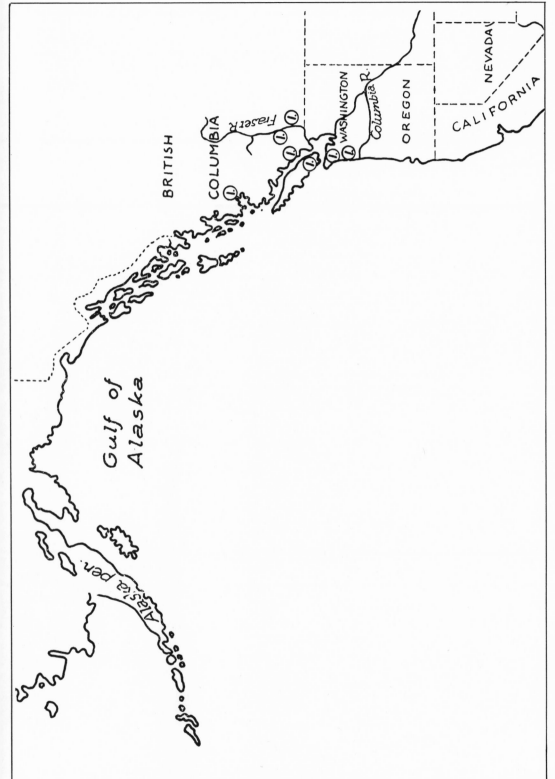

Map. 1   Northwest Coast of America

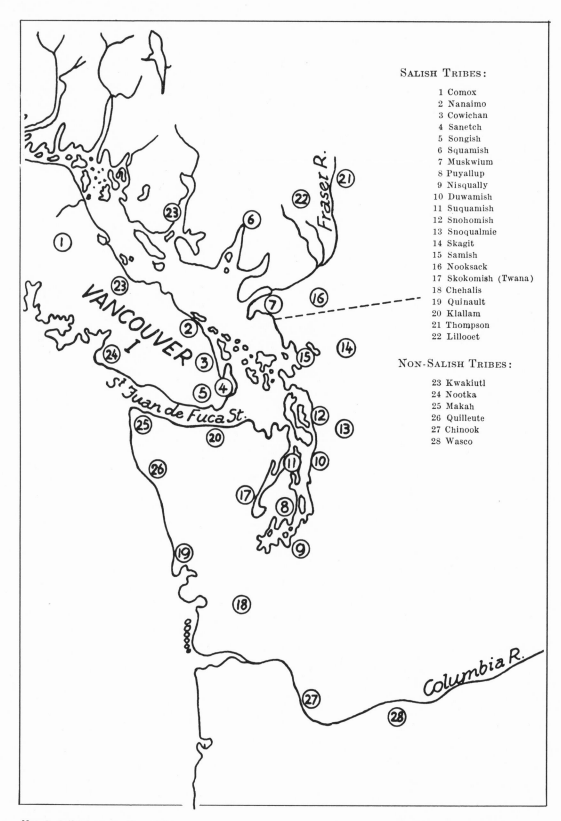

SALISH TRIBES:

1 Comox
2 Nanaimo
3 Cowichan
4 Sanetch
5 Songish
6 Squamish
7 Muskwium
8 Puyallup
9 Nisqually
10 Duwamish
11 Suquamish
12 Snohomish
13 Snoqualmie
14 Skagit
15 Samish
16 Nooksack
17 Skokomish (Twana)
18 Chehalis
19 Quinault
20 Klallam
21 Thompson
22 Lillooet

NON-SALISH TRIBES:

23 Kwakiutl
24 Nootka
25 Makah
26 Quilleute
27 Chinook
28 Wasco

Map. 2 Salish Area, location of tribes

Introduction

THE ART of the North American Indian reaches a climax in the spectacular wood carvings of the Northwest Coast. This region, extending from Alaska to Oregon, has become best known for its great carved and painted masks, house fronts, and totem poles. Human and animal figures are treated in highly characteristic fashion. Once seen they can be recognized anywhere. Typical Northwest Coast art is unique among the world's art traditions. Scientific and popular studies have been written about it and many fine examples of the art are in natural history museums and private collections the world over. But the Northwest Coast was originally peopled by a number of Indian tribes, not all of whom produced art of this kind. The Salish, for example, who occupied the southern part of the area, developed a distinctive style of carving that differs notably from the typical Northwest Coast style of historic times.

No area of North American Indian art is in greater need of careful study than that of the Northwest Coast. Relatively few attempts have been made, however, to interpret and characterize its art styles in careful detail. The present volume establishes these styles for the southern portion of the coast, for Salish wood carvings of the historic period. It is thus a pioneering work. Every effort has been made in the use of the objects themselves, and the literature pertaining to the region, to allow the styles to emerge in the context of their culture so that they may be seen in proper perspective. With this in mind, the analyses upon which the conclusions are based have been thorough.

It seemed desirable for several reasons to restrict the scope of this initial monograph to the southern part of the Coast. The comparatively simple culture of this area has produced less complicated and diversified wood carvings than the more northern regions, and the lack of the mid-nineteenth century florescence which developed in the north under the stimulus of metal tools makes Salish sculpture more representative of earlier basic styles. The important influences exerted by these southern styles on those to the north are merely suggested here. They should serve as subject for a future monograph. The present paper makes a careful analysis of a primitive art in order to discover what values can be derived both for the anthropologist and for the art historian. The details of the analysis are included in Chapters 3 and 4. The general reader may wish to pass over these in favor of Chapter 5 where the results of the analysis are synthesized.

Although Salish sculpture is on exhibition in various natural history museums[1], and several anthropological studies of it have been published[2], it is but imperfectly known. Until the large exhibition of "Indian Art of the United States" at the Museum of Modern Art in New York in the spring of 1941[3], it had never been given the prominence its high aesthetic qualities deserve.

The people who produced this art occupied small villages in a continuous area extending from Vancouver Island and the adjoining mainland of British Columbia south to the Columbia River. Strictly speaking, "Salish" is a linguistic term referring to a group of related languages and dialects. To the north, another Salishan group lived at the heads of the long inlets in the upper part of British Columbia where they were surrounded by non-Salishan peoples[4], and south of the Columbia River lived other scattered Salish peoples, but none of these made objects in the art style here designated "Salish". The main body of the Salish may be arranged into five sub-groups: the *Coast Salish* of (1) the Straits of Georgia, (2) the lower and middle Fraser River, up to and including Yale, (3) Puget Sound[5] and Hoods Canal and (4) the Olympic Peninsula, and (5) the *Interior Salish* of the upper Fraser River drainage, British Columbia[6].

This Salish region, in common with that of the entire Northwest Coast, is characterized by a high degree of humidity and a heavy rainfall. The climate is equitable. Native economy was based upon the spectacular wealth of river and marine life, and the art of sculpture developed from a fine tradition of woodwork in cedar. This tree, in fact, had for the Indians the importance of the coconut palm for the South Sea Islanders; and largely because of it this area was one of the great centers of aboriginal woodcarving. Shell, stone, and bone provided the tools for the craftsmen until metal tools replaced them late in the 18th and early in the 19th centuries. Although stemming from a relatively similar economic and social background, the ceremonials for which many of the carvings were made varied considerably from region to region, and even from village to village.

---

[1] Notably, the Chicago Natural History Museum; the American Museum of Natural History in New York; and the Museum of the American Indian, the Heye Foundation, in New York.

[2] cf. Bibliography.

[3] This exhibition was arranged for the Museum, and the excellent accompanying handbook by the same title was written by René d'Harnoncourt and Frederic H. Douglas.

[4] These are the Bella Coola Indians. Their art is more closely related to that of their neighbors than to that of their kinsmen to the south, and it will therefore not be included in this study.

[5] Strictly speaking, "Puget Sound is the body of water above Admiralty Inlet and Possession Sound in the neighborhood of Seattle and southward" ... but the term is "used by geographers as well as anthropologists to refer to the entire water region| from the inlets south of Olympia, Washington, to the bays south of Vancouver, Canada...." (Smith, M.W., 1941, p. 197).

[6] Cf. Boas, 1897, pp. 320—321; Smith, M.W., 1941, pp. 199—203; and verbally.

Politically the Salish had no coordinated structure, such as the more northern peoples of the Coast, which would, strictly speaking, permit them to be called tribes[7]. Rather, they were small semi-sedentary groups who lived in permanent winter villages of plank houses and in temporary summer encampments. The tribal names under which the ethnic groups are now known are extensions of local terms, but the villages, or at most small groups of villages, were autonomous. The following "tribes" are important for this study: among the Coast Salish of the Straits of Georgia, the *Comox* on the eastern coast of Vancouver Island at the head of the Straits (see Fig. 1), the *Nanaimo, Cowichan,* and *Sanetch* on the southeastern coast of the Island, the *Songish* on the southernmost part of the eastern coast of the Island, and the *Suguamish* on the mainland coast of British Columbia at the head of Howe Inlet; the *Muskwium* at the very mouth of the Fraser River; among the Coast Salish of Puget Sound, the *Puyallup* and *Nisqually* of the southern part, the *Duwamish, Suquamish, Snohomish* of the central part, the *Snoqualmie, Skagit, Samish, Nooksack* of the inland part of the Sound, the *Twana (Skokomish)* of Hoods Canal, and the *Chehalis* north of the Middle Columbia River region; among the Coast Salish of the Olympic Peninsula, the *Quinault* of the Pacific coastal region, and the *Klallam* facing the Straits of Juan de Fuca; and for the Interior Salish, the *Thompson* and *Lillooet* of the upper reaches and tributaries of the Fraser River in British Columbia.

The wood sculpture of these Salish tribes is distinctive; and yet, as even a cursory consideration would show, it bears an important relationship to that of their non-Salishan neighbors. It is therefore necessary for an understanding of Salish art to give due attention to that of these neighbors. They include the various *Kwakiutl* tribes on the northern part of Vancouver Island and on the mainland of British Columbia, the *Nootkan* tribes of the southern and western parts of Vancouver Island and their close relatives the *Makah* who lived directly across the Straits of Juan de Fuca along the coast of Cape Flattery in Washington, the *Quilleute* farther south on the Pacific coast of Washington, and the various *Chinookan* tribes along the lower Columbia River. The very differences as well as certain similarities in the sculptures of these peoples when compared with those of the Salish are of considerable significance, since they indicate possible diffusion and sources of style, and thereby help appreciably to fix upon and to characterize more completely Salish style and its relationships.

The Northwest Coast began to attract the attention of European nations in the 18th century. Before the revolution of the American colonies, the Rus-

---

[7] Gibbs, 1877, pp. 169, 184—185; Smith, M.W., 1941, pp. 197—198. Although Barnett speaks only of the Coast Salish of Canada when he says that "the whole group... had no inclusive name for itself, no head chief..."(1938, p.119), it would appear that this is basically true of all the Salish.

sians, inspired by the quest for furs, came down along the coast from Alaska[8]. Two voyages of exploration were later made by the Spanish, who embarked from ports in California, in 1774 and 1775, and touched at different points along the coast from, probably, the mouth of the Columbia River to the Queen Charlotte Islands. The English were the next to arrive on the Coast when Captain Cook by accident came into Nootka Sound in 1778 while on the third and last of his famous voyages, this one in quest of a northwest passage[9]. As a result of the published accounts of this voyage a maritime fur trade was inaugurated in the southern part of the Coast by the Englishman John Meares who voyaged there for that purpose in 1786—87. Almost immediately American and French ships entered the trade, in 1788 and 1790 respectively. Meanwhile the French had reached the Coast, not only by the famous voyage of La Perouse in 1785, but also, at about the same time or even earlier, by an overland route through inland waterways from the east. An immensely profitable enterprise, the fur trade, grew rapidly, with the result that by the early years of the 19th century contact had been made with most of the Indians of this southern area. Descriptions of the various cultures and their implements appeared sporadically during the 19th century; and although they are important, their value is often minimized by the fact that they are vague and prejudiced[10]. Only during the closing years of the last century and throughout the present one have properly trained investigators been conducting scholarly researches among these Indians. It is largely from their studies that our knowledge of the proper functioning of sculptured objects within the various environments derives.

The specimens of wood carvings collected from this Salish area provide more than adequate material for the study of a non-European art. For the present paper, all available examples were examined, and from them those specimens were selected for illustrations which would present all of the various types and styles of carving. In every case, care was taken to choose representative objects for which there was available documentation or reliability of provenience. Documentation of Salish sculpture is sometimes very meager. This is at best merely the field-notes and records of travellers or investigators and it includes, when most complete, the source, function and date when the example was collected. With few exceptions, the majority of objects were obtained during the last decade of the 19th century. Although occasionally some idea of when the work was done is recorded, no more precise dating can

---

[8] For an account of these explorations see Howay, 1924, pp. 1—31; Goddard, 1934, p. 20.

[9] For a complete account of the history of the opening up of the Northwest Coast, see Bancroft, 1884, 1, pp. 137—310, 343—377, 666—703; Underhill, 1945; pp. 201—211.

[10] cf. Bibliography: Lewis and Clark, 1804—6 (Thwaites, 1904—5); Jewitt, 1815; Wilkes, 1845; Hale, 1846; Swan, 1857, 1869; Willoughby, 1889; etc.

be given for any of these carvings. Some specimens were old when they were collected, others had been made recently. A determined effort was made to secure as many old objects as possible, and, at the same time, more recent specimens of the same type, in order to examine possible style changes. For similar reasons, the choice was not limited to examples showing the finest technique, but some carvings of a considerably cruder handling were included.

When art styles are carefully studied and are considered in conjunction with historical and anthropological material, it becomes possible to establish certain centers and to arrive at the dynamics lying behind their development. Within the ordinary materials of a fine art, such as European, the wealth of material available and the size of the geographical area covered make it most difficult to isolate important trends. In dealing with European art, moreover, it is almost impossible to divorce oneself from one's appreciation of the art. In the materials handled in this paper, however, the historical development may be just as intricate, but the number of objects was definitely limited by the relatively few artists produced by the small Salish population[11]; and the materials can be handled objectively in their own terms with as little as possible of the subjective element entering in.

No art can be fully understood when it is isolated from its cultural environment; and no art can be intelligently comprehended when considered merely as a group of objects in an ascending historical series, that is, in a vertical sequence. Rather, before such historical patterns can become important, the complete milieu of an art object must be considered in what amounts to an horizontal cross-cut of a culture at a given moment. When regarded in this manner, the true vitality and vigor of tradition implicit in an art is revealed. The method adopted in handling these Salish materials is, therefore, not only valuable for aboriginal arts, but may be fruitfully applied to all studies of the dynamic development of a fine art.

---

[11] For population estimates, see: Gibbs, 1877, pp. 181—183; Smith. M.W., 1940 b, pp. 7—11.

CHAPTER ONE

THE SCULPTURES AND THEIR SIGNIFICANCE

To CONSIDER only the formal aspects in a work of sculpture — the essentials
of its design, the relationships of lines, surfaces and shapes — is comparable
to reading poetry for its metre and balance without giving any thought to the
meaning conveyed by the words. The appreciation of sculpture, as of all art,
is enhanced by an understanding of the meaning embodied in a work and by
a knowledge of the purpose for which it was intended. It is now no longer
denied or doubted that aborigines have a developed aesthetic sense and that
this is manifested in their sculpture. But, due to its close integration with their
beliefs and customs, it is essential to understand as completely as possible the
meaning and purpose of an aboriginal carving.

Crude beginnings and many fumblings mark the primitive stage in the evo-
lution of any art tradition. From these develop sophisticated styles which
adequately convey the intended meaning and wholly satisfy the aesthetic de-
mands of both artist and audience. Salish sculpture shows every indication
of having developed a mature and highly sophisticated art style. In it, as in
all art styles of every age, country, and cultural level, the good artist created
masterpieces, but the poor artist carved inferior objects. Yet he worked in
the same tradition. It is, therefore, necessary to distinguish in Salish sculpture,
as in that of all peoples, the products of the artist from those of the expert
craftsmen, who are not able to give their carvings the strong conceptualization
and the vitality of expression so evident in the sculpture of the true artist.

Salish wood sculpture consists of carvings in the round and in relief. Human
and animal forms are most frequently represented and these range in size from
figurines to large house posts. Between these two extremes are found half to
two-thirds life size figures and figures of life size or a little over. Relief carvings
also vary from small to large, but masks are usually of impressive scale.

It is unfortunate that Salish culture had begun to disintegrate and, in fact,
had all but disappeared in many areas, before scientists had a chance to record
those aspects which bear upon the meaning of their sculptures. Towards this
end, information acquired by early travellers is both meager and of too general
a nature to be of much value[1]. The most reliable and specific interpretation

[1] The failure of many of these travellers to make any inquiry about the carvings
they saw was largely because they considered them crude and of little interest
or value (cf. Willoughby, 1889, p. 275; Gibbs, 1877, pp. 201—3; Lewis and
Clark, Thwaites, 1904—5, p. 166). It is probable also that, especially in the

of content has come from the oldest Indians, who remember old beliefs, practices, and technologies, and serve as informants for the trained investigators. Enough information has, therefore, been recorded by anthropologists to permit a comprehensive and, in some cases, even a detailed understanding of the meanings implicit in Salish carvings.

Three basic categories of subject matter are common to all sculpture. These are religious, social, and decorative. In religious carvings, although in some parts of the world the artist creates an image in the likeness of the concept of his god, he is more occupied with carving ritualistic objects of a traditional form. When used in conjunction with the proper dance and/or song patterns, these objects bring about either a direct manifestation of or direct contact with the supernatural forces governing life. Sometimes they symbolize personal relationships with the supernatural. Sometimes they are regarded as constantly sacred or even dangerous, and sometimes they are only considered so when they are in use. Tradition also determines the essential shape and character of the carvings which are mainly of social significance. These sculptures indicate or enhance the social position of their owners. Convention frequently dictates that they *must* be made or the prestige of an individual or family or clan suffers. Many carvings are entirely decorative, their sole purpose being to enrich an object. Among the Salish, although some carvings fit the social and decorative categories, the main group is predominantly religious.

The fundamental concept which lay behind all Salish religious sculpture was that of a partnership set up between the world of men and the supernatural world. To induce or to create circumstances favorable for the establishment of such a partnership, individuals, preferably although not necessarily in their youth, would follow a rigid and often severe pattern of exposure, fasting, and hardship in a deliberate quest for a "vision" in which the relationship with the supernatural world would be established[2]. The purpose of this quest and the resulting partnership was to obtain thereby extra skills and abilities. The word best fitted in English to describe these, and the word English-speaking Salish Indians now use, is "power"[3]. The concept was personalized and one can therefore speak, and the Indians do speak of powers in semi-personal terms. This is sometimes referred to in the literature as a guardian or a spirit, but both of these terms are somewhat misnomers. After it was obtained, power was so

Puget Sound area, early travellers did not even see the finest carvings, due to the practice of hiding these objects, when not in use, in the forest at a distance from the villages (Waterman, 1930, p. 49).

[2] Youth was the most propitious time for the setting up of a relationship with the supernatural, but this was possible at any age. The "vision" as it existed among the Salish differed in many respects from the "vision" as described for other North American areas, such as the Plains. (cf. Gunther, 1927, pp.289–290; Stern, 1934, p. 8; Olson, 1936, p. 141; Barnett, 1938, p. 135, 1942, p. 387; Smith, M.W., 1940a, p. 56, 1940b, p. 15).

[3] Smith, M. W., verbally.

much a part of the individual that anything that happened to it affected the individual, and illness or even death might result.

The ties between a person and his power were socially expressed through ceremony. He was instructed by the supernatural during the quest as to the visible attributes of the power, such as, song, details of costume, and ritual paraphernalia, including various sculptures, among which were sometimes anthropomorphic figures[4]. These attributes subsequently formed his ceremonial objects and were used whenever he participated in ceremony or expressed his power socially. The carved figures therefore were not representations of the appearance of a god, and no sacrifices were ever made to them. In fact, they were never worshipped in any sense of the word. Indeed, the notion that they could be supplicated and would in turn intercede with the supernatural in behalf of a human would have been considered absurd. Their existence and activity were among the tangible expressions of a cooperation already established between the supernatural and the individual.

One of the more important uses of sculptures in the Puget Sound area was in a highly dramatic curing ceremony involving a journey to the land of the dead to recover souls. Designed to reëstablish perfect rapport between the individual and his power or powers, the purpose of this ceremonial journey was the recapture of souls or of powers that had been stolen by the dead. If these could be recovered, the sick would be restored to health[5]. In order to perform this cure, shamans whose ritual objects included carved figures and painted boards, associated with the requisite powers, made the journey in an imaginary canoe. This was represented by sticking the figures and the boards in the ground in such a way as to outline the rough shape of a canoe[6]. Since the way to the land of the dead was beset with many dangers that had to be overcome, the success of the trip depended upon the operation of the shamans powers, the visible evidences of these being the paintings on the boards (Plate 16.1—4) and the carved figures (Plates 8—11; 13—15; 17—21). The entire ceremony was conducted in pantomine, the shamans being aided frequently by the spectators who acted out in this world the events as they took place in the spirit world. At one moment in the dramatic performance, it is recorded that the shaman picked up his carved figure and pointed it head foremost towards the

---

[4] Waterman, 1930, pp. 37—41; Olson, 1936, pp. 141, 145; Smith, M.W., 1940a, pp. 99, 115.

[5] This ceremony was performed throughout the Puget Sound area except by the northern inland groups, the Skagit and the Nooksack, and the northern group, the Samish. (cf. Dorsey, 1902, pp. 234—237; Haeberlin, 1918a, p. 249; Waterman, 1930, pp. 3—4; Smith, M.W., 1940a, p. 98; 1941, p. 205.)

[6] Not all regions of the Sound used a canoe in this quest. The Suquamish, for instance, followed a land trail and only used a canoe, which was then made by outlining it with a cedar rope, to go around certain obstacles (Smith, M.W., verbally; Stern, 1934, p. 80).

danger[7]. In this way, his power was brought immediately to bear upon the danger.

Detailed records are available in print of two such ceremonies. Models of the figures used in these have also been obtained (Plates 18—21). Waterman says in connection with a description of four of these (Plates 18—19) that they "always represent a certain definite class of spirits, the 'ground-beings' "[8], that from them the seeker receives his power, and that during a trance-like state these powers talk to him thus: "This is I. This is the way I look. This is my rig. This is the way my hands look. This is my song[9]." Following these instructions, the man "paints his ceremonial objects just that way"[10]. The implication is that similar instructions were given for the carving of the figures. Waterman thus indicates that the figures commemorate the personal experience of the individual with the supernatural, and remain a vital part of the complex through which the power is used[11]. It should be thoroughly understood that once the power was obtained, it was used and demonstrated and worked with *as a partner*[12]. It was never propitiated for continued favor, nor sacrificed to in any fashion. There was no doubt of its capabilities, or any fear of it[13]. In fact, the figure was even given a good "bawling out" if the power did not accomplish satisfactory results. It should be noted also that some powers were stronger than others and that these would enable men to manifest greater skills and to achieve greater results than the weaker powers.

Although somewhat meager, the information given Waterman about four figures now in the Museum of the American Indian is of considerable importance for an understanding of content in these Puget Sound power figures. Plate 18.1 is identified as a female earth being who gave Doctor Bill "power to go to the underworld", but no reasons are given for its shape or iconography[14]. Possibly

---

[7] Smith, M.W., verbally from field notes (Suquamish).

[8] Waterman, 1930, p. 37.

[9] *Op. cit.* p. 38.

[10] *Ibid.*

[11] This complex includes songs, dances or ceremonies, and ritual objects, such as the carved and painted figures, dance sticks or wands, etc. (see Waterman, 1930, pp. 15—19; Dorsey, 1902, p. 228; etc.)

[12] That the "final criterion of power was always achievement, that is, the power demonstrated", indicates to what extent it was a positive, tangible quantity (Smith, M.W., 1940 *a*, p. 58).

[13] There is no record in the literature on the subject of any feeling of fear being associated with these figures or in their use, although in their use there was often a good deal of danger involved, since the forces against which the power was used were often tricky and had power of their own — hence a stronger power was needed to overcome them. It was felt, however, that "power hung around its objects and was dangerous to persons who did not have it, that is, did not have a sufficient power of his own strong enough to withstand danger of handling ceremonial objects" (Smith, M.W., 1940 *a*, p. 102).

[14] Waterman, 1930, p. 39, Fig. 44.

the painted design at the top of the torso depicts the gullet and heart, which in company with the dots were meant to express the transparency of the supernatural being. This interpretation is supported by the statement that "the horizontal band painted below the heart" on Plate 18.2, a male earth being, "represents the diaphragm"[15]. A slightly larger variation of the same design appears on the torso of Plate 19.1, which represents a male supernatural being who was encountered by Bill Tetctatctld on a log jam as it was looking into the water for fish[16]. The being gave Bill great power with the spear, and, since it had only one eye, the carving also had only one eye. The fourth figure, Plate 19.2 likewise a male earth being, lived in a blackened tree stump, and "for this reason they used to paint the carven figure black with charcoal".[17] He was said to be a "friend worth having".

Although this interpretative material secured by Waterman is scant, it is nevertheless sufficiently confirmed by additional information[18] to warrant the conclusion that the iconography of these figures was not important in itself and that the painted details did not constitute symbols of any sort. The object was important in its entirety, and only in relation to its use. It is obvious that the general form of the carvings, the shapes and their composition, follow conventions which were both localized and individualized.

Not all power figures in the Puget Sound region were put to the same use. In some sections, where the soul recovery ceremony was not performed, single power figures were used in other ways. Among the Samish, for instance, they were set up and their owner sang his power song in order to get the full cooperation of his power for a cure[19]; while among the Puyallup-Nisqually single figures were "set before the doors of some of the houses in the fall as protection against the dead who at this season were very active in their quest for souls".[20] Figures used in this way should not be interpreted as "guardian", since the "protection" came from the fact that they exercised their power against that of the dead.

The small Quinault shamans' wands comprise another important group of Salish religious carvings (Plates 1—5). These have also been called "guardian spirit" figures, but it is obvious that they too were power figures, acquired and used in a manner similar to those of the Puget Sound region[21]. Their

---

[15] *Op. cit.* p. 39, Fig. 45 on p. 40.

[16] *Op. cit.*, pp. 39—41, Fig. 45 on p. 41.

[17] *Op. cit.* pp. 41, Fig. 47 on p. 42. The figure is now however painted entirely white. Perhaps this was an underpainting over which the black charcoal was laid.

[18] Smith, M.W., verbally from field notes.

[19] *Ibid.*

[20] Smith, M.W., 1940 *a*, p. 115.

[21] Among the Quinault, shamans were those persons who possessed very potent powers. Every one from his youth on went in quest of spirits, since the acquisition and control of supernatural power was necessary for success in life. Only

particular function was also in a curing performance which involved a journey to the land of the dead to secure stolen souls[22]. The ceremony here was relatively simple and was usually performed by a single shaman and a helper[23], although in difficult cases, or if perhaps the patient were an important person, more than one shaman took part. The carved wands served as tangible evidence of the power which enabled the shaman through its use, together with that of the accompanying power songs, to travel along the road to the land of the dead, to overcome specific dangers along the way, and to recapture the pilfered soul. The additional protective character of these figurines, frequently mentioned in connection with their function, should be interpreted as a further use to which the owner put his power.

The earliest expression of these conclusions comes from the data obtained by Willoughby from Sammy in 1886. Sammy was the owner of the Quinault wand now in the National Museum in Washington[24]. The carving was called a "Se-quan figure", se-quan meaning a mole, or as Sammy called it in English, "my doctor". It was Sammy's belief, Willoughby affirms, that the image told him if any one were sick or dying at a distance; that, "if any one dies the se-quan disappears from the house and goes down into the ground", travelling from place to place[25]. Attributes of his power, which could "not see much, but has great will power", were expressed by small eyes and mouth in the carving[26].

---

through aid of this sort could one achieve success. The climax came when a person, through an induced trance-like state, experienced a vision, during which and in the sleep which followed the "guardian spirit" appeared. It then taught him the songs and dances to use in invoking and using its power, and gave him directions as to what type of carved wand to make. If not made by the person himself, this carving was usually made by a friend or relative according to his instructions (Olsen, 1936, pp. 141, 145).

[22] As among the Sound peoples, the same belief prevailed here: that sickness or bad luck could be caused by the loss of the soul or of the power of the individual due to theft by a ghost of the dead, who then proceeded to carry it to the land of the dead; and that if the soul could be recaptured before it had been carried into the land of the dead, and returned to its owner, his health would be restored or his bad luck dispelled. It was therefore necessary that the shaman, to effect a recapture, have a greater power than that used by the dead. Sickness could also be caused by the presence in the body of a disease object, that is, by intrusion (*op. cit.*, pp. 158—160).

[23] The role of the helper was to hold the wand and to help in singing the song of the spirit (power), through which the "spirit came to and became one with the shaman and the search was on," (*op. cit.* p. 160).

[24] Catalogue no. 127 864. Repeated requests were made to various Museum officials for a photograph of this important Salish carving. Unfortunately these requests were all to no avail. The carving somewhat resembles the specimen on Pl. 1, the most significant exception being that the arms are not attached but hang free of the body.

[25] Willoughby, 1889, p. 278.

[26] *Ibid.* "In doctoring, the figure sings, but only the medicine man, its owner, can hear it; while if a patient is about to die, it warns the doctor" (that is, the power

Sammy further told Willoughby that the deer-hoof rattles which were hung on the figure, were the "rattling bones of the image". This suggests again that the power figure represents a transparent supernatural being[27].

Quinault figurines do not appear to have had the painted personal iconographic designs which constitute such a striking feature of Puget Sound power figures. It seems, in fact, that, although differences in proportion and shapes are discernible among examples of these shamans' wands, they are less individualized in content and follow a more formalized pattern than their Puget Sound counterparts[28].

The subject matter of the relief carving described as a "large Tamanous board" (Plate 7) associates it with that of all Salish religious sculptures. This is no doubt an example of the boards set up by the shaman near his bed as an expression of his power[29]. They are not known to have been used in any ceremony. Evidences of a personal iconography seem more pronounced on these boards than on the shaman figurines.

In the northern part of the Salish area, house posts are sometimes carved with figures which seem to combine a social with a religious subject matter.

---

of the shaman makes him realize when a patient is going to die). "At night, when not in use, the figure stands in the middle of the floor of Sammy's house and sings and protects it" (thus the power is constantly in operation and is protecting against other power).

[27] The possibility that this might have referred to a skeletalized being receives support from the carved indications of rib structure on two specimens (Plates 3, 6). Painted and carved designs on some of the Puget Sound figures (Plates 13.2, 14, 20, 21) and decorative carvings (Plate 24) have similar character. The suggestion has been advanced that such treatment may have had to do with a "cult of the dead" (Strong, W.D., 1945, pp. 244—261).

[28] Of significance in this respect is the fact that Farrand calls one specimen (Plate 2) a "shaman's seqwa'nc," apparently the same Indian word transliterated by Willoughby as "se-quan". (cf. Catalogue of Illustrations, p. 130 below). This implies two things: (1) that this was the generic term for these figures, the form of them likewise following a type; and (2) that Sammy did not divulge to Willoughby the personal elements of his power, or how they were embodied in his carving. Disclosing certain features of the association between the individual and his power was believed to lead to the illness or even dead of the individual. So it is small wonder that certain reticences were observed.

[29] "Beside the bed of every shaman stood a post or thick plank... representing his vision" (Curtis, 1907—30, 9, p. 109). Early travellers in the Columbia River-Washington coastal areas mention the number of carved and painted boards then in evidence. Lewis and Clark make numerous reference to them (Thwaites, 1904—5, 3, pp. 166, 185); Gibbs says that there was the custom of placing "the tamahno-us board of the owner" near his grave after his death (Gibbs, 1877, p. 203). Wilkes was so impressed by them that he had Mr. Eld make drawings of some of them (Plate 7), although he was unsuccessful in his efforts to secure any information about them, merely stating that they were "placed upright, and nothing could be learned of their origin. The colors were exceedingly bright, of a kind of red pigment" (Wilkes, 1845, 5, pp. 128—129).

An anthropomorphic form, frequently represented holding an animal, is identified by rather meager and unsatisfactory documentation as the "owner's
guardian spirit" and the animals as mythological beings known as "skawichens"
or "scowmidgeons" (Plates 45; 46; 52, a, b; 53; 55). Although differing somewhat in species, these animals are always represented in action which the human
figures strive to restrain. This suggests that the figure expresses a strong power
in combat with a slightly weaker power expressed by the animals: that is,
that the entire carving is a dramatic demonstration of the potency of a man's
power. But the similar use of like animals on grave post carvings[30], which were
commemorative or so-called portrait figures, tends to refute this interpretation;
and it seems more likely that the house posts represented in generic fashion
the owner, his power and his control over it. It would seem therefore that the
social and religious content of these carvings were of almost equal importance[31].

Salish funerary sculptures that use the single human figure (Plates 27, 39.1)
are largely social in content. It has been reported that these carvings were set
up "on practically all graves of adults" and that rows of them stood in front
of every grave-house. It is also affirmed that they represented the deceased,
"bearing as much as possible his likeness". This implies that they were portrait
figures. The fact that they were "dressed in the clothes of the deceased"
(Plate 30.5) and had the face painted in his favorite manner[32] shows however
that the likeness lay in secondary features and the carving may have been
a consistent type. To this type also belong the grave posts and figures carved
to represent persons wearing masks (Plates 28, 37). Since the right to wear a
mask was the privilege of only certain families of high social position, these
carvings therefore indicate that the deceased was a member of a socially
prominent family.

But another type of grave figure (Plate 29) appears to combine religious with
social content in a manner comparable to that of the house posts. A kneeling
figure restrains the upward movement of a mythical animal, part fish, part
mink. Since the mink was one of the "shamans' guardian spirits"[33], it seems
likely that this was a "portrait" figure placed by the grave of a shaman, with
the animal depicting his power. It should be noted that the dynamic action
of the figures, the lashing about of the animal and the force with which it is
restrained, strongly implies a story or narrative content. The carving may,

---

[30] Cf. p. 14.

[31] This identification of content is further supported by the fact that such house-
post carvings were of relatively late development, and that they probably show
the adaptation of carvings with different content, such as grave figures, to this
new type and function. The social content would therefore be a survival of a
type of carving in which it was the dominant content, or an introduction from
an area in which it was dominant, such as Nootka and Kwakiutl.

[32] Teit, 1906, p. 273.

[33] *Op. cit.*, p. 283.

in fact, have referred to an incident in the relationship of the shaman with his supernatural helper, or to a mythological happening connected with the power.

The appearance of animals on house posts and funerary carvings indicates that in this north Salish area, an animal represents not so much the power itself as the narrative incidents through which its nature is revealed. This contrasts with the direct expression of power in the Puget Sound-Washington region, and with the concept that power resulted from personal contact with the supernatural. The northern carvings show the owner demonstrating his control over an animal which is in actuality a proxy for the power, and which could therefore with more justification be called a helper or guardian spirit. It is probable that two of the small figures on the Cowichan drum (Plates 44.1, 44.2 a, d) had similar subject matter[34].

Still another type of north Salish funerary carvings shows social meaning. (Plates 33.1, 2, 39.2, 58.2). These are mundane in feeling. They emphasize the personal peculiarities of the deceased, his portliness, tallness, facial features, and often, through the use of such iconographic details as "coppers"[35], represent him as having been a wealthy man of high social position. Although it is evident that types also existed among these figures, they nevertheless contain an individual, momentary, emotional quality which suggests that they were so closely related to a specific event in life as to make them practically historical chronicles. In meaning they are essentially narrative and have no parallels among more characteristically Salish sculptures[36].

---

[34] On the other hand, these carvings may have referred to mythological beings of the tribe whose presence was desired at the winter ceremonials when these drums were used. They may, for instance, have represented the mythological being Qäls, the great transformer, who changed the original inhabitants of the earth into animals, depicted here as holding or creating the mink, which played "an important part in the mythology of this (the Cowichan and Nanaimo) tribe" (Boas, 1889, p. 326). Even this interpretation would however associate these carvings with the supernatural.

[35] "All along the North Pacific Coast from Yakutat to Comox curiously shaped copper plates are in use" (Boas, 1895, p. 344). These were "shield-shaped with a rib running across the middle and from the center to one end" (Goddard, 1934, p. 89), the upper part frequently containing an etched design. They were objects of great value, "each had a name and a well-known history" and they functioned as "bank notes of high denomination" (Boas, op. cit., pp. 344—346, Goddard, op. cit., pp. 89—91).

[36] It should be noted that these carvings do not record in photographic fashion all details and all idiosyncracies of their subjects, but are based on the selection and dramatization of the most pertinent elements. In their subject-matter and treatment these figures resemble the carvings made by the Kwakiutl to be exhibited during a potlatch and afterwards frequently to be set up on the roof of the house to commemorate the event and the elevated social position of the chief (Boas, 1897, p. 390).

Masks are the most strongly social of all Salish carvings (Plates 34; 35; 36a, b; 38; 42.1, 2; 43; 48.1, 2; 49a, b). Variously transliterated as swaixwe, xwai-xwai, xoae'xoe, sqo'aeqoe, qa'eqoe, swaihwe, skway-whay, they are said to have functioned as "the crest of certain families" and were believed to represent "a supernatural people living in lakes", whose protection a person successful in bringing one of them to the surface of the water acquired for himself and his descendants, together with the right to wear the mask[37]. Although they were obtained in a personal encounter with a supernatural being, that is, through a religious experience, it is quite clear that these masks were never used in winter ceremonial dances, which were essentially religious, but were "one of the privileged exhibitions" worn "to enhance the impressiveness of an intrinsically profane occasion such as a marriage, a potlatch, or the reception of visitors"[38]. In other words, their function was entirely of a social nature: to heighten the prestige of the family who had the right to possess and use such an object. But, since the mask was acquired from the supernatural and represented this contact, it gave the family "protection". Reference to the supernatural, it seems certain, appears in the basic design patterns of the masks. These were traditionally associated with certain areas. The use of animal and bird forms may possibly have come from the northern concept of power or supernatural help as operating through animals. The carved forms of these masks seem therefore to be no more personal in their expression of content than those of the house-posts and funerary figures. A revealing comment comes from an Indian informant who stated that the masks were "painted with one's own paint" which "made the mask one's own"[39]. Ownership was thus shown through the colors used to paint a traditional type of object. It is possible that the color of the paint was believed to have been the tangible evidence of personal contact with the supernatural. In brief, these masks seem to have had a double content: (1) that of the carving, which referred to a basic experience and function, and (2) that of the painting, which expressed a personal experience and ownership[40]. In both cases, it seems certain that

---

[37] Boas, 1894, p. 455.

[38] Barnett, 1938, p. 138; 1939, p. 293.

[39] Smith, M.W., verbally from field notes from the Chilliwack, a Salish people who lived near the Fraser River.

[40] This duality of meaning seems common to the majority of Salish sculptures; while the carvings which differ from it, such as the narrative type of funerary figures, reflect considerable outside or non-Salish influence.... An alternate interpretation of the use of bird or animal heads on the masks is that they were intended to associate the privilege of wearing the mask with specific groups. Towards this end, the animals or birds would be emblematic of the gentes who possessed these masks, which Boas implies in his first account of them when he states that they represented "either beavers, or ducks, and spring salmon" (Boas, 1889, p. 324); while Barnett states that the "variations in the nose of the swaihwe made it owl, beaver, raven, etc." (Barnett, 1939, p. 293).

the mask was semi-religious in character and functioned entirely in a profane manner as a symbol of privilege.

Little is known of the meaning or significance of subject matter in Salish decorative carvings (Plates 23.1, 2 ;24. 2 ; 41.1, 2 ; 47.1, 2). An attempt to interpret them, in view of the complete absence of information, would be at best only a conjecture and would have no real importance. It would appear, however, that, since in design and style these decorative works agree with the more significant socio-religious objects, they were carved by the same craftsmen, who in turn used for these less important, purely decorative sculptures the designs and styles with which they were familiar. The manner of handling these significant motives, on the other hand, suggests a lightness of touch, an aesthetic interest in effect, shown by the adaptation of the design to the object. It is possible, of course, that entirely new meanings were given to these forms when they were used in decorative carvings; but it is just as possible that they were without content and used merely as ornamentation. The answer might conceivably fall between these two conjectures: that is, some decorative carvings had important meaning, and others had not.

The sculpture of these Indians, therefore, centers essentially in the recording or displaying of contacts and relationships with the supernatural. Although this subject matter was sometimes used in a social, sometimes in a decorative context, the major interest was in a highly individualized religious expression. The personal element which differentiated between otherwise similar objects was originally very strong; but since it was frequently represented in perishable surface paint, evidences of it have in many cases disappeared.

Chapter two

Classification and Analysis of Styles

Certain common features are distinguishable in all Salish sculpture. With few exceptions the material used was cedar. Compositions were most frequently based on the human figure, which was represented without sex characteristics, and greatly simplified. Sometimes the figures were combined with animals; but compositions involving more than one human figure occur only rarely. Although proportions for the human figure varied considerably from area to area, the most frequent distortions were the elongation of the torso and the enlargement of the head. On the other hand, animals, which were occasionally represented by themselves in groups of two or four, were always depicted naturalistically. All carvings were painted, the colors appearing most often being red, white and black. Very often, too, such materials as horsehair, shredded cedar bark, and shell were used for hair and eyes.

From the aesthetic standpoint these carvings are diversified and can be grouped according to styles within each of six classes: figurines, large figures, house posts, post figures, figure reliefs, and masks. This procedure may appear arbitrary because of the possible overlapping of a work in two or more groups, but study of the whole of Salish sculpture has led to this method as the most practical. A classification and analysis of styles follows.

FIGURINES

This class embraces specimens ranging from twelve to twenty-four inches high. Four types appear among these carvings: figurines on wands, combs, and drums, and small heads carved in the round but unattached to any object.

Type A[1]

Quinault power wands make up this important homogeneous group of small carvings (Plates 1—5,25). They are commonly cut from a single piece of cedar and consist of three parts: a circular handle surmounted by a horizontal crosspiece which supports a human figure carved in the round.[2] No constant proportion is maintained between the handle and the figure, but in the majority

---

[1] Cf. chart 1, opp. p. 18 for a tabulation of types and styles by classes.

[2] The crosspiece, rectangular or circular in cross-section, may or may not have a diameter larger than that of the cross-section of the handle on which it rests.

CHART 1 — TYPES AND STYLES BY CLASSES

Class of Object	Types and Styles
1. Figurines	Type A: Style 1: 1, 2, 3 Style 2: 4, 5.1, 2, 25 Type B: Style 1: 23.1, 2 Style 2: (2701, 2703) Type C: 44.1a, b, c, d Type D: 26.1, 2
2. Large Figures	Type A: Style 1: 8, 9, 10.1, 2 Type B: Group 1: 6, 22 11.1, 2 Group 2: 27, 29, 12, 13.1 50.1, Style 2: 13.2, 14, 15, 50.2, 17 30.1–5, Style 3: 18.1, 2, 31 19.1, 2, Group 3: 33.1, 2, 19.1a, 2a 39.2, Style 4: 20.1, 2, 21.1, 2 58.1 Style 5: 16. 1–4
3. House Posts	Type A: 45, 46, 53.3, 55.1 Type B: 51, 52, 53.2, 55.2 Type C: 50.1a, 50.2, 53.1, 40.2, 3, 56.1, 2
4. Post Figures	Type A: 39.1, 58.2 Type B: 28, 37 Type C: 41.1, 2, 47.1, 2
5. Figure Reliefs	Type A: 32, 40.1, 2, 3, 50.1b, 50.2, 57 Type B: 7.1, 2 Type C: 24.1, 2
6. Masks	Type A: Group 1: 35, 42.1, 42.2, 43, 48.1 Group 2: 34, 48.2, 49 Group 3: 38 Type B: 36

of specimens the latter occupies more than half of the total length. Besides this similarity, the wands have in common the following features: vestiges of red and black coloration which clearly show that they were originally painted in whole or in part; the use of inlay materials for eyes; the suspension, either on the chest or around the neck, of a sizable group of dried deer dew-claws to serve as rattles[3]; and the simulation of long bushy hair by the use of shredded cedarbark or black horsehair. It is therefore evident that the original effectiveness of these objects did not derive from the carved wooden forms alone, but also resulted from the use of important extraneous materials.

[3] These are termed "deer-hoofs" by Olsen (1936, p. 148) and deer's toenails by Willoughby who further says, as already mentioned, that they represent the "rattling bones of the images" (1889, p. 278).

Design and style characteristics further relate the figurines in Type A to one tradition. A static, frontal pose, wherein parts are disposed symmetrically to either side of an implied vertical axis, focuses attention upon the disproportionately large head. The shape of the head varies within oval forms; but the faces are composed of flat or concave planes to either side of a straight, high nose and of a small mouth, and large round eyes set close to the nose under overhanging, accented brows. From this facial design an alert, intense, almost menacing expression results. The nude, sexless figures are reduced to the simplest geometric forms, and are characterized by straight shoulders and elongated torso. They are slightly concave in profile, with arms cut free of the body but usually attached at the hips, and short, heavy legs carved in the round with a slight knee articulation. Further suggestion of joints appears in the shoulders and arms. The resultant design is compact and lucid, and shows within the enclosing contour a strongly balanced arrangement of solids and voids.

Important variations in the interpretation of this general design make it possible to differentiate two styles: Style 1 is represented by Plates 1, 2, 3, and Style 2 by Plates 4, 5, 25[4].

Style 1. A functional rendering of the essential parts of the human form is characteristic of Style 1. Whether the figures have the squat proportions of those on Plates 1 and 3, or the elongated ones on Plate 2, the primary purpose of each simplified part is at once apparent. The flexed legs, for instance, are treated as supporting members in which is felt the downward weight exerted by the torso; the rigid vertical character of the torso, emphasized by the flanking arms, expresses this downward pressure; and the shoulders integrate arms and torso into one unified part upon which the neck is set as a support for the head.

The most distinctive elements of Style 1, however, are the ovoid shaping of the head and the designing of the face. The back and sides of the head are defined by a continuous convex plane; while the face is divided by two horizontal lines into three zones: the upper one, containing the high forehead, is marked off by a wide depression below the brows[5]; the middle zone, including the eyes and the nose, is terminated by a shallow depression on a line with the end of the nose; and the lower area contains the mouth and the pointed chin.

---

[4] For data concerning all of the plates, see Catalogue of Illustrations, pp. 130–144 below. Another excellent example of Style 1 is in the National Museum in Washington (127 864).

[5] Although eyebrows are indicated in the three figures, in Plates 1 and 3 the cutting below the brow is horizontal and in Plate 2 it is slightly curved. The treatment of the forehead in Plate 3 is identical with that of the other two, a fact unfortunately hidden in the photograph by the shredded cedar bark hair, which the Chicago Natural History Museum was reluctant to remove when the photograph was made because of the almost impossible task of putting it back afterwards.

The use of strongly marked horizontals in this facial pattern accents their importance in the upper part of the design of the figure as a whole, where they arrest and effectively balance the upward movement provided by the legs, torso, and arms.

The three arch-like openings which separate the forms emphasize their verticality and give to the figures a significant pattern of solids and voids. This pattern stresses not only the structural unity of the figures, but also, by closely relating the active pose of the flexed legs and arms with the dominating head, the expressive unity as well.

Style 2. In comparison, the figures representing Style 2 (Plate 5.1, 2) are weaker in structure and expression[6]. Although composed of distinct parts (arms, torso, legs, head) the forms are weakly articulated. For example, scarcely a suggestion of knees appears in the legs; while the hips are only attached to the torso in the pelvic region. The schematic manner in which these parts are shaped and composed further diminishes an expression of structure. The arms are thin and widely separated from the body and the shapeless legs are so attached to the hips, which extend at right angles beyond the outline of the torso, that a tall arch appears directly below the torso. To support the weight of the body above this arch, the projecting hips function as buttresses. These "buttresses" are further strengthened by attaching to their outer surfaces the hands, which exert an inward pressure. This is most apparent in the figure on Plate 5.1, where, in fact, the three openings between the limbs are so prominent that the pattern of the body becomes a perforated one.

The treatment of the heads in the figurines of this style is also conspicuously different from that of Style 1. In shape they approximate a pointed oval. The face is composed of two major surfaces, a convex one for the forehead, and a slightly concave one for the area below the deeply recessed eyes. Although the projecting brows create a marked horizontal which parallels that of the shoulders, these facial designs are not as strongly correlated with that of the body as they are in Style 1. The pointed head of the figure on Plate 5.1, however, does repeat the pointed arches of the openings between the limbs, giving thereby a degree of unity to the design.

Of the two figures representing Style 2 that of Plate 5.2 is somewhat less rigid and schematic, partly due to its rather rubbery forms, but largely because of the greater contrast in the proportioning of parts than in the figure on Plate 5.1, where they have an absolute equality.

All of the carvings of Type A are power figures and this appears to have had some influence on their design and style. Of particular significance was the

---

[6] Two other carvings, Plates 4, 25, also seem related to this style. Although Plate 4 has some points in common with Style 1, such as a structural handling of the forms of the body and the shape of the head, these are not integrated. A similar factor relates Plate 25, in spite of the three-zoned design of the face, with Style 2.

belief that the land of the dead lay underground. Hence the figurines expressive of the power that guided the shaman along the dangerous subterranean pathway have small penetrating eyes, enabling the power to see underground. These piercing eyes, moreover, express a tenseness which permeates the entire figure and reveals in dramatic and concentrated fashion the fearful dangers involved in this quest[7].

Type B

In contrast with the significance of the wand figurines of Type A, the small figurative carvings on wooden combs are essentially decorative. Carved combs were made throughout the entire Northwest Coast area. They seem to have been used extensively as objects of personal adornment; but they were also used "to comb the hair" and "to separate nettle fibres from cellular portion of the stalk and to card the hair of mountain-goats[8]. Although the carving was decorative and in no way an outgrowth from or related to use or function, it may originally have had some greater significance. This is suggested by the fact that it is so closely related in style and design to sculptures with established religious and social significance.

Carved from a flat piece of dry, hard yew wood, the entire comb averages seven inches high and the carving about four inches. Despite the actual smallness of the latter, the simplification of shapes and the compactness of design create an impression of far greater size. On some of the combs the carvings are nicely integrated with the hilt and the teeth below; but there is so great a variety in these objects that each specimen tends towards uniqueness, indicating that their design was not restricted by any strong tradition.

Style 1. Two examples represent Style 1. That shown on Plate 23.1 has the stronger technique and the better unified design. It depicts a half-length figure growing out of a wedge-shaped base which in turn rests on the wide curved top of the comb. The figure wears a low, flat-crowned hat with a wide straight brim, seems to have a shawl wrapped around its head, the end hanging down over the chest, and has a blanket or cloak held tightly around its body[9]. The sculptor cut boldly into his material to define the surfaces of these shapes as contrasts in depth. This technique produces a tactile effect and a sense of volume which is considerably emphasized by the absence of any descriptive detail. The careful

---

[7] The concept that shining eyes capable of seeing in the dark characterize spirits appears in many widely separated aboriginal areas, such as the Solomon Islands north central New Guinea, Gabun in West Africa, etc.

[8] Curtis, 1913, 9, p. 65. While this reference concerns the Quinault, it would apply to other tribes as well. It is surprising that so little mention has been made of combs in anthropological monographs dealing with the material culture of the Northwest Coast.

[9] This costume suggests that the figure may represent a white man, or at least may show the influence of the white man's dress.

interrelationship of shapes is characteristic of this style. Their composition in groups or sets of curved and horizontal lines lead the eye upward to the head and give the figure a dignified, calm expression.

The second example of this style, Plate 23.2, has a more rugged technique. Rounded forms are rigorously expressed. The figure has an active pose, and the heavy legs, widely spread in the shape of an inverted V, form the top of the comb. The design of the carving is thus a part of the shape of the object. The downward pressure of the legs on the teeth of the comb is counteracted by the movement developing upward along the profile of the two arms of the V; while the diagonal volumes of the legs converge at the waist into the columnar shape of the torso above, the weight of which part they carry down and distribute along the greater width of the comb below. The torso flares out below the narrow shoulders into stubby arms and then tapers in sharply above the shoulders to form a thick neck. A squarish-shaped head sits abruptly on the neck, and a large, high-crowned hat rests on top of the head. These two parts, the head and the hat, do not satisfactorily combine with the forms below; rather, they are shapes piled one on top of the other.

Style 2. Two examples of combs in the National Museum in Washington, D. C., (cf. figs. 2,3, 2701, 2703), of which photographs could not be procured, show a different style. The designs are schematic, and the forms have little feeling for nature. The small carvings, one representing a head, the other a human figure, are moreover unrelated to the shape of the combs which they surmount.

Type C

A single object, a large Cowichan plank drum with four figures carved in the round (Plate 44.1), represents Type C of the Figurine Class. In spite of certain differences, the four carvings are essentially similar: the two end figures, which appear to be male forms holding an otter-like animal between their legs, are practically identical (Plate 44.2a, d); and the two center ones, which because of their enveloping costume may be female figures, are very closely alike (Plate 44,2b, c). All four of the carvings retain clear evidences that they were originally painted, black and red being the two colors used throughout, with some white appearing on the two center figures.

A basically similar design is shared by the four specimens. This may be described, due to the narrowing at the waist of the figures, as dominantly spool-like, with loops formed at either side by the position of the arms. There is a continuous flow of movement along the outlines of these curvilinear shapes, to which the flexion of the arms at the elbows, providing an angle of force, gives both an inward direction and a degree of energy. Large rectilinear heads, with somewhat similar facial features, act as a contrast to the curved shapes below and impart an appearance of heaviness, largely because, in the male figures, they rest directly on the shoulders and, in the female ones, on short powerful necks. An area of deep shadow on the upper chest, provided by the overhang of the squared jaws, contributes appreciably to this effect. Technically the carving varies from small, fairly evenly spaced tool marks to long, vigorous, uneven cuts. There is practically no evidence that surfaces were re-worked to achieve a regularity and elegance of finish.

Important differences, however, appear in the treatment of the heads. Those of the male figures, for example (Plate 44.2 a, d) are rectangular in shape, the frontal profiles forming unbroken convex curves that indicate very low and broad cheekbones. A flat, hat-like object surmounts and projects slightly beyond the limits of the head. This creates a strong horizontal which is substantially repeated below in the line of the eyes, nose and chin[10]. Widely spaced and large, sharply pointed oval eyes are rendered by a deeply incised outline which catches the shadow and produces the desired effect. The consistently rounded surface of these heads, which the features of the face cut into but do not destroy, establishes them as generalized shapes reduced to their structural and expressive essentials, comparable to the shapes of the forms below. A similar style appears in the handling of the animal forms[11].

Even more drastically simplified, the female figures (Plates. 44.2b, c) have a somewhat different treatment of the head. A trapezoidal shape results from the flat top and straight converging sides of what appears to be hair or a headdress. The facial features are similar to those of the male figures, although not so vigorously carved. The face, however, is of slightly different proportions. It is short and very broad, with a low forehead and less distinct structure. The eyes, moreover, are not carved but were painted on the surface, evidently in white; while the incised creases at either side of the mouth were also marked with white paint. Of interest likewise is the flat area on the breast directly below the over-hanging face. Painted red, this has an inverted triangular shape with the apex developing downward towards the hands, a treatment which effectively sugg-ests that the figure is heavily draped.

All four figures, in spite of these differences, have the same feeling for simple shapes and rounded forms with a minimum of descriptive detail. The effect is not representational, but is sculpturally expressive, each figure having a sturdy

---

[10] The flat "hat" is suggestive of a similar form which appears on the housepost carvings between the head of the figure and the impost block (cf. Plates 46, 55.1). Perhaps here this was actually meant to represent a hat; but it may show a form deriving directly from the houseposts, where it may have had a different significance or function.

[11] These mythical animals, with their long snouts and flat heads pointing upward, have generalized rounded forms and express an energy comparable to the human figures. From the point of view of design, their forms, plastically fused with those of the human figures, furnish a rich counterfoil to the heavy legs between which they are held and have a strong upward movement that focuses attention on the head of the human figure.

plastic unity. Although their purpose is not clear, it is likely that they were power figures of the narrative type.

Type D

Six small crudely carved wooden heads from the Thompson Indians of British Columbia constitute Type D (Plates 26.1, 2a, b)[12]. They are four-sided in plan and seem carved to be seen from the front. The faces are rather broad with long, narrowing chins, high foreheads and beetling brows which indicate in prominent fashion the orbital structure. A horizontal band of deep shadow across the width of the face results from the deep recession of the eye areas, but no eyes are represented on any of the specimens. The facial planes are flat and slope outward at an angle to form the prognathous chin. A straight, triangularly shaped nose extends downward practically on a line with the brows; while in some cases the end of the nose is marked by a straight, horizontal cutting extending across the width of the face. Not far below the nose a crude gouging marks a small mouth. This facial design is reminiscent of the three-zoned type previously noted in other objects of the figurine class. In these small heads the narrowness of the central zone brings the features of the face into close relationship and emphasizes the length of the chin and the height of the forehead.

The sides of the heads are shaped as an inverted triangle, with the apex at the point of the projecting chin and the base on a line with the brows. Some specimens have very large flat ear-like forms set high on the head and the arm of the triangle farthest from the face undercut sharply to represent the line of the jaw. A long columnar neck supports the head. Although these carvings vary slightly from specimen to specimen, they all have essentially the same design.

Surfaces are handled in such a way that the heads not only have a strong frontality, but also a relief-like character. Forms project, planes recede and flatten out, sharp angle under-cuttings create areas of deep shadow — and outlines mark off the limits of the relief and offer no intimation of a rounded three-dimensional form to the back. This relief style, moreover, is entirely and strongly, if crudely sculptural[13], and because of it these small heads constitute an important group of objects.

LARGE FIGURES

A number of extremely important Salish carvings belong to this class. In general, they average from three to four feet high and vary considerably in

---

[12] Only two of these heads are illustrated here, the other four (American Museum of Natural History 16/8010, 8011, 8012, 8013) being very similar in size, design, and style.

[13] Traces remain on practically all of these specimens to show that they were originally smeared with red paint, although there are no suggestions that the eyes were painted in. The surfaces on some of them also have a patterned arrangement of parallel horizontal or diagonal lines or shallow grooves, these perhaps representing face-painting designs of the area (cf. Plate 26.1).

design, technique and intent. On the basis of broad stylistic similarities, they fall into two types.

Type A

Type A comprises the Puget Sound power figures that were used in the spirit canoe ceremony. Although they disclose four styles, these objects are nevertheless a remarkably homogeneous type. They consistently represent half-figures that are composed of four parts, a head, neck, torso and supporting stake-end. These are carved as simplified geometric shapes. Some variation in proportions is found, but the head is usually rather large, the neck very small, the torso in most cases considerably elongated, and the stake small in diameter, and short. While important differences appear in the handling of the features of the face, the back of the head is generally given a finely shaped half-spherical surface. No ears are represented on any of the figures. The heads terminate in a horizontal line in place of a defined lower jaw; and the neck is usually represented by one of four types: a projecting, spool-like form (Plate 9), a depressed ring (Plate 10.1), or a columnar form (Plate 18,1). In a fourth type no neck is carved at all (Plate 12.a). The torso is an elongated hexagon, although in some specimens this has deteriorated, and in others, the four long sides give way to unbroken curves. The stake-end is always crudely shaped, since this was normally hidden from view. In the design of these sculptures bilateral symmetry is emphasized through the strict frontality of pose.

Style 1. Six of the carvings are much alike in style (Plates 8; 9; 10.1,2; 11.1,2; 12a, b; 13.1). Extreme simplicity of form and compactness of design are distinctive of the figures of this group. For example, the heads and torsos are variations of essentially similar geometric shapes in which flat, concave and rounded surfaces meet in sharp contours. An interesting rhythmic relationship therefore closely unifies these two parts. A unity is also achieved through the expression of a contained force in all of the forms, as though the entire figure were tightly wrapped in an encircling blanket. This effect is largely the result of the way in which the shapes are arranged at different angles one to the other. The carving of these figures strongly implies the existence of such anatomical parts as the arms, which are conspicuous by their absence. The heads, averaging between a half and a third the height of the torso, are large and dominating, but are finely proportioned. Although linked together by these general style features, important variations in design and treatment exist among the objects of this group.

A three-quarter frontal view is necessary, for instance, to perceive the strongly sculptured shapes of Plate 9, which represents the simplest type of Puget Sound power figure. The front planes, broken only by the spool-like projecting coelar, are entirely flat. Arranged at different angles, these planes impart a degree of depth and movement. The head is posed so that the face tilts slightly down-

ward; while the torso appears to lean backward, largely because of the treatment of its flat surface as two convex, sloping planes which fuse to form a
projection at the point of its greatest width. From the side, the outlines of the
head and torso are long curves, but from the front they are irregular and
angular. Since both of these parts are truncated at top and bottom, four
parallel horizontals are created which are strong enough to stabilize any
vertical movement[14]. This design represents in succinctly sculptural shapes
an erect figure peering intently at the ground[15].

The most carefully designed and carved example of Style 1 is that figured on
Plate 8. A frontal view shows the rounded character of the forms and the
hexagonal shapes of the front planes of the torso and head. The irregular
hexagon of the head, with the base twice the width of the top, is projected in
depth, so that the shape of the head is prismatic. The figure is painted an allover
brownish-orange color with no traces of any other surface painting, although it
seems likely that the arms were indicated on the surface of the torso, as they
were in other carvings in this group.

A particularly sophisticated feature of the face is the handling of the forehead.
This has the shape of a triangle, the apex truncated and flaring out slightly,
and the base, which forms the brows, curving out over each eye to describe orbital
structure. Below the brows the planes of the face are sunk, the surface of the
forehead continued around this area as a narrow rim. Of the facial features, all
of which are carved, a large angular nose stands out prominently; two small
holes, set close to the nose and high up well within the area of shadow cast by
the brows, indicate the eyes; and a small rectangular depression represents the
mouth.

The high neck or collar is more developed and more important in the design
of Plate 8 than in that of any other Puget Sound figure. It repeats, in reduced
size, the shape of the head, with, however, the lower half being considerably
curtailed[16]. Since the torso is an attentuated rendering of the same shape, it is
apparent that the collar acts as a unifying part in a rhythmical sequence of
similar forms.

---

[14] Plates 10.2 and 11.1, 2 are similar in design, although they differ in the use of a
depressed neck-like part instead of a spool-like form. Plate 10.1 is also similar but
it has no carved neck.

[15] The fact that painted surface details, such as the arms, have become so obliter-
ated as to be negligible factors in the total expression shows to what extent this
was achieved by simple sculptural means. A heavy band of shredded cedarbark
was originally wrapped around the forehead and cast a deep shadow across the
eyes, thus enhancing the expressiveness of the figure. A tight band of cedarbark
was also tied around the upper part of the torso just below the neck.

[16] A cedarbark band was originally wrapped around the upper part of the torso
at the base of this collar. Thus the illusion was created that the hexagonal shape
was completed under this band.

In its proportions, Plate 8 also differs from others in this group. Both the head and the torso are shorter, due to the greater size of the collar[17]. A similar ratio of a little less than 1:2 exists between the height of the head and that of the torso and collar combined, and between the collar and the head. This set of proportions enriches the compact design of these three forms and effectively focuses attention on the head. The projection of the wide head beyond the collar and of the collar beyond the "shoulders" of the torso dramatically emphasizes the parts and their relationships.

This figure is stylistically associated with the one illustrated on Plate 12.a,b, although the latter is carved with a much cruder technique[18]. Strong similarities appear in the general shape of the head, in its slight angle of inclination, and, most obviously, in the depressed carving of the face. Another important resemblance is seen in the three-dimensional rendering of form. The front surface of the torso of both carvings has planes sloping away from a median ridge.

Of the differences in design, the most significant one is the lack in the figure on Plate 12 of a neck or collar[19]. Without this part the proportions are changed considerably. The figure is two and three-quarter instead of three and one-quarter heads high, the head therefore being much larger in proportion to the total height. But measurements disclose the important fact that in both carvings the torso is approximately one and three-quarter heads high. This indicates that, although the collar part is omitted from the design of Plate 12, it maintains the same proportionate height of head to torso as Plate 8. The attenuation and shaping of the torso in Plate 12, however, hides this relationship. Certain differences should also be noted in the treatment of the head. The top of the head, for instance, is not truncated but ends in a point and the brow-line, instead of being straight, is arched, repeating in somewhat flattened form the profile of the top of the head. A unique feature is the carving of the back of the head as a flat surface which reproduces the outline of the front of the head. Likewise distinctive of this design is the shaping of the torso: the widest part is near the top and therefore more effectively suggests the shoulders of a human form than the geometric shape of the torso of Plate 8.

A further difference between these two carvings is the closer association of the simpler forms of Plate 12 with the shape of the log from which it was carved. In its coarse technique, there is the implication that the carver lacked

---

[17] The head is less than a third and the torso only a little more than a half of the total height. In other words, the collar is one-eighth and the head and torso combined are seven-eighths of the height of the figure.

[18] Specific evidences of dark red and white paint have survived: red covers the entire facial area, the back of the head, and the curious rounded knob on the back, and white the rest of the figure above the stake end.

[19] This figure may well have worn originally, like some of the other examples, a cedarbark collar, which would have masked the lack of a carved neck or collar.

the skill necessary to secure finer shapes and surfaces, or that, as the alternative, he had no interest in such refinements. That the latter was the case seems especially borne out by the rough but strong planes and outlines of the head[20]. The more expressive handling of the parts as simplified human forms further substantiates this interpretation. The artist had as his goal plain, forceful statement, not elaboration of phraseology.

A less distinguished example of this style is represented by Plate 13.1. This figure shows certain similarities with Plates 8 and 9. For example, it resembles Plate 9 in the shape of its four major parts and in their proportions; in the emphasis on frontal outlines, suggesting no third-dimension; and in the way in which the arms are painted on the torso, the left one placed above the right. The arms, as well as the constricting band around the top of the head, the collar, the outlines of the eyes and mouth, and the entire back are painted a dull black; the rest of the figure is white. It therefore differs in coloration from the brown and black of Plate 9 and from the orange-black of Plate 8. Only in the slightly depressed carving of the face does Plate 13.1 at all resemble Plate 8. This figure has, through the formality of its pattern and the dull shaping of its parts, some relationship with the carvings of Style 2. It is, in fact, largely transitional between Styles 1 and 2.

Style 2. In comparison with the above group, a greater realism characterizes the four figures representing Style 2 (Plates 13.2; 14; 15; 17). Carved arms and a suggestion of body structure are distinctive features. But equally characteristic are the weak designing of component shapes and a looseness of composition. The unity of the figure is broken up by a rendering of its parts as separate and distinct elements. Proportions vary from carving to carving; while almost as great a diversity is found within a meager technique. The dramatic expressiveness and the sculptural qualities of Style 1 are faintly recalled in the figures of this group.

Plate 14a, b[21] represents a work that is related to both styles. The deeply depressed treatment of the face and the general shaping of the head recall similar features of Plate 8, and the configuration of the collar and torso those of Plate 13.1. But the head is more geometric and the sunken face more stylized than in either of these two; while deep grooves mark off sharply head, collar and torso as individual parts. A greater number of planes than in Style 1 figures are used to describe surfaces, where the smaller marks of the carver's tools demonstrate a technique lacking vigor and breadth.

---

[20] Attention should be called to the protruding rounded area on the back, approximately on a line with the greatest width of the figure. This area was painted red. Perhaps the fact that it is a knot in the wood and presented difficulties with which the carver either could not or did not care to cope is sufficient explanation of it.

[21] The original paint on this figure is unusually well preserved, black, white and a reddish-brown ochre being apparent.

The most notable features that link this figure with Style 2 are the carved arms. These are crossed over the front of the torso in the same manner as the painted arms on Plates 9 and 13.1, the left one above the right. They are carved in high relief and there is no suggestion that they are articulated to any shoulder structure, although such realistic details as elbows and hands are represented. The very presence of the arms and the sharp flexion of them provide a second center of interest which draws the eye away from the head towards the torso.

Attention is further attracted to this part of the figure by the series of painted bands or stripes which continue the chevron-like design formed by the angles of the arms. These stripes, possibly indicating skeletal structure, are strikingly painted in a sequence of black, white, yellow and white. Above the V of the left arm, which is repeated in the striping on the back, the torso is painted white and light pink, with a series of irregularly placed round spots of pink-red. The collar is painted yellow; the face, white; and the large eyes outlined in black. The entire surface appears to have been first painted white and the other colors then painted over this background. The stripes are continued around the sides and back of the torso, while diagonals of similar color are painted on the sides and back of the head. This use of color gives to the figure a unity which the composition of the carved shapes does not have.

In comparison with Plate 14, the power figure illustrated on Plate 13.2 is weaker both in technique and design. Surfaces are relatively flat; details are coarsely carved; and component parts are more attenuated in shape. The head and torso, for example, have outlines of truncated ovals; while the long stake-end, unique in this specimen, is a wedge-shaped part, oval in cross-section[22]. Proportions are somewhat more naturalistic than those of Plate 14. The torso is almost two and a half, as compared to less than two heads high, thus considerably reducing the size of the head. In width, the proportioning sets each part off one from the other. The top of the stake is wider than the lower part of the torso, and the top of the torso is wider than the lower part of the head, from which it is separated by a narrow collar. This treatment further emphasizes the slenderness of these parts. It also accents the rhythmic sequence of their vertical profiles.

There is more carved detail than in Plate 14 and it is of a more descriptive and realistic character. All of the facial features are carved, the sinking of the facial area being very slight. On the upper part of the torso, above the arms, a U-shaped design is carved in high relief: this may have been meant to represent a water-proof garment, frequently worn by the Salish of this region. The arms and hands are arranged similarly to those on Plate 14; but the arms are rounded

---

[22] Although slightly more elongated, it resembles the supporting parts of the large painted boards used with these figures in the performance of the spirit canoe ceremony (cf. Plate 16.1–4).

and their upper ends are enlarged and flattened in such a way as to imply an articulation with the torso. The reduced diameter of the collar gives additional evidence of the greater realism in this figure.

That the original appearance of the carving was to an extent modified by surface painting is obvious from the traces of paint that have survived. The use of color, however, differs considerably from that of Plate 14. A dark red seems originally to have covered the entire surface, with the other colors painted over it. This is especially evident on the face where a good deal of the white over-painting has flaked off. Traces of white also appear above and around the arms and on the collar; dark red, on the arms; and black, on the U-shaped part at the top of the torso. A bluish color appears to have been applied in and around the eyes and on the forehead. Although the design on the back is indistinct, clear traces of black and red are to be seen. Horizontal stripings of white, black and red on the lower part of the torso bear comparison with the painted designs on Plate 14, although they appear to have been limited to the front surface of the torso and show no design relationship with that of the flexed arms. The horizontal stripes repeat the carved horizontals in the design and, when freshly painted, may have slightly counteracted the upward movement of the slender forms.

The meager technique so characteristic of Style 2 carvings is conspicuous in Plate 15, where small knife-marks show a niggling treatment. Although the parts traditional to this type of figure appear in the design, they consist of crude shapes, roughly defined and abruptly related. This specimen, though fully within the Salish tradition, lacks much of its force.

An enormously proportioned ovoid head dominates the carving. The whole figure is less than two and a half heads high and the torso only a little more than one and a quarter heads high. Since the greatest width of the head is almost equalled by that of the torso, these proportions are heavy and squat. A very short cranium is represented by a meagerly convex surface, while angular facial features, mainly similar to those on Plate 13.2, are crudely shaped and widely spaced on the large, flat plane of the face. The slight curve of the lower jaw approximates nature more closely in the delineation of this part of the face than any figure of Style 1. A similar degree of naturalism appears in the shaping of the neck[23] and torso; while an unmistakable rendering of elbow joints, muscular structure, and shoulder articulation give the arms a weak lifelikeness, which is conclusive proof of the sculptor's greater concern with natural forms than with conventional stylization. This is also seen in the arrangement of the arms which gives to the figure an expressive unity by directing attention to the head as a single center of interest.

No evidence remains of any elaborate schematic surface painting. The collar was painted white; the front of the torso and head, a yellowish-red; and the back

[23] The neck is columnar in cross-section and has a slight frontal depression. A heavy collar of shredded cedarbark was originally hung around the neck.

of these parts, black and red. This simple use of color offers no distraction from the carved shapes and details.

An important example of Style 2 is represented by Plate 17[24]. The original surface is much damaged and evidently no traces of paint remain[25]. Although the technique is rough, the figure is strongly three-dimensional. Carved descriptive detail, such as arms, shoulders, clavicle structure and hips give this work an even greater life-like quality than the carving on Plate 15.

Plate 17, in fact, is only related to other Style 2 examples by such general similarities as the hollowing out of facial planes and the straight cutting of the brows. The long oval of the head, for instance, is unique. Great care was taken in the designing of the face. A sharp median ridge is formed in the forehead by the meeting of the slightly convex surfaces at either side and continues downward into a long, thin, straight nose. This creates within the oval outline a strong bisecting vertical, which together with the horizontal line of the brows forms a cross-shaped design. The simple boldness of the pattern gives scale to the features and integrates them into an expressive whole. This effect is furthered by the treatment of the mouth which is cut as a projection of almost equal height as the end of the nose.

In the nearly realistic representation of anatomical parts, the body differs strikingly from that of any other figure of this type, while the proportioning of the slender body to the large head is almost identical to that of the Style 1 example illustrated on Plate 12. A rigid pose gives to the arms, shoulders and clavicle structure a marked horizontal and vertical pattern which repeats that of the face. This carving ranks high among Salish sculptures because of the richness of its design and the simple vigor of its style.

Style 3. A homogeneity in design, shape, size, and proportion characterizes the four figures of Style 3 (Plates 18.1, 2; 19.1, 2; 19.1 a, 2a). They are all roughly carved in a coarsegrained cedar and show evidences that such tools as the saw were used in their creation. Essential parts are rendered as geometric shapes that are crude in design and in configuration when compared with those of Style 1 carvings which they most nearly resemble. Front surfaces are flat and two-dimensional in appearance, while rounded planes give to the sides and backs a three-dimensional quality. Although the length of the torso and neck vary somewhat, the size of the heads and the coarse rendering of facial features are similar. A lack variety is, in fact, distinctive of these figures. This is due to the limitations imposed by the meagerness of their style elements. Combinations of identical shapes therefore appear in more than one design.

The torsos of the figures represented on Plate 18.1 and 2, for example, are carved as long vertical rectangles, the upper corners bevelled off and the lower

[24] This specimen is comparatively large for a spirit canoe figure: four feet, two inches high.

[25] I have not had the opportunity to examine this work, nor the catalogue for information regarding it. I am indebted for my knowledge to H. F. Barnett.

part tapered abruptly near the end. But the long columnar neck and the angular outlines of the head of Plate 18.2 differ from the treatment of these parts in Plate 18.1; instead, they resemble those of Plate 19, while the more regular curvilinear profiles of the dead of Plate 18.1 agree with those of Plate 19.1a, 2a. The truncated top of the head of Plate 18.1 is similar to that of Plate 19.1, 2, and the rounded top of the head of Plate 18.2 to that of Plate 19.1a, 2a. The torsos of the figures on Plate 19, however, have the same truncated oval shape.

In the shaping of the back of the head in Plate 18.1 and 19.1a, 2a the rounded surface continues downward as an unbroken curve to the upper edge of the torso; while in Plate 18.2 and 19.1, 2 this surface is terminated by a sharp horizontal as it approaches the neck, similarly to the treatment of the squared off lower edge of the face in all four figures.

It seems certain that the elements which contribute most effectively to the distinctive characterization of each figure come from the painted designs rather than from the carved forms. This can be seen most clearly by comparing the drawings made by Waterman before the figures had lost part of their painted designs with photographs taken recently[26].

In contrast to the remains of color found on some of the examples discussed above, these carvings are poorly painted with a chalk-like earth pigment that rubs off easily. Light, weak colors were used, such as a light pinkish-red, a delicate pinkish-white, a black-green, and traces of black and white. The fragile nature of the pigments is evidenced by the fact that the three figures which have for some time been on exhibition within the protection of a glass-enclosed case have retained more of their color and design than the one (Plate 18.1) which has been in storage and so handled more often[27]. The painted designs are quite different from those still visible on Style 1 and 2 figures and they are restricted to the front surfaces of the head and torso.

Style 4. The four carvings comprising Style 4 (Plates 20, 21) are spectacularly painted and are significant examples of the importance of painting for Type A figures. The profusely painted designs are more noteworthy than the carved forms. The head and torso are, with one exception[28], represented by foursided shapes which provide flat surfaces to accommodate these painted designs. Even the traditional projection of the forehead and recession of facial planes are so slightly carved that they are barely apparent.

Sculpturally these figures are schematic in design and rudimentary in technique. The front and back outlines of the head, for instance, describe octagons which are formed by bevelling off the corners of rectangles. The neck

---

[26] cf. Waterman, 1930, Figs. 44—47 and Plates 18.1, 2; 19.
[27] cf. Waterman, 1930, pp. 38—39.
[28] Only on Plate 21.1, where two vertical planes meet in a projecting ridge, is there any break in the flat planes of the torso.

is a thick, post-like form; while the torso in three of the carvings is thin and somewhat attenuated, the exception being that on Plate 20.1 where the proportions are rather wide and squat. All of the torsos taper from top to bottom, and the upper corners of those on Plate 20,2 and 21,1 are bevelled, in the fashion of that on Plate 18. The frontal profiles have a very slight convexity, this being most apparent in Plate 21.1 and least in Plate 21.2. As in the carvings of Styles 1 and 3, these figures do not possess carved arms, nor is there any indication, as in Style 2, of painted arms. In this respect they resemble most closely Style 3 carvings. The proportions of all four figures are almost identical, the head being about one-half the total height of the torso and neck combined. Characteristically they have a rigid pose and an alert expression; but only basically do the sculptured parts contribute to this effect, since it is apparent that without the survival of surface painting, a very great part of this quality would have been lost. These figures show only a faint understanding of poorly remembered features of an old tradition.

The painting therefore merits careful attention. Three colors are used, red, black and white. The designs are all varied and suggest analogies with carved and painted designs found variously on examples of Styles 1, 2 and 3. In Plate 21.1, for instance, the design on the upper part of the torso is similar to that on Plate 18.1 and 2; while the curved lines immediately below it resemble the carved arms and the painted lines on Plate 13.2 and 14. Perhaps the relief at the top of the torso on Plate 13.2, which agrees in shape with the painted portion at the top of the torso on Plate 21.1 originally had a like motive painted on the surface.

The eyes of all of the figures, especially those of Plate 21, may be compared with the painted eyes on Plate 13.1 and 14; but they are unique in having pupil and iris represented[29]. Much of the painting, in fact, seems to be descriptive. This is seen in Plate 21.1 in the way hair is represented at the sides and back of the head by a black area which is terminated near the neck by a red line, while a similar red line near the top of the sides and back of the torso indicates the shoulder area. The design on the torso is painted black on white, with the exception of this red line and the row of large red dots above it. Two rows of red dots are also painted around the neck and one row around the lower part of the head; the design on the face is likewise black on white, although the mouth is realistically red. The range of broad verticals at the base of the torso is without parallel, but the painted design above was probably meant to represent, as in Plate 18 and 19, inner organs and bony structure. This seems even more strongly implicit in the design on the torso of Plate 21.2.

---

[29] The pupil in all of the figures is depicted with white paint, with the outline of the eye in black; while in Plates 21.1 and 21.2 the iris seems to be indicated by a fine point of black paint, and in Plates. 20.1 and 20.2 it appears to be marked by a small hole.

A close parallel is apparent between the painted details on Plates 19 and 20.1. Both have only one eye, which has painted eyelashes, an eyebrow above and a horizontal line below. Unique to Plate 20.1 are the white on black vertical striping of the neck and the large semicircular design at the top of the torso which consists of crossing broad red lines against a white ground[30]. The rest of the torso and the back of the head are painted black; while the forehead, right side and lower portion of the face are also black, the nose and mouth red, and the left side of the face white with the eye, eyebrow and design in black.

The painting on Plate 20.2 is of particular interest. Aside from the general similarities, only the painting of the face shows parallels with other figures of this type: the painted eyelashes and the square cut mouth which is connected with the painted zone at the bottom of the face are somewhat comparable to like features on Plate 18.2. The large and conspicuous design on the torso is the most important feature in the painting on this figure. It distracts attention from the head and creates an equally important center of interest. In shape it suggests the ceremonial object called "skudi'litc";[31] but the appearance of features on the upper portion, with tablike ears projecting at either side, associates it in style with the representation of power found on the painted planks used in the spirit canoe ceremony (Plate 16.1—4). Further similarities with these planks are the painting of eyelashes and the appearance of many dots. It appears therefore that in this figure there is a fusion or confusion of concepts and iconography related to both the spirit canoe power figures and the painted planks. This implies that at least some of the traditional significance of the carved shapes has been lost sight of in this figure. In color, all of the designs painted on the front surface stand out vividly as red against white. Black is only used for the back of the head.

Type B

Type B of the Large Figure Class may be divided according to function into three sub-types or groups of carvings, shaman, commemorative-funerary, and narrative-funerary. Although there are similarities of content and style among objects within each group, the type as a whole is a heterogeneous one. Perhaps the only important feature which the figures all share in common is an almost complete reliance upon sculptural means to achieve the desired effect. Some show traces of paint and others use extraneous materials; but in every case these are secondary in importance to the carved shapes, surfaces and details.

---

[30] Perhaps this design is a window-like opening showing the inner bony structure of the figure.

[31] This consist of an ovoid-shaped cedar plank cut with handholds at either side and painted in a manner "revealed by the spirit... Power entered these things during certain ceremonies, and they dragged people about, causing them to quiver and shake... It is considered a most powerful form of 'help'" (Waterman, 1930, pp. 26—27, 57, and Fig. 49 on p. 46).

Vigorous expression is characteristic of all of these figures, while the technique is usually strong.

Group I: Shaman Figures. Two of the carvings of this class (Plates 6;22) represent shaman power figures. A large head, long neck and torso, and short legs give them very similar proportions[32]. In both, the shoulders are wide and rounded, the torso has concave profiles, and the arms, carved in the round, are held rigidly at either side and attached at the hips. The two figures also have a number of stylistic elements in common, such as the bold cutting of the features of the face and the emphatic rendering of shoulder, elbow, wrist, hip and knee joints. Further similarities are apparent in their technique. Surfaces are not smoothly finished but show numerous and analagous tool marks, while incised detail is filled with color and some inlay is used[33]. These objects differ nevertheless in many respects. This is most evident in the handling of shapes and surfaces, and in the specific treatment of detail.

An impressive carving of facial features occurs in Plate 6. These are designed in the three-zoned pattern previously noted in figurine carvings and are framed by the long oval of the head, which tapers almost to a point at the chin. A carefully shaped forehead, on which curved eyebrows are carved in high relief, overhangs deeply indented eyes of shell inlay. The nose is high, thin and straight. The mouth, narrow and crescent-shaped, is set with small pieces of ivory in simulation of teeth.

The treatment of the planes of the face is the most notable element in the style of this figure. Two planes slope sharply outward from the deeply depressed eye area to near the end of the nose where they abruptly slope downward, forming angles which express low cheekbones. This dramatic design is further intensified by the handling of the lower zone of the face. The angle of the long prognathous jaw repeats that of the planes immediately below the eyes, while the shape of this area is an inverted variant of that of the forehead. With the exception of the slightly convex surface of the forehead, all of the facial planes are flat. Depth or roundness of forms is however emphatically implied by the forward and backward movement of these planes.

Unlike the head, the surfaces of the figure below the thin neck lie practically in one plane. This is only slightly broken by the low relief carving of hands, by the horizontal depressions below the hips, which suggest a groin line, and by the knob-like projections of the knees. But the bevelled edges of the torso show that the sculptor had a rounded form in mind. Many details of the entire lower part of the figure, in fact, are strongly descriptive, such as the shaping of shoulder,

---

[32] Although the lower portion of the legs on Plate 22 are missing, it seems certain that, on the basis of a comparison of the surviving upper legs with those of Plate 6, the legs of both figures were of similar proportions.

[33] From a close examination of Plate 22, it is apparent that the now empty eyes and mouth had originally held inlays, probably like those found in Plate 6.

elbow and wrist joints and the carving of hands and fingers, feet and toes. Muscular parts are suggested in the profiles of the arms, especially of the forearms, while at the upper part of the chest clavicle bones are clearly apparent. A striking feature of the torso is the representation of rib structure by five inverted V-shaped incisions filled in with white paint. Perhaps this is again a stylization of a skeletal form.

The style of the figure as a whole seems at first glance to be full of inconsistencies. For example, the strongly schematic head, with its remarkable contrast of planes, differs considerably from the flatter surfaces of the forms below, where plentiful evidence suggests naturalistic representation. Closer examination shows that a feeling for roundness and for light and shade effects also appear in the treatment of the torso and legs. The flat surfaces of these parts, therefore, seem to be imposed on shapes conceived as fundamentally three-dimensional. Aside from the horizontal depth appearing in the head and the implication of depth in arms and torso, only the neck and the legs are actually carved as rounded forms; although the back is defined by completely rounded planes.

The dramatic expression so clearly evident in this figure centers in the large head to which the V-shaped incisions on the torso direct attention. All parts of the figure, however, assist in the attainment of this effect. The piercing intensity of the facial expression is strengthened by the rigid pose of the body. This is emphasized by the squaring of the shoulders, the flattening of the surfaces of the torso, and the placing of the arms and hands. The component parts of the body form an essentially symmetrical pattern of verticals and horizontals which perform important roles in the design of the figure as a whole. The downward movement of the long oval of the head, for instance, is stabilized by the upward movement created by the inverted V-incisions on the torso; while the profiles of this oval find their rhythmical counterparts in the long reverse curves of the torso. Other sequences of curves appear in those of the eyebrows and mouth, in the slight curve at the top of the torso and those at either side of the nose; and in the outlines of the arms and torso. Although vertical elements dominate in the design, they are largely balanced by a number of strongly stated horizontals. This gives to the forms a tension which is fundamental to the expression of a potential power, menacing and alert, but kept in restraint.

In comparison, Plate 22 is less dramatic. The bold pattern of Plate 6 is tempered by a stronger feeling for three-dimensional form; while descriptive details, rendered in low relief, are both more numerous and smaller in scale. The curious diagonal incisions on the upper arms and the three parallel horizontal grooves just below the hips at first glance suggest that the figure is represented as clothed, an interpretation clearly ruled out by its apparent nudity[34]. Low

[34] If the notched-like projection at the base of the torso was intended to represent male genitalia, as seems apparent, this is unique in Salish sculpture, where, as

relief carving marks the clavicle bones, an eye-like motive appears on each shoulder, and a vertical line of notched reliefs on the neck continues down the chest where it has smaller scale and seemingly ends in a pendant. It is possible that this latter design may have been intended to denote the trachea and heart, previously observed as painted on some of the Puget Sound power figures. The parallel lines on the face just below each eye are also rendered in low relief.

In its basically ovoid shape the head differs from that of Plate 6. The face is wide and short and narrows abruptly to a sharp point at the chin, while the forehead, high and truncated, has a slight reverse curve in its tapering profile. More important differences appear in the flattened surface of the forehead and in the comparatively slight projection of the brows. The flat planes of the face, deploying downward to the slightly protruberant chin, are sunk very little below the surface of the curvilinear areas under the eyes, which are roughly on a line with the end of the nose. This treatment seems to be a modification of the three-zoned design.

The rounded torso has a slenderness of proportion which is emphasized by the ample spacing between the arms and by the width of the shoulders. The latter are so high that a shallow V-shaped depression is formed into which the very large columnar neck sets. Less attention was paid to abstract rhythms of line pattern than in Plate 6 and more to the development of three-dimensional shapes. As an example, the hands are now attached at the sides and not to the front of the hips. Movement flows primarily around the forms and develops secondarily in depth, forward and backward, over the surface, as in the face, neck, upper torso and shoulders.

The function of this carving also appears to have differed slightly from that of Plate 6, since the tenon-like cutting on the top of the head and the flat treatment of the back suggest that it was probably mortised in place at the top and adossed to a board or post[35]. Few precedents for thus placing a figure are known, although a similar treatment was resorted to in setting up carved power boards, which in some areas stood beside the head of a shaman's bed[36].

Olsen notes among the Quinault, "most spirits and powers personified were ageless, usually sexless" (Olsen, 1936, p. 142).

[35] The groovings down the back and the pegholes in the back of the head, if original, make it difficult to determine the kind of member or members to which it was attached. From the cutting of the lower part of the torso, however, it seems that the head was attached to a wide plank and the neck and central part of the torso to a relatively narrow one. The rounding of the shoulders and the shaping of the arms, legs and sides of the torso support this contention. It is possible, however, that the tenon-like cutting at the top may simply have provided a surface for attaching a cedarbark wrapping, as noted among Puget Sound power figures.

[36] Curtis mentions that these boards were placed with their bases "on the ground and the top bound by spruce withes to a board running the length of the house" (Curtis, 1913, 9, p. 109).

Group II: Commemorative-Funerary Figures. A degree of lifelikeness unusual
among Salish sculptures characterize the nine carvings in this group (Plates
27; 30.1—5; 31; 29; 50.1 a, b). Although these figures differ somewhat one from
another in meaning, design, and the quality of their technique, they are all
nevertheless alike in the essential elements of their style. Simplified three-
dimensional shapes represent anatomical parts that are integrated in a naturalistic manner. No schematic surface detail appears on the forms. With the
exception of those on Plate 31, the arms are carved in the round and flexed
strongly at the elbows, forming loop-like projections at the sides of the torso;
while the hands are held against the front of the figure, where they at times
hold something, or are stuck in "trouser pockets" at the sides. This treatment
of the arms is the most distinctive feature in the design of these carvings. It
imparts vitality to otherwise stiff poses and implies a movement kept in
restraint. As grave monuments, these objects are dignified and impressive.

The simplest of these figures in design and in technique is represented on
Plate 27. In a manner resembling that of certain Puget Sound power figures,
the head and thick neck are carved as a single form, on the surface of which the
lower part of the face is in high relief[37]. The upper part of the chest is carved to
show clavicle bones and breasts; while the arms and shoulders fuse to form bold
projecting loops. A slight irregularity in the profile of the arms indicates elbows,
and on the large heavy hands knuckles plainly appear on the carefully cut
fingers. In contrast, the torso below the breasts and the lower part of the figure
are practically flat, and although a slight narrowing at the waist prevents the
sides from being straight, the shape becomes four-sided as it nears the base.
This treatment of the lower part, together with the indication of breasts,
suggests that the carving represents a female[38]. The surface of the entire back
of the figure is flat and implies that, like Plate 50.1, it may originally have
stood against a support or formed a part of the architectural structure of a
grave house[39]. The style is simple and direct. Forms and surfaces are summary
in treatment, and although the head is rather large, the figure has nearly human
proportions. The facial features in their configuration and proportioning are also
more lifelike; while the technique throughout is coarse but vigorous.

This carving shares a stylistic relationship, particularly in its proportions and
in the design of the face, with Plate 29. The latter has a far stronger technique,

---

[37] In this connection it should be noted that the rounded chin of this figure is
never found among Puget Sound power figures, where the chin is squared off
(cf. Plate 10).

[38] Grave figures were set up on practically all graves of adults, i. e., male and
female alike (Teit, 1906, p. 273).

[39] Teit, in fact, refers thus to the carved grave posts: "four posts rising from the
corners of grave-box, with cross-poles and a roof of cedarbark"... with the
"corner posts carved with totem of the clan of the deceased" (op. cit., p. 272).
Plate 27 is obviously not a totem carving; but it may have been used, as suggested, above, in the manner of Plate 50.

however, and is, in fact, one of the most important Salish sculptures. It depicts a kneeling three-quarter length figure which is holding in restraint against its midriff a mythical animal[40]. The head, wide and rectangular in shape, shows a heavy jaw and low forehead; while the hair is deeply undercut and forms a band of shadow across the top and at the sides of the face. Unusual in Salish sculpture is this representation of hair, described by a smooth surface, parted in the middle, and hanging down the back. The eyebrows are cut in very high relief and furnish a heavy area of shadow above the eyes. Shadow also marks the curved edges which, extending from the nose to the jaw, set off the depressed lower part of the face. The mouth is carefully shaped, as are also the slightly pointed circles of the eyes and the flattened plane on the chin.

The large rounded forms of the body are summarily rendered, but clear articulation is given to the shoulders and arms. The deep shadow caused by the projection of the head suggests a short thick neck. Of great importance in the expression and design of this figure is the sharp flexing of the arms. It not only keeps an implied movement entirely within the carving, but also aids in focusing attention on the head either by allowing the eye to move rapidly upward from the animal, or by carrying the eye down to the animal. In either case, the arms integrate the two centers of interest; and the animal form, infused with movement, directs attention instantly upward. Details of the animal are handled with almost the same care as those of the head of the figure, the obvious desire being to create descriptive shapes such as the snout, head, body and tail, while the pelt is represented by fine diagonal incisions. It is significant that, in order not to divert interest from the animal and thus interrupt the flow of movement, the sculptor suppressed all details of the hands. The clear and economical statement of the purpose of these strong sculptural forms make it one of the most effective Salish figures.

Certain stylistic similarities are apparent between this carving and the one shown on Plate 50.1. The latter is an architectural figure made for the front of a grave house. The rotted condition of the base suggests that the carving was originally sunk in the ground up to the feet of the figure, so that the plinth-like "hat" functioned as a support for the front horizontal beam. Seated on his haunches, the figure rests his hands on his knees, the flexed arms looped at the sides. On the chest, the forepart of an animal, similar in species to the one on Plate 29, is suspended from the heavy collar. Other resemblances with Plate 29 are seen in the designing of facial features, in the use of undercutting with the resulting areas of shadow, and in the bold shaping of the forms of the body.

A number of individual style features, however, characterize Plate 50.1. Large tab-like ears, for instance, project from either side of the head and

---

[40] Funerary figures in varied poses were common to British Columbia, and Teit states that Lillooet grave figures were "carved in many attitudes" (op. cit. p. 273). The animal, appearing here as part fish, part mink, probably represents the mythical being called variously "scowmidgeon" or "squa-mit-chen".

introduce descriptive details not found on Plates 27 and 29. The face is short and wide, the chin slightly pointed, and broad strap-like designs in low relief, which follow the line of the jaw, extend from the temples almost to the mouth. Oval eyes are carved in low relief: a center hole marks the pupil and gives an aggressive expression to the features. The carved collar is not found in any other of the nine examples in this group. A quality of restlessness is also distinctive of this figure. Again, the animal is a secondary center of interest and is closely related in design to the face. But the pose of the animal creates a movement away from the face. The sturdy character of the legs serves partially to counteract this and, through the loops of the arms, leads the eye up to the face. Here, attention is soon carried away by the downward swing of the animal, to begin the cycle all over again. An open, nervous movement therefore pervades the carving. This may be resolved into the forward thrusts of the head, the animal, the forearms, and the knees, and the backward thrusts of the upper legs and the arms. The forward thrusts dominate, although the arms do much to balance them and, more importantly, to keep the two centers of interest in constant relationship. This is the most dramatic type of funerary figure; and, although the cedar is now badly split and decayed, the carving shows sufficient evidences of a vigorous, if somewhat crude technique.

Five figures are represented in front of an old grave house on Plate 30.1—5. They all depict full length standing figures with comparative lifelikeness; but the summary handling of parts and the patterning of features clearly show that this is only relative. In conformity with tradition all of the objects are represented as clothed, in the small ones by carving, two in trousers and top hat and two, perhaps females, in long skirt-like dresses[41]; and in the large one by real clothes, an old sweater and polka-dot cloth trousers[42]. From the photograph, it appears that three of them are carved with feet, and as though wearing shoes. The five figures have the characteristic loop-like arrangement of arms, but there is no tension in the pose; three are represented with their hands in their trouser pockets, and two with them held against their chests. In every case a relaxed, contained, calm expression prevails.

Two general types appear in these figures: the smaller ones have stocky proportions and large heads, and the larger one has more realistic proportions. All show wide and rounded shoulders, a slightly constricted waist, and the usual frontality of pose. The heads also reveal two general types: (1) those with wide and square jaws, and (2) those with oval faces and a narrow chin; while the facial features and the tab-like ears, noted in Plate 50.1 are similarly handled in all five specimens.

---

[41] Good examples of these small male and female figures are to be found in the American Museum of Natural History (cf. 16—7081, 16—7079).

[42] Grave figures were frequently, if not customarily dressed in the clothes of the deceased. This was one means of identifying the carving, and it was a sign of respect for the descendants to keep the carved figure well clothed (cf. Teit, 1906, p. 273).

The carving illustrated on Plate 31 has the most realistic treatment of any figure in this group. Large protruding eyes, cut in low relief and set almost on a level with the faintly indicated brows, are represented by a circle inscribed within a wide, sharply pointed oval. Below, a depression produces an area of shadow. This treatment is practically the reverse of the usual Salish rendering of brows, eyes and face planes; and it is closer to actuality. The shaping of the large ears, kept flat to the head, the straight, full-lipped mouth, and the carving of a low neck are further evidences of a more realistic attitude.

In conception, the shapes of the large rectangular head and the parts of the body below are distinctly three-dimensional. Narrow, sloping shoulders continue downward to fuse with the long and heavy arms, which, almost as long as the body, are cut free only at the waist. A disproportionately long torso tapers to the hips where it joins the short, heavy legs. These are carved with no indication of feet, but are posed with a wide stance and shaped to imply a flexion of the knees. Throughout the forms, volumes and surfaces flow without interruption; while their essential structure and function is simply but directly disclosed.

The pose of this carving differs significantly from that of other funerary figures. Frotalinty is here relaxed. The lower, sloping right shoulder, for instance, together with the slight projection of the left leg, show a movement or twist from left to right[43]. That this effect was intentional and not merely fortuitous is evident in the raised left shoulder and in the diagonal line at the waist, while both arms are placed at the back of the legs, a position they would naturally assume to agree with this movement. In contrast, the head is turned towards the left and is very slightly tilted to the right, causing diagonals to be formed by the mutilated brim of the plug hat, by the line of the eyes and jaw, and by the placing of the left ear higher than the right. It is therefore apparent that the intention of the sculptor was to embody in his carving both vitality and mobility.

The purpose or function of this figure is not known, but it seems likely that it was a funerary work. Like the figures on Plate 30, it stands on a plank-like base from which it is not carved free. The mutilated top of this base also discloses that it originally projected over the plank below[44]. Traces of color remain to show that the carving, unlike others in this group, was painted, black appearing throughout, with suggestions of red visible on the face.

Group III: Narrative-Funerary Figures. The realism manifested in the above carvings receives its greatest development in the four examples of this group shown on Plates 33.1, 2; 39.2; 58.1. It is most apparent in the contorted facial features which are arranged in an expressive mobility. An open mouth represents

---

[43] Left and right are here used and will be used throughout this paper with respect to the figure; thus they are right and left respectively on the illustration.

[44] The possibility should be noted that there may have been some indication here of feet, this being suggested by the rounded corner at the left side of the base.

a person in the act of talking forcibly or shouting, an interpretation confirmed by the inflated cheeks and the high arched brows. The energetic poses of the figures and even the shaping of parts, which are carved with a vigorous, three-dimensional technique, are in realistic agreement with the dramatic and momentary expression of the faces. It is apparent that these carvings were designed to stand alone as figures in the round. A single style is evident in the four objects of this group, but each one has its own proportions, pose and distinctive treatment.

Numerous similarities however show a close stylistic relationship between Plate 33.1 and 2. For example, both have long oval heads, thin columnar necks and sloping shoulders. Both also have tapering torsos, well marked groin lines, and similarly carved hands and fingers. But the nearest resemblances are found in the rendering of facial features. These suggest that, due to the appearance of such individualistic details as the high pointed nose and deep creases at the sides of the mouth on Plate 33.1 and the higher forehead and long broken nose on Plate 33.2, the sculptor may have carved them as life-like characterizations.

Although large, full-volumed shapes show a like feeling in the two figures for the structural parts of the body, yet the design and proportions of these shapes are different. In Plate 33.1, the legs are long and widely spaced, the torso narrow, and the arms heavy, cut free of the torso and attached to the sides of the hips. The voids between the limbs give this figure an open design; while the emphasized joints of the arms and the spindle-like shapes of the legs divide the body into a number of closely integrated parts. This treatment is effectively evident in the angular rhythms of the outline. In comparison, Plate 33.2 has a compact design. The only open space is the meager one between the short and sturdy legs, even the feet being connected to form a block-like base. The thin arms are carved in high relief on the long torso; and the head is much larger in proportion. The body is more summary in treatment, even the joints being merely suggestions, and smooth vertical and curvilinear rhythmus mark the outline.

The individualization given by facial features in Plate 33.1, 2 appears in the realistic carving of the body in the example represented on Plate 39.2. This figure is partially composite in technique, the long arms having been carved separately and attached by tenons. A greater lifelikeness than is usually found in Salish sculpture distinguishes the explicit form of the parts of the body, such as the legs, arms and buttocks. Even the navel and the finger nails are carefully rendered. In the shaping of the large protruding belly, however, an individualistic element is introduced, suggesting that this may have been a portrait statue. Moreover the heavy squat proportions, the rectangular shape of the head, and the handling of facial features are strikingly unlike those of other Type B large figures.

This figure is carved in one of the most three-dimensional styles of the entire Northwest Coast. Broad, strongly carved planes, evident in the smooth curves of contours, describe the large heavy forms and express their volume. For example, the girth of the large torso and its heavy weight bearing down on the sturdy truncated legs are graphically represented. In profile, the flexion of the knees, indentation of the waist, protrusion of the belly, and the acute projection of nose, mouth and chin show vigor of form and expression. This is intensified by the tilt of the head and the wide spacing of the truncated legs, which tend to give balance to the figure and to create a slight twist, thus departing from a strict frontality. Small tool marks are apparent throughout the carving, no attempt having been made to remove them and to smooth out the surface. These add a texture to the surface which is not found on Plate 33.1, 2.

For its dramatic expression of movement, Plate 58.1 is unique among Salish sculpture. The pose is dynamic. The left arm is bent sharply at the elbow and pressed tightly against the chest and the right arm is held back of the body, the hand resting in the small of the back. To conform with these gestures, the right shoulder is lowered and brought forward, and the body is twisted at the waist. The widely spaced legs support and balance the movement of the forms above.

Contrasts of light and shade considerably augment this expression of movement. Deep undercutting provides an area of shadow around the perimeter of the face and in the mouth. This treatment emphasizes the face and focuses attention upon the open mouth as the center of interest[45]. The position of the left arm serves a similar purpose and integrates expressively the dramatic vocalization of the mouth with the movement of the forms below. The meager shaping of the component parts of this figure suggests that the sculptor was more absorbed with the problem of movement than with that of form. Although he was far from successful, his greatest attention was obviously given to the rendering of the difficult pose of the shoulders and the arrangement of the arms.

In technique, the figure is rough and uneven. No care was given to the smoothness of surfaces, or to the finish of detail.

HOUSE POSTS

Carved house posts measuring from six to twelve feet high are the most monumental of Salish sculptures. The majority of them were wall posts designed to be seen only from the front and sides; while the survival of paint on many

---

[45] Only a sight suggestion of projection appears in the brows, and the eyes, set close to the nose in an area of shadow, are moderately sized incised circles with pointed ends. Thus the eyes are only at best secondary centers of interest and as such are placed in shadow, hence not distracting from the mouth. Since the eye is a shallow depression, it does not seem likely that there was originally any inlay; rather the eye was probably painted, as faint traces of red seem to indicate.

examples suggests that they were all originally painted. These carvings, on the basis of stylistic resemblances, may be divided into three types.

Type A

The five examples of this type represent standing figures holding an animal (Plates 45; 46; 53.3; 55.1). With the exception of Plate 45, they have a number of similar style elements. A wide curvilinear abacus-like form rests on the head and supports a high impost block in such a way that it carries the weight of the house beams down through the head to the heavy forms below. The rectangularly shaped heads have slightly pointed chins and large tab-like ears. Facial features are characterized by low curved brows, small round eyes and narrow mouths. All five figures have their arms flexed in a similar manner and hold the animal so that it forms a diagonal across the torso, its head resting against the right arm and pointing upward. Elbow and wrist joints are shown in every case and fingers are delineated by incised lines on the small hands. The animals, except the one on Plate 45, are small quadripeds. Of these carvings, the three illustrated by Plates 46 and 55.1 are similar in design and treatment; while those on Plates 45 and 67 have their own distinctive style elements.

Two of the posts are shown in situ on Plate 55.1[46]. The upper part of each seems almost identical in design and in proportion to that represented on Plate 46[47]. Large heads, carved entirely in the round, are supported by short, heavy necks. Square, hunched-up shoulders repeat the horizontal line of the abacus above. The torsos are long and narrow, and the figures are so short-waisted that the measurements from the hips to the crotch are almost equal to those from the hips to the shoulders. Very short arms emphasize this proportioning of the torso.

The lower part of these three posts differs somewhat. Those on Plate 55.1 have heavy, cylindrical legs, short below and very long above the knees due to the high placing of the hips, and roughly carved feet which appear to stand on a base. The one on Plate 46 seems to have its similarly shaped heavy legs truncated just below the knees[48]. Also characteristic of these figures is the carving of bone and muscle structure. For example, the clavicle bones and the vertical channel between the ribs are shaped, and the muscles of the upper

---

[46] A notch cut in the impost block provides accommodation for the cross beam, the wall beam appearing to rest on the top of this.

[47] I have not had the opportunity to examine the three carvings on Plates 46 and 55.1. Since the photograph from which Plate 55.1 was made was unfortunately of poor quality, a more complete analysis of the style of these figures is not possible.

[48] It is impossible to tell from the photograph whether the legs were originally terminated in this manner, or whether they were cut off when the figure was moved from its original position in the interior to the exterior of, probably, another house. The plinth block has also apparently been cut down in size.

arm, which are tense as though an effort were required to support or restrain the animal, are carefully modelled. The details give the carvings a strong quality of naturalism[49].

As caryatid or supporting figures they are effectively composed. The horizontals of the abacus and shoulders are strongly supported by the vertical masses of head, neck, torso and legs. It is important to note that in Plate 46 the width of the shoulders agrees with the diameter of the abacus block, that this width is retained in the outline of the arms, and that it is considerably increased in the sturdy columnar legs. The heavy forms, proportioning of parts, and unity of design make these three figures appear more than adequate for the weight they have to support. In style they are so nearly alike that they may well have been made in the same locality.

A weaker style and technique characterize the carving which appears on Plate 53.3. The proportions are more attenuated, and the head and abacus block greatly reduced in size. As a further distinctive feature, the figure is represented as clothed in a short tunic, belted in at the waist, the skirt of the tunic and the belt both depicted sculpturally. The parts of the upper half of the carving are poorly shaped, weakly integrated: the arms, chest and shoulders are almost flat, and the thick neck is joined with the back of the head in such a way that the face seems carved in high relief[50]. Very large tab-like ears are set far down at either side of the head, a distortion in size and shape of those found on Plate 46. The forms of the lower part of the figure are a little more successfully rendered. The waist and skirt of the tunic are columnar in treatment, and the legs are meagerly shaped, four-sided forms with the edges bevelled off[51]. The knees are defined by circular projections carved in relief on the flat surface. As a work of sculpture, this figure has poor quality and, as a supporting post, it appears weak and ineffectual.

The carving on Plate 45 is different in design and style from the other four examples of this type. It apparently represents a half-length figure and is composed of four distinctive parts: head, neck, torso and base. Descriptive detail is rendered in relief on the rounded surfaces of these shapes, which rest compactly one on top of the other. Emphasis in the design is placed on the diagrammatic balancing of horizontals and verticals, the preponderance of strongly marked horizontals in the upper part contributing effectively to the expression of weight and stability. The semi-circular character of the base

---

[49] Male sex organs seem to be represented on the right figure on Plate 55.1 and on that on Plate 46, although it is difficult to ascertain from the photograph the accuracy of this observation.

[50] The neck and upper torso have split, and the shoulders now contain three pieces of wood added to strengthen them. It is therefore apparent that this considerably detracts from the original appearance of the figure; but the basic shapes and relationships were not changed in making these repairs.'

[51] Faint evidence of paint has survived to show that this carving, as others of its type, was painted.

defines the broad surfaces of the parts above and imprints upon the finished figure an agreement with the original shape of the half-log from which it was carved.

The modelling of surfaces and the treatment of detail does not detract from the nearly geometric shaping of the four parts. The head is large in proportion, truncated at top and bottom, and divided into two horizontal halves by the hat-like design of the upper part. A curvilinear geometric design carved in relief decorates the front of this part, which contains no suggestion of orbital structure but is handled as a tight, constricting surface. The face is described by a single plane which rounds out to indicate the cheekbones; and the large facial features are set closely together. The eyes are emphasized by an incised delineation and by the use of black and white paint. A small tongue hangs limply out of the crescent-shaped mouth, the interior of which is picked out in white paint. Also unique to figures of this type is the absence of ears and the broad red band around the lower edge of the face with its sharp zigzag design carved in low relief and painted alternately red and black. The thick neck is likewise painted white.

The torso is dominated by the animal whose snout extends to the very top of the chest. Lacking feet and with a long crocodile-like head, this animal is of different species than those depicted on other house posts. It is carved in high relief and painted red, black, and white against the white background of the figure. The thin arms, carved in high relief on the surface of the torso, are without shoulder articulation; while the lower are slightly more modelled than the upper arms[52]. As a secondary center of interest, the animal so effectively carries the eye of the observer up to the head of the figure that these two focal points are brought into close relationship. This expressive integration compensates for the lack of an organic connection between the shapes of the carving. A broad red band encircles the bottom of the torso, while the base itself is painted black. Very little modelling, other than that of the parts in relief, appears on the torso.

Type B

Four of the five examples of this type of post (Plates 51a, b; 52a, b; 53.2) are shaped with the following parts: the architectural members of plinth and abacus, a human head and neck, and a large geometric planklike form below. The other example (Plate 55.2) does not have a plinth. All of these posts retain traces of an original polychromy. Although differences in proportion, style and technique are found in each of them, those represented on Plates 52, 53.2 and 55.2

---

[52] The speckled design painted on the hands seems to have too close an affiliation with that of the animal to have any descriptive or expressive association with the hands themselves.

appear to belong to one common tradition, and those on Plate 51.a and b to another.

The carving shown on Plate 53.2 has in the treatment of the head, facial features, neck and shoulders close stylistic resemblances to the one on Plate 53.3 (cf. also Plate 54, 1—4). This is further seen in the painted horizontal stripes around the neck and in the design on the face. The latter, now faint and almost indistinct on Plate 53.3 (cf. Plate 54), forms an angular pattern around the mouth and chin. From there it spreads over both sides of the face, this being quite apparent on Plate 53.2. It should be noted that in the latter design a thin moustache-like pattern appears around the mouth and extends down beyond the corners of the mouth to the chin.

In both examples the rendering of the animated animals is similar. The single one on Plate 53.3, although more elongated, seems to be of the same species as the two pair moving in opposition up and down the plank on Plate 53.2. In both cases these little figures are carved in very high relief, with directness and vigor of form.

The design of the post on Plate 53.2 shows a more complex subject matter than that of Plate 53.3. There are apparently three centers of interest: the confronted animals, the head of the human figure and the now mutilated half-figure carved in high relief on the face of the tall impost block. While the verticals discernible in the design of the latter and in the treatment of the animal forms tend to focus attention on the head, yet the eye soon wanders away, if to return again. This creates a nervous movement, as well as a diffusion of interest. It seems likely that the intention was to represent the owner of the post and the power or powers possessed by him[53]. It is nevertheless obvious that these centers of interest were of more importance separately than as parts of an organic figure.

More rugged in technique, the carving illustrated by Plate 52 a, b resembles the forgoing in the shaping of facial features and in the proportioning of the neck. But the ears are set farther back on the head, the jaw is square and both the head and the neck appear more columnar in shape and more structurally related. The design of the face painting on these two works also differs considerably. That on Plate 52 has a basic pattern of large dots, with some evidence surviving to suggest that at least some of these were connected by broad lines.

---

[53] The meager catalogue description of this post only partially supports this interpretation: "... spirit seen by the owner in the woods when preparing for secret society Tiyi'-wan" (cf. Boas, 1891, p. 564). This does not make it clear whether the entire carving represents the spirit or merely some detail, such as the animals. On the other hand, it is possible that the face painting may indicate the owner's membership in the secret society and that the carving on the impost-block may be in the nature of a crest, thus indicating the wealth and prestige of the owner. Barnett mentions that crests were purchased in this area (1942, p. 387). If this were the case, the post would certainly be both religious and social.

Only in the marking off of the zone of the mouth and in the horizontal stripes in the neck is there any similarity of painted designs.

The plank base or "body" of this post differs strikingly from others of the group. At the base of the neck a curious octagonal bolt-like collar fits tightly, its outer face cut with a flat surface and a greater projection than the neck, and its lower side continued as a long, tapering high relief shape almost to the bottom of the post. To either side of this collar "shoulders" are cut comparable to those on Plate 53.2. In conjunction with a curvilinear cut below, to either side of the collar "handle", these shoulders form a geometric design in low relief having the shape of an irregular octagon. When seen from the front, this design, together with the vertical "handle" of the collar, has something of the nature of a double-ax motive. It should be noted, moreover, that the curved lower sides of the "ax" repeat to an extent the curves of the lower sides of the collar. Slightly below the center on the base of the post two rectangular projecting surfaces are cut, each of which supports an animal finely carved in very high relief. The surface of this base has therefore a depth of relief carving. With the exception of the animal forms, the geometric shapes of the base suggest that the subject matter of this post may have been more symbolic than that of most other house posts.

The focal point of the compact design is the head. The upward movement of the animals and their proximity to the vertical axis of the geometric forms lead up to and relate these forms with the head. But in the composition of the design, the sculptor kept in mind that he was carving an architectural supporting member. Thus the heavy, columnar head and neck rest solidly on the "collar" which appears to distribute this weight to the rectangular plank below.

Design elements somewhat similar to the geometric forms of the lower part of this post also appear on the short post figured on Plate 55.2,[54]. These are carved however in a higher relief and have a slightly different shape: the collar-like form, for example, now encircles a thick, naturalistic neck, its long extension is in bold relief, and the flanking forms on the "shoulders" more nearly resemble a double-ax motive. The surface of the collar and its pendant are decorated with circular pits which appear to have been made with an auger; while there are no animals on the flat plank base.

The upper part of this post is unlike that of the four other Type B house posts. A widely overhanging block, its under surface concave, suggests by its shape a native hat and replaces the defined architectural forms of abacus and impost block. The head, facial features and ears have a strong lifelikeness in their delineation and modelling. These are in contrast to the geometric shapes

---

[54] It would seem that only the upper portion of the original post has survived but again, I am unable to say that this is so, since I have not had the opportunity to examine the carving. Several of this type of post have recently been acquired by the Provincial Museum in Victoria, B.C.

of the base. In style, this post therefore combines in a pedantic manner naturalistic and plastic with conventionalized forms.

A similar type of post, resembling somewhat in its design that found on Plate 53.2, appears on Plate 51a, b. The head and neck, carved in the round, rest on a simple rectangular base and support architectural forms so mutilated that it is difficult to determine accurately their original character. The thick base is four-sided and only a bevelling of the "shoulders" suggests any sculptural treatment. A simple cylindrical shape represents the neck, and the head, comparatively small and round, is terminated abruptly just below the mouth. Faint traces of an indistinguishable light and dark coloration remain on what appears to be fragments of a shallow abacus and a large impost block to show that they were originally painted.

The facial features of these two carvings are stylistically similar. Three rounded, inflated areas mark the forehead and cheeks, and three adjacent sunken areas set off the eyes and mouth. The eyebrows slant sharply upward from the bridge of a short, straight nose of moderate height. It is apparent therefore that light and shade are important elements in this style. In technique, surface modelling is summary and the delineation of such features as the eyes and mouth is crude, although the expression of volume gives these heads a strong sculptural quality.

Type C

Type C consists of a number of house posts with geometric carvings (Plates 40.2, 3; 50.1, 2; 53.1; 56.1, 2). They are all shaped from a log bisected vertically. The rounded front surface is divided into three parts, a flat rectangular lower section and two superimposed barrel-shaped sections always separated by a deeply depressed collar. Sometimes a like collar marks off the lower section, as on Plate 53.1. The upper sections in frontal profile describe carefully shaped truncated ovals which in cross-section are segments of a circle. The top section is usually larger and more attenuated than the sections below. In proportion the rectangular base appears to have been designed to harmonize with the profiles of the rounded shapes above, thus the narrow and tall base on Plate 53.1 and the wide and squat one on Plate 50.1. An additional rounded section was added to the top of the larger posts (Plate 56.1), while a similar rounded section is sometimes found at the top of posts carved with human figures (Plate 54.1, 2).

Independently of their sculptural and architectural character, portions of the various sections were frequently decorated with painted designs (Plate 53.1). Carved surface decoration also appears on some of the shapes, such as the zigzag depressed pattern bordering the two sides of the base of the latter specimen, the large coffer-like vertical rectangles ranged in parallel rows on the rounded sections of the posts on Plate 50.1, and the sunken circular decorations also spaced in rows on the top sections of the two posts to the left on Plate 54. All of these surface carvings are geometric; and, while they give a degree of depth, especially on Plate 50.1, they do not disturb the large shapes into which the posts are divided. It is this feeling for bold simple shapes and clarity of outline, plus the balancing of their vertical and horizontal rhythms that make these geometric posts important examples of Salish style.

POST FIGURES

The eight specimens representative of this class are stylistically and functionally different from the carved house posts. Due to their divergent form and style, no generalities can be drawn for the class as a whole. These carvings may be divided on the basis of size and purpose into three types.

Type A

Two examples, Plates 39.1, 58.2, illustrate this type. The one figured on Plate 58.2 somewhat resembles in the elements of its style an architectural sculpture, such as a house post. Carved from a segment of a log, the shape of which is retained in the cylindrical drum at the base, the figure is attached to a plank background, part of the form being rendered in high relief and part practically in the round. A flat cap-like form, composed of two low overlapping sections, fits tightly on the head and furnishes a comparatively flat surface which could have supported a horizontal architectural member. If such were the case, it is unlikely that it was thus used as an interior post, since a beam resting on the head would have cast a dark shadow, thereby obscuring the features of the face. It is more reasonable to suppose that this was an exterior post. Several hypothetical interpretations of content suggest just such an architectural function. On the basis of pose and proportions it may have been (1) a commemorative funerary carving, either set up at the site of the grave or inserted into the structure of a grave house as a trumeau figure (cf. Plate 50.1), or (2) a power figure and as such inserted in the exterior wall of a house as a "crest"[55]. In either case the position of the hands and the mutilated portion of the torso below them suggest that the figure originally held something, probably an animal. This would substantiate either interpretation.

Heavy, full-volumed forms characterize the almost naturalistic proportions of the carving. Joints and muscle structure are well modelled in the upper part of the body, although the short legs are generalized shapes that swing forward and down from the hips in an unbroken volume, only the curvature of the outline implying knee joints. The abrupt termination of the legs and the roughly shaped and now mutilated ankles and feet indicate that the sculptor

---

[55] cf. Barnett, 1938, p. 128.
[56] A similar treatment has been noted above in the specimens shown on Pl. 30.

may have represented the figure as wearing trousers[56]. Long exposure to the elements has given the surface a weathered appearance and practically all traces of color have disappeared, only a light discoloration remaining in the triangular area around the mouth. No part of the figure is carved in the round, but deep undercutting between the arms and the torso and around the forms gives the carving a strong threedimensional appearance. This is the work of an accomplished sculptor whose technique gave him almost complete command of his medium. His treatment of human form is not stylized, nor is it realistic, but it is rather a simplified expression in terms of the material and of an established naturalistic convention.

The figure shown on Plate 39.1, although carved in the round and lacking the realistic details noted in the example on Plate 58.2, has a similar feeling for compact, full-volumed forms. It represents however in its simpler design, its proportions and facial features, a stylization that emphasizes the large rounded head.

Type B

Similar heavy, simplified forms characterize the two examples of the second type in this class (Plates 28; 37)[57]. Both represent grave effigies wearing the swaixwe mask. They therefore commemorate the privileged right of the deceased. In contrast to the figures of Type A, the example illustrated on Plate 28 has an active pose. The rounded forms of the body have a kneeling posture suggesting the representation of a pose in a dance. Although the forms are generalized, emphasis is placed on the rendering of joints, and the short, heavily proportioned parts convey the impression of a strong muscular body. The left arm forms a loop at the side, the hand resting on the thigh, and the right arm is sharply flexed, the hand gripping the tongue in the act of holding the mask in place. All details of the swaixwe mask are given: peg eyes, animal-head nose, protruding tongue, and such details of costume as the surmounting feathers. A curious feature is that only one animal head is carved on top instead of the usual two. The detailed carving of the mask contrasts with the simplified handling of the body and indicates the greater importance of that part of the figure. In the excellence of its technique and the naturalism of its forms and pose, this carving equals if it does not surpass those qualities noted in Plate 58.2.

The second of these masked post figures (Plate 37) is a static, frontally posed half-figure. The body is relatively flat and highly stylized, and the mask differs in type from that of Plate 28. The details of costume and the animal heads are missing, while the peg eyes, their deep hollows, and the protruding tongue are larger in scale and carved with great boldness. No recognizable human forms appear in this post. It lacks the naturalism of expression of the

---

[57] These two plates show single examples of identical pairs of carvings in the American Museum of Natural History. The two not illustrated are numbered 16—7075 and 16— 4693.

figure on Plate 28, but it has in common with the latter a simplification of design, emphasis on heavy volumes, and a concentration on bold, dramatic detail.

Type C

The four examples of the third type in this class are small carvings made as decorations for the top of loom posts. Two of them (Plate 47.1, 2) represent human heads slightly under lifesize on thick columnar necks. In style they are stiff and formalized. Expanding surface planes describe the volumes of forehead, coiffure or hat, cheeks and chin, while the mouth and nose protrude from depressed areas. The eyes are delineated by deep incised lines, and the straight brows parallel the horizontal line of the jaw. The surface of the loom post is decorated with an incised geometric pattern and the top is rounded, as though in simulation of the shoulders of a human figure. Thus the heads seem functionally related in design to the posts below. It is unlikely that these were more than decorative carvings handled in the style idiom common to the region or tribe of their origin.

The other two loom post decorations (Plate 41.1, 2) are more important examples of Salish sculpture. Although small in size, they are carved in a vigorous style.

The one illustrated on Plate 41.1 represents a small human figure dressed apparently in a cloak, arms held akimbo, sitting on the top of a small post. A circular spool-like form is carved at the top of the flat loom post, while a crown-like form rests on top of it and serves as a base into which the small post and its surmounting figure fit. The carved figure is therefore not related in design to the loom post below. Very general shapes describe the essential parts of the little figure. The legs, carved in relief, are bent at the knees and have small, block-like feet, and the flexed arms under the drapery form a diamond-shaped background against which the torso is carved in high relief. A proportionately large, square head overhangs the long neck which forms the upper part of the diamond design below. A small, flat cap, deeply undercut all around, sits well down on the head. Of the facial features, only the nose is carved and faint survivals of color show that the eyes and probably the mouth were rendered in paint.

Comparable to this figure in style and in the naturalness of its pose, a small animal, similar to those found in so many Salish carvings, decorates the loom post on Plate 41.2. This animal, placed as though crawling downward, is carved practically in the round against a thin rectangular background. Between the carving and the top of the loom post there are four spindle-shaped, geometric forms of which the lower one is reversed in position and serves to check the downward movement created by the jagged profiles of the three above. Considerable care was therefore given to insure a design that would not seem to bear down too heavily on the loom plank below.

The animal form is reduced to a few easily recognizable essential shapes. These are not described realistically but are rendered as simplified sculptural parts which through their integration express the animal organically. Paint was used to mark off the shapes and to give such descriptive details as the eyes. Enough of the original paint remains to show that the basic color was a reddish-pink. A white collar was painted about the neck, the eyes were picked out with white, and black lines marked off the area of the face. This small figure has all of the animation usually found in Salish animal carvings.

FIGURE RELIEFS

Frequent references have been made above to the use of relief in the rendering of parts of some figures in the round. Numerous examples also show that the Salish often carved entirely in relief. As a class this is not homogeneous in style, subject matter or size; but similarities of concept and technique make it possible to group these carvings as high, low and incised relief.

Type A: High Relief

Animal forms, already discussed in connection with house posts[58], constitute an important group of high relief carvings. They were sometimes used independently of the human figure to decorate the flat planks that served as siding for grave houses. Six of them are represented (Plates 50.1, 2)[59]. The animals crawl up the heavy planks, the long claws of the widely splayed feet clinging to the surface and the rigid tail supporting the movement. The open mouth, as though the animal were crying out, is further evidence of animation. All six of these carvings have long rounded bodies, snout-like heads, and high prominent cranium bumps. Although considerably weathered, they still retain a vigorous, naturalistic quality.

The two animals shown on Plate 50.1b differ in style and in species from the other four. The head and snout are long and broad and are attached to the body without any indication of a neck, and the short feet grow directly out of the body which is continued by a very long, thick tail. All of the forms are simplified and, with the exception of the upper jaw, they are not cut free of the board. Although the parts are differentiated, they are so unified by the continuous volume that flows uninterruptedly throughout the figure that the form of the animal as a whole is more important than its component parts. The suggestion of bony structure and of articulation is therefore restricted to the skull and snout and to the four feet. In technique, broad surfaces give ef-

---

[58] cf. Plates 53.1, 52, 53.2 and the small figure on Plate 41.2.

[59] The grave house shown on Plate 50.1, now in the Museum of the American Indian, is also illustrated on Plate 50.2 as it was assembled "in the field" together with parts from other grave houses. It is apparent that the house as reassembled in the Museum of the American Indian is not a completed structure.

fective definition to the outlined forms, but little variation appears in the depth of the carving. Thus the relief lies within a few planes.

In contrast, the four animals illustrated by Plate 50.2 have short snouts and heads, long thick necks and thin round tails. The legs have well described joints and the forelegs are attached to the surface of the body by flat plate-like forms carved in a low relief[60]. This treatment separates them from the continuous volume that unifies all other parts of the figure. The four legs are carved in a lower relief than the rounded body; while the head with the half-open snout is carved in the round. All parts of these animals are carefully formed so that their nature and structure are defined, as, for example, in the treatment of muscle in the hindlegs and in the shaping of the under surface of the snout and neck. Planes are likewise kept broad, but considerable undercutting appears in the carving of the feet, while the forms themselves are in high relief and the surfaces rounded. In concept these animals are more descriptive, less generalized, and in technique more developed than those of Plate 50.1b.

Four other animal forms are shown on Plate 32. With the exception of the feet and tail, they are carved entirely in the round[61]. They also represent a different species of animal, one more nearly related in form and structure to a bear than to the lizard or mink-like mythological animals usually found in Salish sculpture. Although they are depicted as walking, not crawling, they show some kinship with the more frequently encountered animal forms in the rendering of the half-open, snout-like mouth, the incised oval eyes[62], and the long heavy tail[63] (cf. Plate 57). But the pointed ears further support their greater bear-like character. It should be observed that the lizard-like forms are almost always rendered without any indication of ears, the one exception being that shown on Plate 29. All parts necessary for an expression of the nature and structure of the animal are carved in sculptural forms that emphasize volume, mass and weight. Although some modelling is apparent, this is so simplified that it does not detract from the organic unity of the figure as a whole. Arranged in an interlocking rhythmical semi-circular design, these animals have a natural animation, a free movement. They are certainly the work of a master sculptor who had no technical limitations and was able to create a sculptural synthesis based on his observations of natural form.

---

[60] This method of attaching the forelegs also appears in the examples shown on Plates. 52, 53.2, 3, where, however, it is likewise used for the hindlegs.

[61] The high relief style of these animals is analogous to that of a large plank in the American Museum of Natural History (16—4653) upon which a full-length human figure is carved.

[62] Two variants seem to have been followed in the placing of the eyes: (1) as here, parallel to the end of the snout, or (2) as in Plate 50.1a, b, at right angles to it.

[63] These tails, only one of which has survived in an undamaged condition, certainly do not appear to be of a bear. In two instances, they are shown as lying flat on the back along the line of the backbone.

Other examples of Salish high relief carving are found on house posts (Plate 40.1—3). These project, sharply outlined, from a slightly convex background, the surface of the carving agreeing in its curvature with that of its background. Remnants of color indicate that, as usual, they were originally painted. In style and technique all three of these reliefs are different.

The one shown on Plate 40.3 represents a person holding a duck-like bird by the neck, its body pressed flatly against that of the figure, its neck held just below the chin and its open wings encircling the hips. The purpose of this carving may be, hypothetically, either to show a man holding a bird that represents his power, or to depict a mythological bird of some tribal or clan legend, in which case it might reveal the source of the prestige or power of a group. The head of the human figure, of the wide, pointed chin type, is outlined by undercutting and is not joined to the body by a carved neck, this probably having been rendered in paint (cf. also Plate 54). Brows, cheeks and chin are slightly modelled, and the eyes are delineated, the pupil formed by incised relief. The ears are small segments of a circle and are placed low and far back on the head, where they are carved in low relief. All parts of the body are executed in high relief, the outer profiles of the arms and legs being undercut. Within the outline of the long, slender arms, the torso is modelled in a lower relief, while the short legs are shaped in a very high relief. Particular care was taken to define the joints and muscular structure in the arms and legs. Parallel incised lines, repeated in the hat worn by the figure, delineate wing and tail feathers on the body of the bird. Varying depths of relief give to this carving important contrasts of light and shade[64]. The pose of the figure is comparable to that of the two figures shown on the two posts to the right on Plate 54.

In contrast, the relief on Plate 40.2 shows a meagerness in shaping the parts of the body and a greater emphasis on descriptive detail. It represents a person wearing a swaixwe mask with appropriate costume and rattle[65], (cf. Plate 42.2). The large mask, as the center of interest, is depicted with considerable accuracy. The parallel groovings, so characteristic of the surface treatment of this .type of mask, are shown by shallow incisions; large round holes suggest that originally pegs may have been inserted in them to depict the customary peg-like eyes; and the upper jaw is undercut to provide the appropriate area of shadow. The feathers worn with the mask are represented at either side by

---

[64] It should be noted that in this carving the post is roughly divided to agree with the divisions¦ of the front surface, thus a block-like base, a rectangular division marking off the body of the figure, a section indicating the area from the shoulders to the top of the head, and two sections above. This treatment suggests a slightly greater integration of the relief with the shape of the post than in the examples on Plate 40.1 and 2.

[65] The description in the museum catalogue corroborates this identification (cf. below, Catalogue of Illustrations, p. 137) cf. Plates 28, 37.

horizontal incisions and above by radiating vertical lines, on which evenly spaced circles describe tufts of down (cf. Plate 42.1). A series of vertical overlapping incisions represent the feathered tunic, here hanging to the knees over the shapeless form underneath; and the small rattle of pecten shells held in the left hand is clearly shown. The figure stands on a semicircular bracket. With the exception of the mask, the relief is not as high as that of Plate 40.3 and a more extensive use is made of shallow incised carving.

The third of these house posts (Plate 40.1) differs from the above two in several important respects. The design, for instance, suggests in the superposition of figures the influence of the totem-pole tradition to the north[66]. The greater use of line, noticeable in the delineation of outlines, in the treatment of the eyes and in the rendering of the upper part of the torsos, is also in the northern tradition. The arms combine with the narrow shoulders to form segments of an oval. A slightly rounded surface defines the narrow, tapering torso of the upper figure, the spaces between it and the flexed arms being depressed to approximately the same depth as the background. An important feature in the rendering of the arms, apparent in all three of these house posts, is the undercutting of the upper outline of the forearms, more striking here in the left than in the right arm. This would help the illusion of roundness by creating a line of shadow, since these large posts would be seen from below, the level of the eye of the observer being about at the hips of the figure. This would also account for the sharp line of the shoulders and the flatness of the upper torso.

The trousered legs are similar in treatment to those of the grave figures on Plate 30.1—5. A projecting hood-like form frames the head, which is square, and repeats, although somewhat more angularly, the curve of the arms and shoulders below. The facial features are modelled, in contrast to the smooth planes of the body. Other distinctive stylistic features are the reduction of the figures to a few large simplified shapes and the delineation of these shapes in a bold, rhythmic design. In content, it suggests the crest or prestige carvings to the north, rather than the power figures of the south[67].

Type B: Low Relief

The shaman power board represented on Plate 7.1 is an excellent example of Salish low relief carving. The technique employed is that of cutting away the material around the form to allow it to project. This process is more arduous

---

[66] Probably for this reason the catalogue identifies this carving as a "totem pole of cedar; two human figures". The only approximation of a similar design previously observed in Salish work appears in the fragment of a half-figure carved in relief on the impost block in Plate 53.2. The design effect, however, is very different.

[67] A carved post of almost identical design and style is to be seen in the American Museum of Natural History (16—4701).

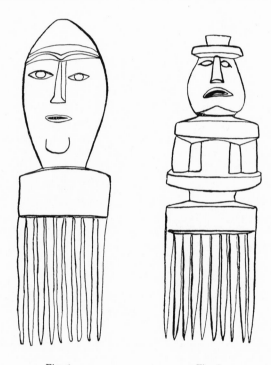

Fig. 1   Fig. 2

than carving in the round and is the same as that used in high reliefs. In this example, the head is carved in high relief, the outline undercut; while the forms below, with the exception of the neck, are rendered in a flat, very shallow relief.

It is obvious that the emphasis here is upon the head. This is carved with much greater care than the other parts of the form and attention is focused on it through the working out of the design. Placed in the upper center of the board, the head is directly beneath the apex of the sharp angle of the geometric design carved in very low relief. The three-zoned arrangement of facial features is strikingly apparent. Elegantly curved eyebrows, flanking a smaller curve over the bridge of the nose, project so far that they cast a dark shadow beneath, in which the close set, inlaid eyes are placed. Cheeks are described by roughly modelled surfaces, where the clearly apparent tool marks show that a smooth surface was not desired; while the outward jutting, flat plane of the lower jaw is marked off by horizontal lines flanking the end of the nose. The head itself is a well shaped ovoid, the widest point of which is at the eyebrow level. Distinctive of this relief is the spectacular treatment of the forehead. It is carfully designed with both lateral and vertical convex curvature and is deeply carved with five parallel horizontal grooves which extend entirely across it.

The long neck, with its slightly rounded surface, serves as a transitional form between the high relief of the head and the flat, low relief of the forms below. With the hands placed on the waist, arms and shoulders combine to form large, wide loops, the curved outlines of which carry the eye quickly up to the head and establish the curvilinear rhythms of the design. Below the waist, the outline spreads out at a sharp angle to left and right, thus repeating the degree of the angle above the head and emphasizing the diagonal rhythms in the pattern. The only details appearing in the lower part of the figure are the delineation of fingers carved in very low relief. A variety in bold design elements, dramatic contrasts in depth of relief, and a controlled technique give the carving its high aesthetic quality and make it an extremely interesting work.

This specimen appears to be a unique example of a very important type of Salish sculpture[68]. Wilkes, during his travels in western Washington Territory, was so struck by the number of "rudely carved painted planks" that he not only mentioned them in his text, but also published wood-cuts of some of them (Plate 7.2). The drawings from which these wood-cuts were made were done by Mr. Eld. Wilkes mentions that the planks were painted and that "the colors were exceedingly bright, of a kind of red pigment". It should be noted

---

[68] So far as I am aware this is the only survivor of these carved boards. To a large extent this may be accounted for by the practice recorded by Gibbs of placing "the tamahno-us board of the owner" near his grave after his death. Thus exposed to the weather and forgotten they would eventually disintegrate (Gibbs 1877, p. 203).

that the color still evident on the Plate 7.1 specimen is a very dark red and black. Meager as the wood-cuts are, they nevertheless reveal such similarities of design and style that there can be no doubt of their association with the type represented by Plate 7.1

Type C: Incised Relief

There are numerous examples of incised relief sculpture. This technique was used extensively to decorate horn and wooden dishes. The incised decorations on these dishes, usually circular in shape, are stylistically similar but show a variety of designs. In shape, the sides slope to a rounded bottom and rectangular sections extend above the lip at either side forming handles. These are continued under the dish as a projecting band and provide a field for combined figurative and geometric carvings (Plates 24.1, 2)[69]. Chevrons, sometimes angular, sometimes wavy in outline were the most frequently used geometric motives. In some specimens (Plate 24.1) they are disposed in parallel rows over the entire surface except that of the handles and their connecting band; and in many cases the chevrons near the rim of the dish have the triangular spaces between them perforated. Full-length skeletalized figures, surrounded by geometric borders, often appear (cf. Plate 24.1), one carved on either side, as decorations on the encircling band. The three-zoned type of face is also frequently used as a design on this part of the dish (cf. Plate 24.2). Pairs of these faces are often disposed in confronted fashion. Other motives are concentric rectangles and chevrons arranged in concentric semicircular rows with the triangular spaces between them deeply recessed.

In the rendering of figurative and geometric designs the same technique was employed. Although working in a relatively hard material, the sculptor did not use exclusively an incised, line technique, but often sunk the background, either by gouging or by sloping planes, thus allowing the design or form to stand out. In some instances, such as in the figure on Plate 24.1, this often crude technique produces an impression of considerable depth. The spacing and variety of design motives give these carved dishes a pleasing decorative quality. .

MASKS

As a class, carved wooden masks do not occupy the same key position in Salish sculpture as in that of other peoples of the Northwest Coast. In fact, instead of the great variety of types found, for instance, among their neighbors the Kwakiutl, the Salish had only two types, both versions of the swaixwe mask. But they are the most elaborately and carefully carved objects made

---

[69] Two excellent examples of Salish carved horn dishes, both from the Quinault tribe, are in the United States National Museum in Washington (127 860, 127 862).

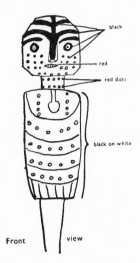
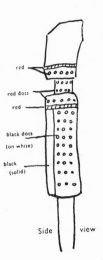
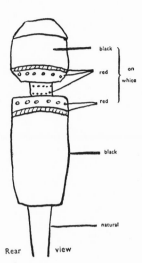

Front view

black

red

red dots

black on white

Side view

red

red dots

red

black dots
(on white)

black
(solid)

Rear view

black

red

red

on
white

black

natural

Fig. 3

Fig. 4

by them. All of their masks have dramatic designs which represent animalistic features and all of them were richly painted.

Type A

The nine examples of Type A are among the most interesting carvings of the entire Northwest Coast (Plates 34; 35; 38; 42.1, 2; 43; 48.1, 2; 49). They combine very naturalistic animal and bird heads with abstract designs to represent a fantastic mythological being. Their impressive forms are carved both in the round and in relief, and red, black and white paint is used to emphasize rhythmic and expressive elements in the design. Although important differences divide these nine specimens into three groups, they all share a number of features in common. A pair of bird or animal heads surmounts a wide round face and seems to represent ears. Large pegs are set as eye pupils in an extensive depressed area. The nose is often a fantastic protruding form. In every case a partly open mouth extends the width of the face, from which hangs a long, wide tongue that is decorated with carved and painted vertical stripes. These masks were worn at a sharp angle, as shown in Plate 42.2, and the open mouth functioned as eye-holes for the wearer. They should therefore be seen at this angle to appreciate their maximum plastic qualities. They should also be visualized with their accompanying costume, of which, judging from accounts, Plate 42.2 is only a poor recent version of a once almost completely feathered dress[70].

Group I. The examples on Plates 35; 42.1, 2; 43 and 48.1 form a stylistically related group. Above the long protruding tongue, the face has the shape of a horizontal ellipse, the sides curved and the top and bottom flattened. It describes a wide jowled animal face, an effect intensified by the treatment of the mouth and tongue. On Plate 43 the large curcular eye pits are almost tangent one with the other and three concentric circles are incised in the center of the low receding forehead. The two animal heads on top of the mask are carved in the round and appear to represent wolf or dog heads, mouths open and tongues hanging out as though the creatures were panting. Simplified and strongly plastic in treatment, these heads are good examples of Salish naturalistic animal style. The oval eye is here also depressed and the pupil carved in higher relief; the top of the cranium is flat; the nostrils are in low relief; and at the sides of the mouth two concentric incisions represent the wrinkles of loose flesh that are formed by the open mouth. The forequarters of a third animal, similar in style and in species to the above two, emerge from the open mouth and form the nose of the mask. The two paws appear to be gripping the edge of the eye rims, as though the small animal were making an effort to

---

[70] cf. Boas, 1894, p. 455.

pull itself out of the mouth[71]. Carved parallel grooves, which follow the rounded contour of the mask, connect this form with the two heads above.

Although similar to this mask in its proportions and design, the one illustrated on Plate 42.1 differs from it in certain significant respects. Two bird heads, identifiable as those of the eagle, now surmount the mask, while a third, carved in high relief and facing downward, forms the nose. To either side of the lower head, a wing pattern is carved. Units of this same pattern appear on the perimeter of the face and on the forehead; while the large crescent motive flanking the "nose" reappears just back of the beaks of the heads on top of the mask. The beaks of all three of the bird heads are depicted as half open. On this mask, the circular depressions of the eye areas are connected by a like depression across the bridge of the "nose". The examples figured on Plates 35, 42.2 and 48.1 are similar to this one in design. Several differences however should be noted. The most important are the carved and painted outlines accenting the upper curves of the eye areas and the curve over the bridge of the nose. The eye areas are also slightly deeper and the bird heads surmounting the mask are of different type: the cranium is rounder, the eyes aslant, the pupil rising out of a slightly depressed area, and the ends of the beak bent downward at a forty-five degree angle.

A precise bilateral symmetry distinguishes the style of the five masks in this group. Striking light and shade effects result from sharp contrasts of projecting forms and flat and sunken surfaces, while variety is also given by the strong vertical and curvilinear elements. Of particular interest is the adaptation of the linear patterns to the carved shapes, the character of which they emphasize. Equally noteworthy is the use of animal or bird forms to function as facial features of the mythological being whose heads the masks represent. These forms may also have served to give to the traditional pattern of the swaixwe mask individualized elements which would help to identify the mask as the prerogative of a specific group of persons whose powers or privileges it represented[72].

Group II. In comparison, the second group of Type A masks (cf. Plates 34, 48.2, 49) shows distinctive variations in shape and detail. Two of these (Plates 48.2, 49) seem to depict beavers. The two incisors are carved as extending in a curve from the upper jaw to a more naturalistic tongue beneath (cf. Plate 49b). In the third example (Plate 34), these teeth or tusks are missing. The upper

---

[71] This animated pose, coupled with the general similarity of form, suggests that these animals may possibly have represented the mythical minks so often encountered in Salish sculpture.

[72] In this connection a similarity should be noted between the proportions of the lower and upper parts of the mask and those of the coppers of the north (cf. note 35, p. 14 above). The vertical striping of the lower part of both objects is the same. The coppers were also symbols of privilege, as well as of great monetary value in their own right.

and lower lips of the mouth are in these three masks completely represented. The head is more angular in shape, wide at the forehead and narrower at the chin. It lacks the sweeping lateral curves which produce so strikingly in Plate 43 a jowl-like effect. The eyes are also carved somewhat differently. The pegs are now pupils and are set within sharply pointed oval eyes which are carved in low relief in the large sunken eye areas. Above the eyes, a narrow rim-like carving describes cranial structure; and below, a large, sharply pointed nose replaces the bird or animal forms of Group I, although in Plate 34 a small bird head seems to be carved on the front of this high, sharp nose. To either side of the nose and extending across the face, a band, carved in Plate 48.2 in high relief, represents wrinkled flesh caused by the partly open mouth. Incised surface designs are few in number and are used descriptively, i. e. the crescents on the front of the nose to indicate nostrils and the lines under the eagle heads to suggest feathers. Contrasts in these masks are less striking than in those of the first group. They lack the richness of design, the depth and vigor of form. In comparison, they seem dull and uninteresting, although their technique is on the same level.

Group III. A third group is represented by Plate 38. In proportion this mask differs from other Type A examples. It is comparatively narrow and the "tongue" is proportionately long. Other important differences appear in the carving of the nose and in the design of the "tongue". The nose is the head of a long snouted animal facing upward, the snout so high and long that it separates the eye areas. To either side of this nose, the forelegs of the animal are carved in relief. The treatment of the eyes and the mouth, with the exception of the "tongue", are somewhat similar to those on Plate 34. The "tongue" however becomes broader near the end and the central vertical relief band on it now has the shape of a tongue and is painted red. Unlike other swaixwe masks of the type the animal heads on top are partly composite: the high cranium and snout are carved separately and attached. The carved and painted surface designs, on the tongue, around the face and across the forehead, have little resemblance to those of other Type A masks. Technically it falls somewhat below the quality of those discussed above.

Type B

A single example represents the Type B mask (Plate 36). It has in common with Type A specimens only such general features as the projecting bird-heads and indications in the partly broken mouth of a protruding tongue. This swaixwe mask was designed to be worn over the face, the slits just below the pegs being eye-holes for the wearer. Unlike those of Type A, it was not carved from a single block, but consists of a number of separately carved and attached parts: the flat, anthropomorphic forms at either side; the bird-heads on the forehead; the small pegs on the cheeks; and the flat, rudely shaped piece along the top, which gives added height to the forehead and thus more adequate coverage for the head of the wearer. The mask appears to depict the mythological swaixwe with human rather than animal features; and in the design therefore the bird heads, as well as the flat carvings at the sides, are distinctly secondary in importance to the features of the face. The nature of this being is thus presented in such descriptive forms as contracted brows and bared teeth, rather than in geometric decorative ones.

The shape of this mask, without the flat pieces at the sides, is a somewhat more angular version of the one on Plate 49. A flat triangular area, with its apex at the notched contraction between the brows, slopes back to form the forehead, to which the bird heads are attached at either side. The large eyebrows are shaped with slightly concave surfaces; the sharp nose has wide nostrils strongly defined in high relief; and the long oval mouth has rounded ends slightly pulled up. A thin rim borders the mouth and represents lips; while stubby, wide teeth are carved in the upper and lower jaws, the latter being interrupted in the center by the thin protruding tongue. Although all of these facial features are carved, it is nevertheless significant that the left eye is painted on the projecting peg, the pupil and iris on the end, the pointed outline of the eye on either side. In comparison with other swaixwe masks, this not only indicates a marked departure in the concept of the peg in relationship to the eye, but it also shows a non-decorative use of paint.

The attached parts are less carefully carved than those of the mask proper. This is especially true of the bird heads, where the technique is quite rough and the greatest attention was given to the shaping of the long, flat bills[73]. The shape of the carved boards at either side of the face suggest full-length standing human figures; but only the flat surface of the head receives any carved definition. The features of the round face are carved in low relief and complement those of the mask proper. The only surface treatment below the heads appears on the right one where a series of roughly semi-circular lines are painted in the center of the board[74].

In the quality of its technique and in the vigor of its style the Salish mask compares favorably with the finest masks from the entire Northwest Coast region.

---

[73] It should be noted that, as in the birds and animals on the other swaixwe masks, the tops of the heads are here also flattened and the ends of the bills are cut in such a way as to imply that they are partly open. These however are not painted nor carved with any descriptive surface detail.

[74] It seems possible that these may be suggestions of skeletalized figures.

CHAPTER THREE

Tribal and Regional Distribution

The provenience of Salish sculpture is, in some instances, difficult to determine because the collector has failed to secure and record all of the facts he could have obtained. Such designations, for example, as "Vancouver Island, British Columbia" or "Coast Salish, British Columbia" give the merest notion of where the object was picked up. Frequently no mention is made as to how the specimen was acquired, whether by purchase from its original owners and so indigenous to the area, or by negotiation with a trader who might have brought it from a distance. This unfortunately also applies to some objects obtained by museums from dealers who had meager information as to their point of origin. But in spite of these deficiencies in information, most of the carvings are provided with sufficient data to place them by either tribe or area so that a characterization of the regional styles becomes possible.

Five major art areas can be perceived in Salish sculpture. They are, in the order in which they will be considered: (1) Western Washington, (2) Puget Sound, (3) Upper Fraser River, (4) Straits of Georgia, and (5) Vancouver Island. For purposes of discussion, this sequence is arbitrarily geographic, from south to north. These art areas should be correlated as follows with the ethnic sub-groups listed above[1]: Area 1, Western Washington, with Group 4, the Coast Salish of the Olympic Peninsula; Area 2, Puget Sound, with Group 3, the Coast Salish of Puget Sound-Hoods Canal; Area 3, Upper Fraser River, with Group 5, the Interior Salish of the Upper Fraser River; Area 4, Straits of Georgia, with Group 2, the Coast Salish of the lower and middle Fraser River; and Area 5, Vancouver Island, with Group 1, the Coast Salish of the Straits of Georgia. Where fully known, specimens will be assigned to their appropriate tribe; otherwise they will be considered in terms of their general area.

WESTERN WASHINGTON

Of the ten carvings from Area 1 (Plates 1—7 and SNM 2701, 2703)[2], all but two (SNM 2701, 2703) are reliably ascribed to the Quinault tribe. These two

---

[1] cf. Ch. 1, pp. 2—4, above.

[2] In this discussion of the distribution of objects by tribes and areas, constant reference should be made to Chart 2, pp. 64—65. Although no photographs pertaining to them are included among the illustrations for this paper, factual material of the two U.S. National Museum objects, SMN 2701, 2703, is listed in the Catalogue of Illustrations. These two objects are merely assigned in the museum catalogue to the Northwest Coast of America.

CHART 2 Distribution of Classes
Areas: 1. Western Washington; 2. Puget Sound; 3. Upper

CLASSES AND STYLES	Area 1: Quinault	Area 2: Duwamish	Snoqualmie	Skokomish	General
		AREAS AND TRIBES			
1. Figurine:					
Type A: Style 1	1, 2, 3				
Style 2	4, 5.1, 2				25
Type B: Style 1				23.1, 2	
Style 2	(2701, 2703)				
Type C:					
Type D:					
2. Large Figures:					
Type A: Style 1		8, 9, 10.1, 2, 11.1, 2, 12, 13.1			12
Style 2		13.2, 14, 15			17
Style 3			18.1, 2, 19.1, 2, 19.1a, 2b		
Style 4			20.1, 2, 21.1, 2		
Style 5		16.1–4			
Type B: Group 1	6			22	
Group 2					
Group 3					
3. House-Posts:					
Type A:					
Type B:					
Type C:					
4. Post Figures:					
Type A:					
Type B:					
Type C:					
5. Figure Reliefs:					
Type A:					
Type B:	7.1 ,2				
Type C:				24.1	24.2
6. Masks:					
Type A: Group 1					
Group 2					
Group 3					
Type B:					

and Styles by Areas and Tribes
Fraser River; 4. Straits of Georgia; 5. Vancouver Island

	Area 3:			Area 4:		Area 5:					
Thompson	Lillooet	General	Mu-skwivm	General	Comox	Nanaimo	Cowichan	Sanetch	Songish	General
26.2 26.1							44.1, 44.2a, b, c, d			
	27	30.1–5 31		29 33.1, 2	39.2			50.1, 2		58.1
						45, 46 40.2,3		51a, b 50.1a, 50.2	53.3 52, 53.2 53.1	55.1 55.2 56.1, 2
	28				39.1 37	41.1, 2	47.1, 2			58.2
			32		40.1	40.2, 3		50.1b, 50.2		57
				35 34 36	38	42.1, 2, 43	48.1 48.2, 49			

are however so close in style as to be almost certainly Quinault work. Three of the six classes of Salish sculpture, figurines, large figures and figure reliefs, are included in these ten carvings. There are no Quinault sculptures of classes 3, 4 and 6, house posts, post figures and masks, since these elements are apparently foreign to fundamental Quinault culture[3]. It is interesting to note that these sculptures fall into two categories, the religious, which includes the representation of shamans' guardian spirits, and the purely decorative[4]. Eight of the carvings belong to the first. This demonstrates the same importance accorded by early travellers and later investigators to the representation of "guardian spirits" among the Quinault[5]. Seven of the eight are carved in the round. Six are small shaman "guardian spirit wands", which constitute all but one of the figurines of Type A as already discussed and one is a large spirit figure (Type B). The eighth carving of this group is a relief figure (Type B), a shaman guardian spirit board.

All of these sculptures are closely related in style as well as content. The two purely decorative figurines (Type B), although showing obvious Quinault style elements, are somewhat less closely related (SNM 2701, 2703).

As a group, these sculptures are remarkably homogeneous in style and show important relationships with objects from the south, north and east.

Quinault Style

The ten examples of sculpture from western Washington are so consistently similar in design, content and technique that it is impossible not to characterize them as Quinault in style.

The carvings from this tribe represent the human figure and are small in size, the largest being thirty-six inches high (Plate 6). They are not architectural, and they were made to be used alone, rather than in combination with other carved objects. The figures have a static, frontal pose. Rudimentary, sometimes four-sided shapes, interpret the sturdy forms of the body, which are unified structurally by the simplified rendering of large joints. Attention is concentrated on the head because of its large proportions and the schematic treatment of its features. These facial features are distinctive of Quinault

---

[3] Swan, Willoughby and Olson make no mention of carved house posts or of large post figures; but Olson states that in the Klo'kwalle Secret Society the leaders (righ men) usually wore masks which represented their own individual guardian spirits (wolf, bear, birds, etc.) and that they used masks in no other rites (1936, pp. 120—121). He affirms moreover that this society existed in only three or four villages (op. cit., p. 12) and that his informants admitted that it came to them through intermarriage with the non-Salish Quilleute and Makah Indians to the north. This implies that the mask forms came with the institution of the Secret Society and that they were probably of the Nootka type which served as the prototype for the Quilleute and Makah masks.

[4] Reference should be made for the distribution of categories of content by areas and tribes to Chart 3, p. 68—69.

[5] cf. Swan, 1857, p.172; Willoughby, 1889, p. 278; Olson, 1936, pp. 141, 145, 148.

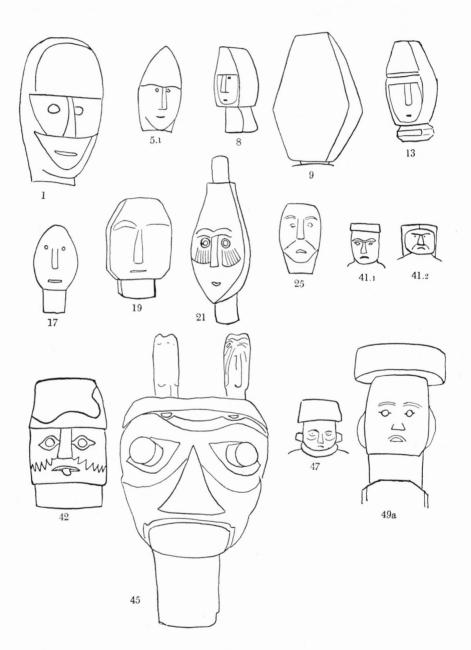

Fig. 5

figure carving. Two types are found: both have prominent brows; in one the lower surface of the face is depressed or dished-out; and in the other, it is given three strongly marked horizontal zones[6]. The spectacular appearance of these figures is enhanced by the use of deerhoof rattles, cedarbark, horse hair, shell inlay and color (cf. pp. 17—18). The way color was rubbed into the incised lines in Plates 6 and 7.1 suggest that it was used almost as an inlay.

Perforations within the design of the figures give depth to the forms and emphasize the verticals in the angular pattern of the body. These contrast with the horizontal line of the shoulders and are repeated in the curves of the outline of the head. The functional role of the bodyparts is made clear by the linear accents in the design, which also stress the expressive importance of the head. This is further accentuated in both facial types through dramatic contrasts of light and shade caused by depth of surface carving. Otherwise, surface planes are usually flat, rarely concave or convex.

Quinault sculpture has little variety in design, and its subject matter is almost entirely limited to the representation of shamans' power. But in technique, whether the forms are coarse and rough or smooth and refined in finish, it manifests a high degree of skill.

Three sub-styles are recognizable in the carvings from this tribe[7]. Of these, style 1 (Plates 1, 2, 3) is the strongest sculpturally and expressively. Since it is composed of all the characteristically Quinault elements, it may in fact be considered the basic tribal style.

By comparison, style 2 figures (Plates 4, 5.1, 2) are more schematic in design. Both the shapes and proportions of their parts are less lifelike. This is particularly evident in the adjustment of weight of the forms and in the pose of the figures. The deeply sunken faces are even less human than the three-zoned arrangement of features so typical of style 1[8].

Style 3 (Plates 6, 7.1, SNM 2701, 2703) comprises the most elaborate carvings of this area (cf. pp. 34, 44—46, 56—58). The three-zoned facial type is conspicuous in their designs, but the figures do not have the structural and expressive unity of those of style 1. A comparison of Plates 6 and 2 shows to what extent these style elements have been exploited, as, for example, in the elongation of the oval of the head, the depth of recession of the face, the pointed

---

[6] This design may possibly have resulted from a stylized rendering of the long, horizontal sticks worn through the nasal septum by the northern peoples of the Northwest Coast (cf. drawing by John Webber made in 1778, in Smithsonian Miscell.Coll., 80, no. 10, Plate 7). Through trade and war contacts with the north, this practice was apparently one of a number of cultural elements acquired by the Quinault. This would thus represent an element of their own culture (cf. Curtis, 1913, 9, pp. 9—11, 42; Olson, 1936, pp. 11—13).

[7] Quinault sub-styles 1 and 2 largely agree with styles 1 and 2 of Type A of the Figurine Class. To this style should be assigned the Quinault wand in the U.S. National Museum, 127 864.

[8] Thus one of the distinguishing Quinault features is not found in style 2 carvings.

CHART 3 Distribution of Categories

	I.	II.			Areas and
	Quinault	Duwamish	Snoqualmie	Skokomish	General
1. Religious: expression of power	1, 2, 3, 4, 5.1, 2, 6, 7.1 7.2	8, 9, 10, 11, 13.1 13.2, 14, 15, 16.1–4	18.1, 2 19.1, 19.2, 19.1a, 19.2a, 20.1, 20.2, 21.1, 2	22	12, 17, 25
2. Socio-Religious: a) Power, owner, control					
b) Commemorative figure with animal (power)					
3. Social: a) Commemorative grave or prestige figure					
b) Narrative funerary					
c) Prestige					
4. Decorative	2701 2703			23.1 23.2 24.1	24.2

jutting chin, and the sloping planes of the face. Detail is here emphasized, as in the toes and hands, the parallel chevrons on the chest and the inlaid teeth. This same style appears in Plate 7.1, which is so analogous in style to Plate 6 that both may originally have come from the same village, if not from the hand of the same sculptor[9]. Style 3, because of its near virtuosity in design and tech-

---

[9] It should be noted that both of these carvings were collected at the same site and at about the same time (cf. Catalogue of Illustrations).

of Content by Areas and Tribes

Tribes

Thompson	Lillooet	General	Muskwium	General	Comox	Nanaimo	Cowichan	Sanetch	Songish	General
III.	III.	III.	IV.	IV.	V.	V.	V.	V.	V.	V.
26.1, 2			32					50.1b, 50.2	53.1	56.1, 2 57
							44.1, 44.2a, b,c,d, 45	51a, b	52, 53.2, 3	55.1, 55.2
				29				50.1, 2		58.2
	27, 28	30 31			37, 39.1 40.1	40.2 40.3				
				33	39.2					58.1
				34 35 36	38	42.1 42.2 43	48.1, 48.2, 49			
						41.1 41.2	47.1, 47.2	50.1a 50.2		

nique and its development of the decorative and dramatic possibilities of other styles in this area, can be considered a Quinault "eclectic" style[10].

---

[10] On the basis of general style features, Plate 3 is related to style 1, but certain parallels between this rather poorly carved figure and that on Plate 6 should be pointed out. The most obvious of these is the elongated shaping of the head. Other similarities are: the high thin nose; the long chin with its flat sloping surface plane; and the coarse parallel incisoins on the upper part of the chest, here reversed in direction.

CHART 4   Tribal and Regional Styles, Influences, Comparisons

AREAS AND TRIBES	Styles	Influences and Comparisons

1. Western
    Washington
    Quinault
	1. 1, 2, 3
	 2. 4, 5.1, 2
	 3. 6, 7.1, 2, (2701, 2703)
		59.1, 62.1, 2
		 59.1, 62.1, 2, 64.1, 2, 59.2
		 59.2, 60.2, 61.1, 62.2

2. Puget Sound
    Duwamish
 	
    Snoqualmie
 	
    Nisqually
    Skokomish
     (Twana)
 	
    Chehalis
    General
	1. 8, 9, 10.1, 2, 11.1, 2,
	    12, 13.1
	 2. 13.2, 14, 15, 16.1–4
	 3. 18.1, 2, 19.1, 2,
	    19.1a, 2a
	 4. 20.1, 2, 21.1, 2
	
	 5. 17
	
	 6. 22,
	 7. 24.1
	 8. 23.1, 2
	 9. 24.2
	 10. 25
		5.1, 2, 59.2, 59.1, 62.1, 2
		
		 62.1, 2, 7.2, 64.1
		 Duwamish styles 1 and 2
		
		 Snoqualmie style 3; 13.1, 2,
		    14, 15, 10.2
		 13.2, 14, 6, 7.1
		
		 5.1, 6, 59.1, 60.2
		 24.2, 61.1
		 16,1–4, 63.2
		 24.1
		 1, 2, 6, 22, 5.1, 2; Snoqual-
		    mie styles 3 and 4

3. Upper Fraser River
    Thompson
    Lillooet
    General
	1. 26.1, 2
	 2. 27
	 3. 30.1–5
	 4. 31
	 5. 28
		2, 3
		 7.1, 15, 18.1, 30.1–5
		 27
		 65.1
		 27, 29, 31, 33.1, 2, 65.1, 67

4. Straits of Georgia
    General
	1. 29
	 2. 33.1, 2
	
	 3. 32
	 4. 36
	 5. 35
	 6. 34
		27, 30.1–5, 28, 66.2, 67.1, 2
		 39.2, 5.1, 65.1, 67.1, 66.2,
		    69.1
		 29
		 69.2, 70.2, 71.1, 2
		 42.2, 48.1, 2, 49
		 36, 42.2, 48.1

5. Vancouver Island
    Comox
	1. 39.2
	 2. 39.1, 40.1
	 3. 37
	 4. 38
		33.1, 2, 67.1, 2, 69.1
		 39.2, 65.1, 67.1, 2
		 39.1, 2, 71.2
		 34, 35, 37, 43, 48.2, 49,
		    69.2, 70.2

Nanaimo	1. 40.2, 3 2. 41.1, 2 3. 42.1, 2 4. 43	40.1, 33.1, 2, 50.1 23.1 48.1, 35 42.1, 48.1, 35, 42.2, 34

AREAS AND TRIBES	Styles	Influences and Comparisons
Cowichan	1. 44.2 a, b, c, d 2. 46, 55.1 3. 45 4. 48.1, 2, 49	30.1–5, 29, 27, 67.1 44.2 a, d 15 42.2, 35, 34
Sanetch	1. 50.1, 2 2. 51 a, b, 3. 50.1 a (50.2)	27, 30.1–5, 29, 13.1 45, 20.1, 29, 13.1, 19.1 a, 21.1 56.1,2, 53.1, 19,2, 19.2 a
Songish	1. 52 a, b 2. 53.2 3. 53.3 (54.3) 4. 53.1	45, 51 a, 53.1, 55.2, 57 52 a, b, 53.1, 57 46, 55.1 56.1, 2, 50.1, 2, 19.2, 19.2 a
General	1. 55.2 2. 56.1, 2 3. 57 4. 58.1, 2	52 a, b 50.1 a, 53.1, 51 a, b 52 a, b

Through travel and trade the Quinault had contacts as far north as Cape Flattery, south to the coastal region of the Columbia River, and inland to the upper reaches of Puget Sound[11]. Although there were "very frequent intermarriages" into groups to the north as well as to the south, it is "puzzling why there were not more northern elements in Quinault culture[12]." Their sculpture, indeed shows little resemblance to northern style, but certain strong similarities with western and southern, particularly that of the Wasco and Chinook tribes of the middle Columbia River[13]. Their manufacture was, in fact, "both aesthetically and practically inferior to that of the tribes to the north, but better than that to the south[14]." In its aesthetic and technical qualities, Quinault sculpture compares favorably with that of their important northern neighbors, the Quilleute and the Makah, while it surpasses the work of the southern tribes, with which it is most nearly analogous.

[11] cf. Olson, 1936, p. 11. The latter contacts were through intermarriage with Lower Chehalis peoples who in turn had very definite north-south contacts (Smith, M. W., 1939, p. 220).

[12] Olson, 1936, p. 13. Among the elements cited by Olson as distinctly northern are the following: whale hunting (they were the southernmost people to engage in this pusuit and then only to a slight extent), and the presence of the tsa'djak and klo'kwalle secret societies (but there again they were near the southern margin of the region in which these societies existed and they were found in only "three or four villages").

[13] Southern elements in their culture included the gable-roofed house, the possession of the horse in pre-European days (they were the most northern tribe to have horses at that time), and a portion of their mythology (cf. op. cit., p. 12).

[14] Op. cit., p. 66.

For example, three Wasco-Chinookan carvings, a small figure (Plate 59.1) and two shaman's wands (Plates 62.1, 2), have the characteristic three-zoned facial type of style 1, but they are cruder technically. The treatment of facial features shown on Plate 62.1, 2 and the pose of the legs on Plate 59.1 are also like those found on Plates 1, 2 and 3 of style 1[15]. Other stylistic affinities between these two groups appear in the shaping of the lower portions of the face, the two Wasco shaman sticks agreeing with those of Plate 3 and those of Plate 59.1 with Plates 1 and 2. But in the three southern examples, the narrow forehead and the tapering, pointed cranium differ from the high, rounded heads of style 1 figures. Another point of similarity is the use of inlay to represent eyes. The shell inlay in Plate 59.1 agrees with Quinault practice, while the single extant bead in Plate 62.2 has its parallel in Plate 1. Traces of reddish color appear on Plate 62.1, 2 and on the Quinault figures.

Numerous resemblances occur between Quinault style 2 carvings and those of other areas. These are clearly apparent. The pointed heads in Plate 5.1, 2, for instance, are similar to that of the Wasco-Chinook figure on Plate 59.1 and the rounded chins to those on Plate 62.1, 2. The shape of the head as a whole, however, is like that of the Quilleute rattle on Plate 64.1; while the sunken face of these style 2 carvings can likewise be compared with Plate 64.1, and with those of the Chinook carvings on Plate 59.2[16] and the Nootka rattle on Plate 64.2.

Similarities are also found between Quinault style 3 carvings and those of the Wasco-Chinook tribes. As an example, the parallel line design on the head of the figure on Plate 7.1 resembles that of the body on Plate 59.2. The use of parallel lines, in fact, is the strongest single characteristic of the middle Columbia River style[17]. Another significant feature of this style is the skeletalized rendering of form[18], of which the incised treatment on Plates 75.1 and 76.1 and the open work handling on Plate 62.2 are good examples. To represent rib structure parallel V-shaped designs are frequently used. Ribs are also indicated in like manner on two Quinault figures, the style 1 carving on Plate 3 and the style 3 example on Plate 6, where the V-shaped incisions are more

---

[15] It should be noted that Pl.59.1 is but slightly smaller than the carvings of style 1, measuring $15^1/_2$ inches long; while the carved portions of the shaman's wands, Pl. 62.1,2, measure only $4^1/_2$ and 9 inches respectively. The upper portion of Pl. 59.1 differs strikingly from the Quinault carvings. Pl. 60.1. should also be compared with respect to the pose and handling of the legs only, since this figure breaks radically from the frontality prevalent in most Salish carvings.

[16] The basic design of this figure, excluding the surface striations, also resembles that of Pl. 5, 1,2.

[17] In this connection attention should be called to the parallel spindle-like shapes at the top of the two shamans' staffs (Pl. 62.1,2) and to the parallel horizontal and vertical chevron designs on Pl. 60.2. The drawings of the boards found during the Wilkes Expedition (Pl. 7.2) along the Columbia River also show an extensive use of parallel groovings or incisions.

[18] cf. Strong, 1945, pp. 245—253.

naturalistically inverted. Other important stylistic analogies appear between the decorative figures on Quinault combs (SNM 2701, 2703) and on small Wasco spoons, particularly in the schematic treatment of forms and in their integration with the objects themselves. Two Quinault decorated dishes[19] may be compared with the Chinook dish (Plate 61.1). In all three instances, skeletalized form is again evident.

Northern elements are also found in style 3 carvings. These are apparent (Plates 6, 7) in the more articulated naturalism of structure, in the long oval shape of the head, the carving of eyebrows and the greater elegance of design. Quilleute, Makah and Nootka influences were probably responsible for these style features.

PUGET SOUND

Twenty-eight of the ninety-eight Salish sculptures examined in this study are attributed to Area 2, the Puget Sound region. Twenty-five of these are allocated to four tribes as follows: Skokomish (Twana), 4; Snoqualmie, 8; Duwamish, 12; and Chehalis, 1[20]. Of the three remaining objects, the provenience of which is not specified, two seem clearly identifiable, one (Plate 12) as Duwamish, and the other (Plate 17) as Nisqually. As in western Washington, these sculptures also include figurines, large figures and figure reliefs; but in Area 2 the majority of the specimens are large figures, the distribution showing 3 figurines, 23 large figures and 2 figure reliefs. That is to say, the majority of the objects from Area 2 are of the larger figure class, while in Area 1 figurines were dominant. But the content of the carvings from both areas falls into the same two general categories, the religious, comprising the representation of shamans' "power", and the purely decorative; although in Area 2 an even greater proportion favors the first of these categories, 24 to 4, as compared with 9 to 4. In both areas power figures constitute the bulk of the surviving sculpture.

Power Representations

Probably all of the twenty-four power representations in the Puget Sound area were definitely associated with the spirit canoe ceremony (pp. 8—11), twenty-one of them with certainty. These are assigned to two tribes, the Duwamish, who lived in the central Sound region, and the Snoqualmie, who inhabited an upriver area contiguous to that of the Duwamish. The figures

---

[19] These are not illustrated in this paper. Two excellent examples are in the U.S. National Museum (127 860, 127 862).

[20] Four spirit canoe boards are included in the twelve Duwamish objects (Plate 16.1–4) because of their age and the fact that they best represent this form of Puget Sound art. Twelve other boards allocated to the Snoqualmie are not included because they are recent and degenerate in design.

constitute the only important carved objects attributable to these two tribes. All of them are in the round, seventeen representing shamans' power figures, and four the shaped power spirit boards. They comprise all but one of the objects (Plate 17) designated as Type A of the large figure class. Two of the remaining three power carvings, one from the Skokomish and one from the Nisqually, are also large figures and the third is a figurine of unknown origin. But in spite of similar content, considerable variety in concept and style characterize these carvings. They are, in fact, an extremely important group of Salish objects.

Decorative Carvings

The four decorative carvings include, as they did in Area 1, two combs and two horn dishes, the combs decorated with small carvings in the round and the dishes with reliefs. Both of the combs come from the Skokomish tribe and are in the figurines class (Type B); while one of the dishes is also Skokomish (Twana), the other, Chehalis, and both are in the figure relief class (Type C). As a group, they are less closely related in style to the power figures than the latter are to each other. Yet the carvings from Area 2 are essentially homogeneous in character and reveal less clearly marked evidences of contact from surrounding areas than occured in Area 1.

In contrast to Area 1, eight styles are recognizable in the sculptures from Puget Sound, Area 2, only four of which can be considered tribal. These are represented by seventeen half-length spirit canoe power figures, the most important objects from this area. Like the Quinault wands, they are tangible evidence of a shaman's power, but they go further in this direction and include the more salient attributes as well as the form of the supernatural helper. Shredded cedar-bark was frequently attached to the figures as hair or collars and paint, used more extensively than by the Quinault, was applied not only to carved parts, but also as flat surface designs. In technique they are not as refined as the figurines of Area 1; little care was given to the carving of detail. These Puget Sound power figures are indeed more or less simple abstractions of the human form without the carved descriptive parts which associate Quinault carvings more closely with human beings. This represents a difference in concept, which, together with the greater importance of surface painting, indicates a more subjective, less impersonal motivation than that of the Quinault. Although they are from two to three times the size of these Area 1 shaman wands and were not meant to be carried, they are also carved with a smaller supporting end, a similarity suggesting that both may be variants of an older prototype.

Distinctive of these seventeen Area 2 power figures is a two-sided concept of form, the front surface flat and the back rounded out. This contrasts with the four-sided forms of Quinault figures. The frontal outline is usually sharp, since the edges of the front surfaces were rarely bevelled. However, some of

9.2   18.2   19   13a   25   5.1

41.1   11a   6a   49   2   47a   43   42   34

Fig. 6

the specimens in this group, in which the back surfaces are defined by angular planes, have an almost four-sided shape (cf. Plates 20—21). No voids or projections appear in the designs of these compact carvings. Heads are rather large, square-jawed; facial areas either slightly sunken (Plates 8, 14) or flat (Plates 9, 10), frequently with a high nose and a rectangularly cut mouth. Except for these facial features, which sometimes include roughly incised eyes, no details are carved. The tool marks visible on the majority of these figures are either long or short vertical cuts which clearly show that the sculptor moved his tool up and down but not from side to side (cf. Plates 8, 14). Hence even in technique emphasis is given to the preponderance of verticals in the design.

The spirit canoe figures form a group of carvings with so many similarities that they could all be considered examples of the same style. But within the common pattern of this style many important variations occur. Four subgroups are therefore easily distinguishable, each with its individual elements strongly enough developed to constitute a separate style. Two of these, styles 1 and 2, were the property of the Duwamish tribe and two, styles 3 and 4, of the Snoqualmie[21].

Duwamish Styles. Of these, style 1 is sculpturally the strongest (Plates 8, 9, 10, 11, 12, 13.1). It represents the basic style of Puget Sound power figures, since it comprises all of their distinctive features. The most elementary and abstract of the six carvings are the three shown on Plates 9 and 10.1, 2. They contain, with the exception of two small holes for eyes on Plate 9, no carved detail whatsoever. Profiles of heads and torsos vary from angular to round; and three collar or neck types are used: the collar type on Plate 9, the neck on Plate 10.2, and no actually carved part at all on Plate 10.1. No close resemblances have been found between these three figures and other Northwest Coast carvings.

The figure illustrated on Plate 13.1 is somewhat similar to them in its forms and proportions; although a regularity of profiles and a symmetry of shapes make it a comparatively dull work. An analogy with Quinault style 2 (cf. Plates 2, 5.1) is seen in the sunken treatment of the face, which, because of the flat rim-like surface surrounding and constricting it, also suggests comparison with such crude Wasco-Chinookan carvings as that figured on Plate 59.2. A similarly despressed face distinguishes the style 1 Duwamish example on Plate 8. Other prominent elements are the tapering of the head, the wide collar and the curved profiles which are especially apparent in the frontal outlines. The projection of the head and collar produce more striking shadow effects than in other spirit canoe figures. The elegance of curves and the feeling for dramatic light and shade effects agree with like features of Quinault style.

---

[21] Although styles 1 and 2 and styles 3 and 4 have more in common one with the other than styles 1 and 4 or 2 and 3, yet they are sufficiently distinctive to justify considering them as different styles.

The sixth figure of this group, Plate 12, displays a coarser technique and simple columnar forms resembling those of a log. A pointed head manifests the straight brow-line common to Puget Sound work (cf. Plates 8, 13.1), which, although somewhat similar to that of the Quinault (cf. Plate 1), finds its nearest parallel among the Wasco-Chinook (cf. Plates 59.1, 2; 62.1, 2).

Unlike style 1, all Duwamish style 2 figures (Plates 13.2, 14, 15) have faces and arms carved, the latter not rendered in the round but in relief on the front of the torso. The finest, Plate 14, is transitional between these two styles. It combines, in fact, the geometric elements of Plates 8 and 13.1 with the more descriptive, life-like forms characteristic of style 2. The other two examples of this style (Plates 13.2, 15) have a weaker handling of forms and a less unified design. Of these, Plate 15 shows by the wide oval of its head and narrow tapering cranium some resemblance to Wasco shaman sticks, Plate 62.1, 2; while the arms carved on the chest may be compared with a similar treatment depicted in Eld's drawings of shaman boards (cf. Plate 7.2, second from left) and with a Quilleute spirit wand, Plate 64.1. In Plate 13.2 curves are conspicuous in the design; but these do not have the vigor of Quinault curves, tending rather towards the decorative. A unique feature of this figure is the use of a wedge-shaped rather than a stake base.

The differences apparent between the two Duwamish styles implies the existence among these people of two traditions: (1) the geometric, with all detail and attributes painted on the forms, and (2) the descriptive, with more carved detail. Although the figures were intended to be used with like objects in a dramatic performance, they were not made as sets, but each one was unique in the particulars of its design as in its meaning[22].

Snoqualmie Styles. The two Snoqualmie styles, Area 2 styles 3 and 4, comprise figures carved more recently than and inferior to those of the Duwamish in technique and design. Although they too differ one from the other, they have a far greater homogeneity, the obvious reason for which is that the four figures of both styles were carved as models at the same time and by the same sculptors. Of the two, style 3 is closer to the general pattern of styles 1 and 2. It has however such distinctive elements as clearly defined necks, which in Plates 18.1 and 19 are long and columnar, and flat front planes of the head and torso. Facial areas are concave in treatment, but the curvature is so slight that it suggests little depth of form. The backs of the heads and torsos are described by rounded surfaces that are also meager in shape. Roughly cut round holes represent eyes and long horizontal incisions mouths. The tool marks show that

---

[22] The diversity of these figures was to a great extent brought about by the fact that the spirit canoe ceremony was "bound to be an intertribal affair" since a number of shamans had to participate and there were never enough in one tribe who "had the sbetetdaq guardian spirit" (Haeberlin, 1918, p. 251; Smith, M.W., field-notes).

the sculptor frequently cut laterally as well as vertically. This by no means implies a lateral movement in the pose of the figures, which are strictly frontal; but it does manifest a breakdown in tradition where concept and technique were closely related. These carvings are indeed comparatively inept versions of the older Duwamish figures.

This is especially apparent in the shapes defined by the frontal outlines of style 3 heads. In styles 1 and 2 three shapes are found: a hexagonal (Plates 8, 10.2), a truncated oval (Plates 9, 13.1), and an incomplete oval with the lower end cut off (Plates 13.2, 15, 17)[23]. Although coarsely formed, all three are recognizable in style 3 carvings: on Plates 18.2 and 19.1a, 2a the incomplete oval; Plate 18.1 the truncated oval; and Plate 19 the hexagon. A comparison with Area 1 is suggested by the use of the incomplete oval shapes, but the halting uneven curves in the Snoqualmie examples show that any Quinault influence was very slight indeed. The important associations are all with the Duwamish.

This is also true of the four figures that represent style 4, Plates 20—21. Their designs, however, are more formalized than those of style 3. Proportions are heavy and short, columnar necks thick, and heads hexagonally shaped. The curves of the frontal outlines of the torsos are now so meager that these parts are almost straight-sided. Like style 3 the front surfaces are flat, while the carved facial features are comparable in treatment. They are also reminiscent of Duwamish styles in certain of their painted details, such as the large round eyes on Plate 21.2 (cf. Plates 13.1 and 14) and the horizontal striations on Plate 21.1, 2 (cf. Plates 13.2 and 14)[24]. It is evident that the component parts of the figures are less important as sculptured forms and more as providing surfaces to be painted. Distinctive of style 4 is the visible columnar axis established by making the lower diameter of the neck approximately the same size as the upper diameter of the supporting stake[25]. On this axis the head rests and to it the torso appears attached. It gives to the torso the possibility of lateral movement not found in other power figures. Together with the strongly pronounced horizontals in the design this effect tends to diminish vertical movement.

---

[23] On the basis of a single example, Plate 12, an irregular shape with a pointed top may be added to these three head shapes.

[24] It may be that this painted design on the figures of styles 2 and 4 depicts skeletal structure, in which case there is suggested an analogy with such representation on Wasco-Chinook and Quinault carvings. In this connection it is important to note that, with the possible exception of the design on Plate 13.2, all such renderings on the spirit canoe figures are either v-shaped or curve downward, thus being similar to the Wasco-Chinookan tradition of designing skeletal structure.

[25] This handling of the neck versus the post, although most marked in style 4, is also apparent in style 3, where however the lack of agreement of the diameters of the neck and stake make it less obvious. Other instances of similar treatment can be noted in Plate 15 of style 2 and Plate 10.2 of style 1.

To recapitulate: on the basis of stylistic comparisons it is evident that the older Puget Sound figures of styles 1 and 2 have few similarities with carvings outside of their own area, these being mainly with those to the south; while the more recent figures of styles 3 and 4 were most strongly influenced by these older styles. No analogous half-length figures have been found in any other region of the Northwest Coast. It is therefore entirely reasonable to deduce that they are indigenous to the Puget Sound area[26].

Painted Boards

The painted boards used with the spirit canoe figures in the same performance[27] are also important for an understanding of the style of this area. They were made of cedar planks with a sharpened, wedge-shaped end to stick in the ground and a simply cut top known as a "head"[28]. Although not carved, these boards have many points in common with the figures. They reveal, for instance, a similar feeling for outlines and shapes, for compact form kept within a continuous, unbroken profile, and for vertical movement. They are also distinctly two-sided; the front and both front and back may be painted with power representations. New boards were made for each performance, and since the ceremony was an inter-tribal affair, it is likely that the boards as well as the figures were of different styles and sizes[29].

Two interesting questions arise in this connection: were there earlier basic tribal styles for boards and figures? Was the inter-tribal conduct of the performances a later development which brought about a disruption of these tribal styles? On the basis of our present knowledge and surviving objects, it would seem that both questions could be answered only in part by an affirmative. For example, there may well have been tribal styles for the boards, since their painted designs and not their shapes were individual manifestations of a shaman's power. But, as stated above, the carved forms as well as the painted

---

[26] The spirit canoe ceremony in which they were used, it should be noted, was unique to the tribes of this region (cf. Ch. 2, p. 13 and note 5, above).

[27] cf. Dorsey, 1902, pp. 228—229; Haeberlin, 1918, p. 253; Waterman, 1930, pp. 19, 20—22.

[28] Smith, M.W., 1946, p. 310.

[29] The shamans met for some days before the performance in order to make and paint the boards as well as to re-paint the figures (cf. Waterman, op. cit., pp. 23, 44). Haeberlin states that not all tribes could cooperate; only those, in fact, who recognized the same land of the dead or trail leading to it. On this basis, he associates the Snohomish, Skokomish and Snoqualmie as one group, the Duwamish and Suquamish as another (op. cit., p. 251). Haeberlin says that the "form of the boards differed somewhat among the various tribes" (op. cit., p. 253); Waterman that "the statement has been made to me by Boas and by my Indian informants that the various tribes had each its own form (op. cit., p. 20); and Marian Smith that "so far as I know, all existent boards are of (one shape)... but a Suquamish informant reported that he had seen other shapes in use" (1946, p. 310, and Fig. 3).

designs of the figures were highly individual and this would have led to variations within a tribal style. That inter-tribal contacts led to a breakdown of
earlier styles may possibly have been true for the boards but not for the personalized figures. Even the figures, however, became types in such recent
examples as those of Snoqualmie style 3 and 4, while the boards are small,
narrow and without the fine curves of the older specimens.

Unlike the spirit canoe figures, all seven of the other carvings from this
area show style resemblances with Area 1. Of these, the one represented on
Plate 17 is probably a Nisqually power figure[30]. It has, because of its use of
carved arms, something in common with Duwamish style 2; but it goes far
beyond that style in its descriptive modelling and articulation of parts. In
design, it belongs to the oval-headed type; while the shaping of the collar is
like that of Plates 13.2 and 14, and the depressed facial area is similar to that
of all style 2 figures[31]. Other equally strong elements suggest Quinault or
Columbia River influences, such as the long narrow oval outline of the head;
the squareness of the shoulders; and the rendering of body structure. Technically the figure is very crude; small, deep and uneven knife-marks resemble
more closely Quinault technique (cf. Plates 6, 7) than that of older Puget Sound
carvings. The rough modelling of the torso, in fact, indicates that the sculptor
was not concerned with providing a smooth surface to accommodate painted
detail; but rather, as in Quinault style, with the carving of form.

This example is one of the most important Puget Sound sculptures. It is
marginal to the styles of both areas 1 and 2, and provides some evidence that
at least in certain regions of the Sound this type was vestigial to the more
formalized, abstract spirit canoe figures. Its stylistic associations confirm a
souther provenience, and this is born out by the fact that it does actually derive
from the Nisqually region.

It should be pointed out that in the spirit canoe figures there appears a
fusion of two media, carving and painting. That painting was an ancient
medium is attested by the profusion of pictographs; while in relief carving
petroglyphs show an early combination of the two media. Both are found
throughout the Salish areas[32]. It is interesting and perhaps worthwhile to
speculate on the possibility that a pictograph-petroglyph technique was native
to the Salish when they penetrated the Puget Sound area, together with a
sculpture technique; and that the former then became transplanted to the
painted boards and the latter to the carved figures, both to be used eventually
in juxtaposition. As a result, the painting technique began to influence that
of the figures, perhaps due to a confusion or a transmutation of concepts and

---

[30] cf. Ch. 3, pp. 49—50, and Smith, M.W., verbally from field-notes.

[31] Aside from the use of the four basic parts, other spirit canoe figure characteristics are: the compact design, the square-cut mouth set far down at the end
of the face, and the truncated lower portion of the head (cf. Plates. 7.2, 14).

[32] cf. Steward, 1937, p. 424.

to a gradual simplification of the sculpture technique. The reasonableness of this hypothesis seems tenable in view of the isolation of this area from those of a more elaborate art to the north.

Skokomish (Twana) Styles. Located on the Hood Canal the Skokomish or Twana were exposed to influences from the central Puget Sound to the east as well as from the south and north[33]. For example, the most important of their extant carvings, a moderately large free-standing figure (Plate 22), has stylistic elements strongly related to those of the Wasco-Chinookan and Quinault traditions. The wide oval of the head terminates in a sharply pointed chin; the surface of the face is flat; a long cylindrical neck is flanked by high rounded shoulders; and openings are cut between the legs and arms and torso, although the arms are held rigidly against the hips. The majority of these elements agree with those of such Quinault carvings as Plates 5.1 and 6; but the treatment of the shoulders and neck distinctly recall Wasco-Chinookan figures, as seen on Plates 59.1 and 60.2. Other Quinault resemblances are found in the facial features; while the modified three-zoned design of the face together with the incised patterns of face and body suggest Columbia River style (cf. also Plates 59.1, 60.2). Few stylistic features in any way connect this figure with those of central Puget Sound, the only important one being the truncating of the head, which evidences an interest in flat surfaced shapes. The formalized head is, in fact, somewhat at variance with the naturalism of the forms below, which in particular are foreign to all central Puget Sound concepts. This naturalism, coupled with greater descriptive detail, are stylistic elements which indicate a knowledge of northern Salish work. In brief, the figure shows many evidences of style influences from other areas; and yet these are not exploited or copied; rather they are combined to produce an original work, virile and sincere. This may be a single extant example of a strong tribal style, or it may be the work of an outstanding sculptor who was capable of the synthesis the object displays.

Three other examples of Skokomish sculpture are decorative in type. Of these the carved horn dish on Plate 24.1 is similar to like objects from other parts of Areas 1 and 2[34]. Conspicuous in its design are such typically Salish motives as parallel chevrons carved in low relief; while the style found on its main decorative zone is characterized by a skeletalized figure with a triangular head. The schematic form of the figure is carved in a low relief which projects above the surface; the open mouth, large eyes and the ribs are roughly incised; and the straight brows and broad flat nose are in higher relief. An enclosing frame, rendered by sloping planes, creates the illusion of greater depth in the

---

[33] cf. Smith, M.W., 1940, p. 21; 1941, p. 202; and verbally.
[34] cf. SNM 127 860, 127 862 from Quinault and Pl. 24.2 from the Chehalis tribes.

shallow relief. The more distinctive features of this dish, therefore, are similar to those of the middle Columbia River style[35].

A second style found on some of these dishes is characterized by a round-headed type of figure, three-zoned treatment of the face, long thin nose, and a technique of rounded sloping planes set within a sharply incised, delineated outline (cf. Plate 24.2 and SNM 127 860). These distinctive elements appear in the heads, the forms below being similar to that discussed above.

Of Skokomish carvings two small decorative comb figures (Plate 23.1, 2) have the closest stylistic analogies with those of central Puget Sound. This appears mainly in the simplified shapes and more particularly on Plate 23.1 in the compact design of the half-length figure and in its wedge-shaped base which recalls those of the spirit canoe boards (cf. Plate 16.1—4). The resemblance is strengthened by the handling of surfaces on the face and shawl, as though to provide a ground for painted detail. Other style elements, especially in Plate 23.2, such as the handling of facial features and the greater rounding of form imply souther contacts, while the fine adaptation of this carving to the shape of the object finds a parallel in the Wasco spoon on Plate 63.2.

On the basis of existing specimens no specific Skokomish style can therefore be formulated. But the carvings have a stronger stylistic affinity with those of the Quinault and middle Columbia River tribes than with those of central Puget Sound. This conclusion is further supported by the known movements and contacts of these peoples[36].

The Salish figurine represented on Plate 25, although it cannot be assigned to any tribe[37], bears a strong resemblance to those of Quinault in style. However, the obvious features of that style, such as the curved outline of the head and the three-zoned facial design, are handled so crudely that they suggest an area marginal to that of the Quinault (cf. Plates 1, 2, 6) as the point of origin for the figure. In so far as it is possible to determine from the photograph[38], the shoulders are square, the neck long and cylindrical, torso and arms rounded, the latter showing low elbow articulation, and the hands are pressed against

---

[35] This is especially true with regard to the diamond-shaped pattern of the head, the upward tilt of the shoulders, the way in which the neck seems to sit down into the torso, and straight brows and broad flat nose (cf. Plate 61.1 etc.).

[36] cf. Curtis, 1913, 9, p. 13.

[37] Aside from the fact that it was purchased "from a private collection in Western Montana in the fall of 1940", nothing is know of its provenience. (cf. Catalogue of Illustrations.)

[38] The "skin clothing over wood" effectively hides important design and style elements. The appearance of this costume does not necessarily mean that it was originally part of the concept; it suggests, in fact, that the figure may have passed from the area of its provenience to one farther east where Plateau influence was strong enough to account for the skin costume. But it could just as easily have been added by its original owners, since Plateau influences had spread as far as southern Puget Sound. The appearance of red paint on the carving implies both the Quinault and Puget Sound areas.

wide hips. Similar design elements are found in the Skokomish example on
Plate 22 and in the two Quinault figures on Plate 5.1, 2.

A further kinship with Area 2 style is also seen in a comparison with Snoqualmie style 3 carvings (Plates 18—19). The most important analogy appears in the
implied central axis which in this example is emphasized by the large diameter
of the neck; while the features of the face, particularly the shape of the nose
and the rough cutting of the brows, are also similar. It would seem therefore
that this figure, if not Snoqualmie, is at least inland Puget Sound in provenience,
showing strong Quinault influence.

In general the styles of Area 2 were not local tribal developments but were
both tribal and regional. The most characteristic style came from central Puget
Sound whence the stronger examples of the simple, semi-geometric tradition
derived; while on the western, southern and eastern perimeter of the area
outside influences from the west and south are evident. In some instances the
latter dominate, in others they fuse with central Sound elements; but in all
cases technique is less elaborate, less developed than in Area 1[39].

UPPER FRASER RIVER

The Upper Fraser River is a very important area and ten specimens definitely
attributable to it were selected for purposes of this study. Eight of these were
assigned by their collectors to the Thompson tribe and two to the Lillooet.
These two interior Salish tribes live in the south-southwestern interior of
British Columbia in the upper drainage of the Fraser and along the Lillooet and
Thompson Rivers. Located as they are to the east and north of the Salish of the
coastal areas, the villages on the lower reaches of the Lillooet and Thompson
came naturally into more direct contact with Coast Salish and are consequently
known as the Lower Thompson and the Lower Lillooet. Teit makes it clear that
only the lower groups of both tribes carved figures and in both they were used
for funerary purposes[40]. He gives no specific indications of separate style
characteristics.

Three classes are represented by these ten objects, the figurine by two, the
large figure by seven, and the post figure by one. All of the carvings are in the
round. The seven large figures, so related in design and style as to be of the
same type, Type C, undoubtedly represent commemorative-funerary sculptures.
These may be safely assigned to the lower villages of the Lillooet and Thompson
even in cases where museum catalogues do not so specify. Their importance is
indicated by the fact that they constitute seven of the nine objects comprising
Type C of the large figure. The post figure on Plate 34 has similar subject-
matter. But the two small wooden heads assigned to the Thompson Indians and

---

[39] The possibility of northern or northeastern influences in the general style of this
    area are discussed below (cf. pp. 112—113).
[40] Teit 1906, pp. 271—273; Teit, 1898—1900, pp. 329, 376.

forming together Type D of the figurine Class 1 present a puzzle. They show only slight stylistic associations with other objects from this Area, and neither Teit nor any other traveller or investigator makes mention of such objects.

Of the upper Fraser River sculpture, these two small Thompson heads (Plate 26.1, 2) are not sufficient proof of a tribal style. They are very coarse technically, without strength of shape, surface, detail or expression[41]. Distinctive stylistic traits are the projection of the brows and the heavy band of shadow across the upper face; the lack of carved eyes; and a flat schematic, and often only partial rendering of the two lower zones of a three-zoned facial design. The latter refers to the Columbia River-Quinault style area, and there is some indication that it may have come to the Thompson Indians from this region[42]. It should be noted that the profuse use of horsehair contrasts with the use in the Puget Sound area shredded cedar-bark for hair; while in some cases the Quinault also used cedar-bark (Plate 3), and in others, horsehair (Plate 2)[43].

The large grave figure from the Lillooet tribe (Plate 27) is, on the other hand, characteristic of an important Salish style. In design the dominating feature is the loop-like arrangement of the arms which gives movement to the outline and depth to the forms. This treatment, although found in the Quinault carved board on Plate 7.1, is foreign to southern Salish design and represents an element found commonly to the west. Forms are defined by simplified shapes, but these shapes are now more naturalistic; while the carving of the face, in relief on the front of the head, suggests a like treatment in Puget Sound figures (cf. Plates 15, 18.1)[44]. The strongest style elements are the shaping of facial

---

[41] In these respects they somewhat resemble the crude and badly weathered grave figure in the American Museum of Natural History (16—1380), published by Teit (1898—1900, p. 329) and identified as a Thompson Indian carving.

[42] In writing of the Middle Columbia Salish, Teit says that the Salish tribe of the Dalles was a distinct tribe, not reckoned by the Columbia River people as one of themselves, but popularly considered as related to the Thompson Indians, or at least to have spoken a similar language; that tradition affirms that, following a quarrel, this tribe divided, some remaining near the Dalles, finally to disappear as a tribe, while others went north, part of them going west to the coast and part, some informants believed, becoming the ancestors of the Thompson Indians. On the other hand, he states that some informants believed that the original home of all the Thompson tribe was in the "central part of the country" (?), and that after a quarrel some went north and became the Thompson Indians, and some went south to become the Salish tribe near the Dalles (Teit, 1928, p. 96). At any rate tradition seems to associate the Middle Columbia Salish with the Thompson Indians.

[43] The use of horsehair presupposes the horse as an important element of culture: Olson states that the Quinault were the "most northern coastal tribe possessing the horse in pre-European days" (1936, p. 12); and Teit says that horses were introduced among the "upper Thompson towards the end of the 18th century... and became common about 1840—50 (Op. cit., p. 257).

[44] This treatment of the head and its shape also have analogies with the Thompson grave figure in the American Museum of Natural History (16—1380).

features, especially the diagonal incisions at either side of the nose, the detailed
carving of the hands, and the effort to give roundness to a fundamentally flat
form. Articulated structure is indicated only in the hands, arms and upper part
of the chest. The figure has a basically simple style, such as might have served
as a prototype for the central Puget Sound carvings, but this has been slightly
influenced by a more elaborate, descriptive style, apparent only in the arms
and hands.

The possible source of the naturalistic influence in this Lillooet figure is
evident when it is compared with the five grave figures shown on Plate 30,1—5.
These undoubtedly came for a region lower down the Fraser where coastal and
Vancouver Island contacts exerted considerable influence. The forms are
rounded and naturalistic, but in all of the figures the arms are looped like those
of the Lillooet at the sides. Other similarities between these figures and that on
Plate 33 are the arched projection of the brows and the downward crescent-
shaped mouth. The expressive facial features and tense pose which are found
in figures from Areas 1 and 2 and are characteristic of Plate 27, are replaced
in Plate 30,1—5 by a relaxed pose and a calm expression. Naturalistic details,
such as the small tab-like ears, the indication of clothing by which sex different-
iation is implied[45], and the rendering of the two head types, one with oval jaw,
narrow face and flat planes, the other with heavy squarish jaw, modelled planes,
are further style peculiarities of these five figures[46]. A relationship, stylistic or
otherwise, between them and carvings of Areas 1 and 2 is practically nonexistent;
only a feeling for light and shade in the delineation of facial features is at all
similar. It therefore seems that the farther down the Fraser one goes the weaker
become the affiliations with Salish areas to the east and south.

The figure on Plate 31, although it differs in important respects from the
above examples, is also typical of the style of this area. It too displays the
greater naturalism prevalent towards the coastal Fraser River region. But, in
comparison, the proportions emphasize the large head, and the heavy shapes of
the body are carved as three-dimensional forms. The pose, particularly the
placing of arms and legs, gives the figure an implied lateral movement, which
contrasts with the restricting vertical and horizontal lines so prominent in the
designs of Areas 1 and 2 and in the majority of those of Area 3. This quality,
together with such style elements as the shaping of the head, the treatment of
facial features, and especially the modelling of the face indicate strong influences
from the west. Similar elements are also characteristic of southern Kwakiutl
carvings, as the Vancouver Island example on Plate 65.1 in which the human
form is interpreted by simplified, heavy rounded shapes. In the Salish figure on

---

[45] This is sharply in conflict with carvings from Areas 1 and 2 where, with one
possible exception (Plate 22), the figures are all sexless.

[46] Grave figures of comparable style in the American Museum of Natural History
(16—7081, 16—7079) are published by Teit as Lower Lillooet (1906, pp. 272,
273).

Plate 31, however, all modelling is concentrated on the head, and the summary treatment of the forms below serve to relate it with Area 3. Other significant style features, unlike those of the figures on Plate 30,1—5, suggest analogies with Areas 1 and 2. The arms, for instance, though cut free are held rigidly at the sides of the body; the legs are rendered as three-dimensional[47]; and a unified design stresses the function of the parts rather than their detail. It should be observed that the hands are merely blocked out and the waist indicated by a tight constriction of the torso. In spite of being mutilated, this remains a satisfying carving, an example of a sturdy sculptural style.

Although identified as Lower Lillooet, the grave figure on Plate 28 manifests a style close to that of the coastal Fraser River region. The heavy three-dimensional forms of the body and the rendering of movement surpasses that of the more simply designed figure on Plate 31 and indicates an even closer analogy with such southern Kwakiutl carvings as that shown on Plate 65.1 and with the Straits of Georgia figure on Plate 29. But like the style of Plate 31, forms are generalized, only a suggestion of muscular structure appearing in the legs. Details are also simplified, even those of the large mask. The dramatic momentary character of the figure is likewise similar to that of coastal (cf. Plates 27, 33.1, 2) and south Kwakiutl carvings (cf. Plate 67.1, 2). This work should therefore be considered as an Upper Fraser River figure, perhaps Lower Lillooet, carved under very strong coastal influences but retaining the essential style elements of Area 3. Technically and aesthetically the figure is very strong being superior to other examples from this area. It was undoubtedly the work of an accomplished sculptor who perhaps came into contact with coastal work through marriage or trade[48].

Elements from both the south, east and west are therefore found in Area 3 style, the farther down-river the provenience, the more naturalistic the intent, the heavier the proportions, the rounder the shapes, and the more the work tends towards that of the coastal people to the west. There is also a noticeable change from the simpler to more elaborate designs and forms.

STRAITS OF GEORGIA

The mainland coastal region of British Columbia lies along the east shore of the Straits of Georgia. This region plus that of the mainland surrounding the lower and middle reaches of the Fraser River have been designated as the

---

[47] Not only does the appearance of these voids suggest Quinault practice, but an informant of the Suquamish, a central Puget Sound tribe, in describing their carved figures says that they were carved in the round "with a face like a man, arms at the side, with hole between body and elbow, and hole between legs to knees, then solid to point where sticks in ground" (Smith, M.W., verbally from field-notes).

[48] cf. Teit, 1906, pp. 231, 252.

Straits of Georgia, Area 4. Three of the seven carvings from this area are not specifically assigned. Only one has known tribal provenience: Plate 32, "Collected at Musquiam, British Columbia". In function and content they show three separate categories: two (Plates 29, 32) are possibly commemorative-funerary, two (Plates 33.1, 2) narrative-funerary, and three (Plates 34, 36, 38) privilege masks. The two commemorative-funerary carvings bear some relationship in style to those from Area 3. Both these and the narrative-funerary figures may combine ideas of power representation and social prestige. The masks are clearly intended to demonstrate the superiority of one family over another in a non-religious sphere[49]. All seven of the objects may therefore be associated in basic intent with the display of individual or group prestige. This would suggest a relationship with the more northern crest tradition; but the style in its fundamental qualities is distinctive of this area. Six of these sculptures are carved in the round, and one in high relief. Grouped by classes, three are large figures (Class 2), one a relief (Class 5), and three masks (Class 6)[50].

Areal but no specific tribal styles can be identified in this sculpture from the Straits of Georgia region. Some examples combine style elements from Vancouver Island with those from the Fraser River Area, but they are more elaborate in design and more proficient in technique than objects from that region. The carvings from Area 4 are also more related in content to those from Vancouver Island than to those from Areas 1, 2 and 3. Instead of the stylized shapes used to express "power" in the majority of examples from the latter three regions, descriptive forms represent momentary emotional states or imply a specific narrative quality[51] (cf. Plates 29, 33.1, 2). These figures therefore, unlike those from the Puget Sound and Quinault regions, seem to have less connection with the supernatural and more with reality. In this respect, northern influences are again evident. These, in fact, often somewhat modified, contributed heavily to the formation of the sculptural styles of Area 4.

One of the most important of these styles appears in the carving on Plate 29. A strong continuous outline gives the figure a contained character, while the well integrated form is composed of simplified shapes, firmly articulated and showing essential, not detailed structure. Many of its stylistic elements are similar to those of the Lillooet carvings on Plates 27 and 28, especially the designing of the broad shoulders and flexed arms, and the features of the face — low forehead, rounded deeply outlined eyes, here flanked by short lateral cuts,

[49] Barnett, 1939, p. 293.

[50] Carved anthropomorphic house-posts, Barnett states, were indigenous to this area. Class 3 objects would therefore be native to this region. (cf. 1938, p. 128; 1939, pp. 242—243).

[51] The difference in concept between this more elaborate and descriptive carving and that of the south is well shown by the attitude of an informant from the Puget Sound area towards this type of work when he scoffed at it and said that an object does not have to be fussy and elaborate to express its content (Smith, M. W., verbally from field-notes).

and carved creases at either side of the crescent-shaped mouth[52]. A further similarity appears in the tendency to flatten out the surface of the heavy forms, except those of the head and the animal, thus emphasizing the silhouette[53]. In this respect and in the shaping of the torso there are suggestions of style 1 of the Quinault. The lack of any carved ears also indicates an association with the tradition of Plate 27 and with that of the south. But the head corresponds in type and in treatment most closely with the square-jawed, short-necked type of Plate 30; while the appearance of the animal and the association of the two forms in a sculptural composition refer to a characteristic trait of Area 5 carvings.

The expression of lateral movement is of particular importance in the style of this figure. It results from the placing of the knees, the implication of a side to side threshing about of the animal, and the statement by the sharp angles of the arms of an active force countering the upward drive of the animal. All of the movement is kept within the closed, angular outline, while the specific disposition of shapes produces a definite and objective, not an implication of movement. This is entirely at variance with the styles of Areas 1 (Western Washington), 2 (Puget Sound), and 3 (upper Fraser River), with the exception of that of Plate 28. The strongest affiliations are with Area 5 (Vancouver Island) and the neighboring Kwakiutl carvings, where the objective rendering of movement, frequently through the expedient of sharply flexed arms, is commonly found[54] (cf. Plates 66.2, 67.1, 2). Other coastal and northern influences appear in the more careful handling of detail and surfaces, and in the inference of narrative content. Although detail is still kept to a minimum and broad shapes and mass are emphasized, the more careful technique, apparent in the carving of the eyebrows and especially in the animal, tend to place this figure within the category of the more elaborate Salish carvings. The compulsion of this northern influence towards more carefully finished and elaborate work has previously been noted in Quinault style 1 (Plate 1); but in the Straits of Georgia Area, due to proximity, it was even greater.

The tense pose of this figure is further developed in the two examples on Plate 33.1, 2, although they have but little similarity to the style of the latter. Rather, the momentary emotional state conveyed through contorted facial

---

[52] As in Plate 27, this treatment suggests a modification of the threezoned arrangement of the face found in Areas 1 and 2. It is possible that in the latter two areas this is a schematic and in Plate 29 a more naturalistic rendering of actuality. It should be noted that in both cases a zone is created of the lower part of the face. The curvilinear nature of the handling of this zone in Plate 29, however, has many parallels in Area 5 carvings, where a similar depression of the mouth area appears.

[53] It should be observed that this treatment of surface differs considerably from the more rounded handling in Plates 30 and 31, also from Area 3.

[54] cf. also the treatment of the hair at the side of the head in Plate 29 with that of the Kwakiutl figure on Plate 61.1.

features points towards Kwakiutl work. This is especially manifested by the wide curve of the brows, the deep depression surrounding the eyes (cf. Plates 65.1, 67.1), and by the almost grotesque personalization of the nose. Other non-Salish style elements are: the long oval delineation of the eyes, the shape of the open mouth (cf. Plates 39.2, 69.1) and the depressed area around it, and a careful, proficient technique showing a regard for surface finish and shaping of detail. But the shape of the heads and the absence of ears differ from the Kwakiutl and suggest Quinault style. A further parallel with Area 1 sculpture is implied by the resemblance of the geometric design of the figure on Plate 33.1 with that on Plate 5.1, though its heavier forms are more life-like. Elements in the design of both of these northern figures in general recall those of the south: for example, in Plate 33.1 the arms held rigidly at the sides are similar in treatment to those in Quinault and Columbia River carvings; while in Plate 33.2 the arms crossed on the torso suggest comparison with certain Puget Sound power figures[55].

Unique among Salish styles, however, is the tense, almost vibrant quality of the angular outlines. This is largely caused by the accentuation of the heavy shapes, and their articulation, which are given on Plate 33.1a perforated pattern and on Plate 33.2 a more compact, closed design of related masses.

The pervading naturalism so strongly apparent in the work of Area 4 becomes the strongest feature in the style of the four animals on the grave box on Plate 32[56]. With a head type and swinging movement comparable to that of the animal on Plate 29, the fully rounded forms are arranged in an interlocking circular composition, again suggesting a story content through the association of the figures in the expression of a momentary action. Only the essential parts of the animal are represented, but, though generalized in treatment, these are given their individual structural and functional character. While it is possible to distinguish several species in Salish animal carvings, the naturalistic concept of the animal is always rendered in sculptural three-dimensional forms. In contrast, among the peoples to the north of the Salish a formalized and realistic concept led to a linear descriptive treatment in which all of the particular details of an animal are included. Frequently however, as on Kwakiutl, Haida and Tlingit totempoles and house-fronts, these details are so stylized that, though they may be carved on the surface of plastic forms, the animal does not have

---

[55] This treatment of the arms should also be compared with the Kwakiutl carving on Plate 66.2 where the right arm is placed, as in Plate 33.2, above the left and where the arms are flexed in similar manner. It should be noted that, when arms appear crossed on the chest in Puget Sound figures, the reverse arrangement prevails, that is, the left arm is placed above the right (cf. Plate 14).

[56] This relief is identified as Muskium and should be compared with the large high relief plank, also from Muskium, in the American Museum of Natural History (16—4653). The latter is carved in the same very high relief technique and has a comparable degree of animation.

the vivid naturalness of those of the Salish[57]. An important analogy in the handling of content should be observed between the animals on Plate 32 and other carvings from Area 4: that is, a momentary pose and expression imparts an almost Baroque quality of becoming, in which movement and change are so strongly implied that they seem actually to exist.

The three swaixwe masks from this Area (Plates 34, 35, 36) represent three variations of this class of sculpture. Two of them are examples of Type A, but one (Plate 35) is Group 1 in style and the other (Plate 34) Group 2. The third (Plate 36) differs considerably in style from the other Salish masks and is the only example of Type B. In its vigorous naturalism, it agrees with other objects from the Straits of Georgia Area, while in style it is closer to the Kwakiutl version of the swaixwe (cf. Plates 69.2, 70.2) than to other Salish examples. Since Area 4 is reputedly the center of origin of the swaixwe[58], perhaps the more naturalistic character of this example represents a closer approximation of the original form than the more schematic coastal and Vancouver Island forms.

Characteristic of Salish style, the shaping of surfaces and parts, such as eyes, nose and mouth, is of far more importance than refinement of finish. To such salient style elements as the peg-eyes, the contraction of the heavy splayed brows, the short hooked nose, and the wide open mouth, must be added the very naturalistic, attached bird-heads and the small flat boards at either side. The flatness of these boards and their summary treatment suggest Puget Sound style; while the bird-heads are clearly in the tradition of the animals discussed above. An unusual Salish feature appears in the composite nature of the mask. The Kwakiutl, on the other hand, frequently composed their masks on this principle (cf. Plates 70.2, 71.1), and it is possible that it represents a Kwakiutl influence. That the reverse might have been the case, moreover, and that it may have been an original feature of the Salish swaixwe mask is suggested by Barnett when he affirms that "the Kwakiutl got the mask (swaixwe) from the Comox"[59]. It is probable, therefore, that the peg-eye, one of the most striking features of the Salish mask, was acquired from them by the Kwakiutl who made such extensive use of it in their masks. But Kwakiutl versions of the swaixwe type are distinguished by realistic surface patterns and elaboration of finish and detail.

Of the two Type A masks Plate 35 of Group 1 is the most typical Salish version of the Swaixwe. With the exception of animal instead of bird heads on top, this specimen is practically identical with the two Vancouver Island masks

---

[57] cf. Boas, 1927, pp. 287—288.

[58] Barnett states that this mask was not of northern origin but probably came from the Fraser River (1938, p. 138), and then again: "curiously, all indications point to an origin either at the mouth of the Fraser River or somewhere up its course" (1939, p. 293).

[59] Barnett, 1939, p. 293. This would not necessarily mean, on the other hand, that the Kwakiutl did not make composite masks until after they had appropriated this type.

shown on Plates 42.2 and 48.1[60]. It would appear therefore that this style was not regional but had wide distribution. Boldly carved forms with incised and carved surface designs give to Plate 35a far more abstract and decorative appearance than that of Plate 36. All of the secondary "actors", such as bird and animal heads, are now equally important as parts of the design and as factors contributing to the final expressive effect. The design consists essentially of finely handled curvilinear elements in the central part and of more angular ones in the upper and lower parts. The latter contrast with and tend to immobilize the movement of the former. In the strength and richness of its abstract plastic design no other type of Northwest Coast mask surpasses it[61].

Although this style of mask is basically Salish, nevertheless, the elaborateness of the design, the finished technique and certain style elements point to Nootka influences. The linear stylization of wings on Plate 35, for instance, has Nootka parallels (cf. Plate 72.2). The concept of an animalistic mask may, in fact, have resulted from a fusion of Salish feeling for naturalistic animal shapes, as evidenced by the bird and animal heads, with the Nootka-Kwakiutl feeling for descriptive, linear realism through stylized surface detail (cf. Plates 42.1, 2, 70.2, 69.2). Comparisons are also suggested by the elegance of the curved profiles with a like quality in Quinault and Puget Sound figures; while the rich use of the parallel line motive recalls both the Columbia River style and that of the non-Salish peoples of Vancouver Island. As a Salish type of carving, this mask, despite its stylistic analogies is unique.

The intermingling of various Salish and non-Salish style elements is also found in the third Straits of Georgia, Area 4, swaixwe mask, Plate 34. An example of Group 2 style of Type A, its design combines the angularity of shape and the naturalistic detail of the Type B mask (Plate 36) with geometric and decorative elements of those of Type A, style Group 1 (Plates 42.2, 48.1). But distinctive of Group 2 are: the treatment of the pegs as pupils which project from within the low relief outline of a long pointed eye; the heavy rolls of flesh across the face just below the eye depressions; and the precise rendering in low relief of the lips, tongue and rim-like band at the top of the head. All of these point towards a descriptive naturalism. This mask, although surfaces are boldly modelled, does not have the angular forms of Type B, nor

---

[60] Another mask of this style is in the Denver Museum (NCow-1-P). Curtis also published two examples of identical style (cf. 9, 1913, op. pp. 114, 116).

[61] It is perhaps worth while to note that, although showing no similarities in design or style, its nearest rival is found in a northern Salish Bella Coola mask, Plate 73, which in turn can, it seems, be related through two other Bella Coola masks, Plates 74.1, 2, to a naturalistic type, the northern Washington Makah "bear" mask, Plate 75. One of the most striking of Kwakiutl masks, Plate 71.1, it appears, combines and develops features of the latter mask with others which seem to point towards the swaixwe type. This however is a composite type of mask, lacking in plastic quality and tending towards the "fussy".

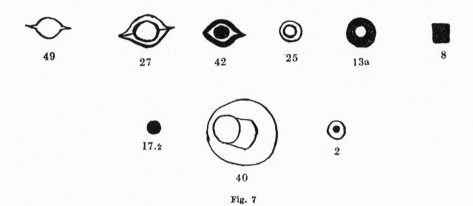

Fig. 7

the curvilinear expanding volume of Group 1 style. Its closest analogy is in fact with the two other examples of its own style group, Plates 48.2 and 49.

Though carvings from Area 4 manifest influences from a number of different regions, a naturalism and an emotional quality are common elements which make it possible to recognize an areal style.

VANCOUVER ISLAND

A large number of specimens have come from Area 5, the eastern and southern parts of Vancouver Island. Thirty-five of the forty-two carvings from this area are specifically assigned to tribes, and seven attributed to the area in general. The fact that all six classes of Salish sculptures are represented shows a variety in content and type. The following distribution by classes is significant: Class 1 (figurines), 4; Class 2 (large figure), 3; Class 3 (house posts), 15; Class 4 (post figures), 7; Class 5 (figure reliefs), 6; and Class 6 (masks), 7. This reveals that the greatest concentration of objects is found in Classes 3 (house posts) and 4 (post figures), with a total of twenty-two carvings. Further, all but one of the sculptures representative of these two classes come from this Area. Since these comprise the most massive Salish carvings, it should be noted that in this Area Salish sculpture achieved its greatest size. To understand fully the ratio of large to small, the four loom-post carvings, which are in themselves small, should be subtracted from the Class 4 (post figures) group; and to the remaining eighteen objects in Classes 3 and 4 should be added the three large figures from Class 2, the six relief carvings from Class 5, and the seven masks from Class 6[62]. The total therefore shows thirty-four large as compared to eight small carvings, with many of the large pieces, such as the house posts, of monumental size.

In function the sculpture of Area 5 appears remarkably diversified, although two fundamental categories seem clear: the socio-religious and the social, with fifteen and sixteen examples respectively[63]. In both cases, however, there exists what may well be a strong undercurrent of mythological-symbolic content. The appearance of this content differentiates the guardian spirit figures here from those in Areas 1 and 2; while on the basis of the few extant specimens a similar content appears to exist in carvings from Area 4. The majority of the sculptures from the Vancouver Island Area were intended either primarily or secondarily as manifestations of privilege or rank. This is of considerable significance. It is the strongest motivation in the carvings of this Area, appearing not only in the funerary but also in the guardian spirit figures. It must be considered therefore as the most important subject matter.

---

[62] It should be observed that these masks are all large in size, averaging more than 18" high.

[63] The socio-religious: Plates 44.2a, b; 44.2,c, d; 45; 46; 50.1; 51.a, b; 52; 53.2, 3; 55.1, 2; 58.2.

The social: Plates 36; 37; 39.1, 2; 40.2, 3; 40.1; 42.1, 2; 43; 48.1, 2; 49; 58.1.

The thirty-five carvings from Area 5 are assigned to five tribes: five to the Comox, nine to the Nanaimo, eleven to the Cowichan, six to the Sanetch, and four to the Songish. Of these tribes, the Comox live to the north and west, and the other four towards the eastern end of the Island. In content, the five Comox carvings belong to the social category and represent four of the six classes of objects: two post figures, and one larger figure, one relief and one mask. The nine Nanaimo objects, of which four large swaixwe masks are the most important, embrace four classes, house posts, post figures, reliefs and masks. With the exception of the two decorated loom-posts, prestige is also a strong motive among these carvings; while it appears to be less evident among the work to the east and south. The eleven Cowichan objects comprise the largest group from Area 5 to be associated with a definite tribe. As a group they show considerable variety and represent four of the six classes, figurines, house posts, post figures and masks, thus ranging from small to large in size, but containing no examples of relief carving, nor of the larger figure class. By virtue of its quality and its relationships with surrounding Salish and non-Salish sculpture, the Cowichan tribal style is of great importance. Seven objects come from the Sanetch who live near the eastern tip of Vancouver Island. Sanetch carvings, although they represent three classes, large figures, house posts and reliefs, show less variety and a relatively simpler style than those from the more northern tribes. In content they are funerary and power carvings, the latter showing a marked difference in concept from like representations to the north. The four sculptures from the Songish, who lived along the south coast to the west of the Sanetch, are also in all probability power representations. The concept here, however, differs from that of their neighbors. Carved as large house-posts, they all belong to Class 3; while the mink-like animals, so prominently displayed, imply a tribal mythological-symbolic meaning combined with the depiction of power. The interpretation among the Songish is therefore more complex than it is among their neighbors, the Sanetch. In general, these thirty-five sculptures of assigned tribal provenience reveal the wide distribution of classes in this area and the extent of tribal variations in content and in concept.

Of the seven objects attributed generally to the Salish of Vancouver Island the range is likewise broad. These include examples of four classes, Class 3 (house posts), represented by four specimens, and Classes 2 (larger figures), 4 (post figures) and 5 (reliefs) by one each[64]. On the basis of style and content, four of these carvings can be allocated to specific tribal groups, especially those of Class 3, and the remaining three are important in determining the style character of the entire area.

In contrast to Area 4, sculptures from Vancouver Island, therefore, have certain well established tribal styles. Typical of the Area is the way in which

---

[64] The exact distribution is as follows: Class 2: Plate 58 (1); Class 3: 55.1,2; 56.1,2; Class 4: Plate 58 (2); and Class 5: Plate 5.

northern elements are adapted to agree with Salish concepts and are trans-
formed into idioms of Salish style. The carvings consequently have an easily
identifiable Salish imprint. Numerous stylistic features require comparison not
only with those of Areas 3 and 4, but also with those of 1 and 2.

Comox

The style of the most northern Vancouver Island group, the Comox, has a
marked likeness to that of the Kwakiutl[65]. The example on Plate 39, for instance, is characterized by a realism at once apparent in the modelling of the
full-volumed forms and in such details as the pot-belly. A momentary expression is given to the face, the large mouth open as though the figure were talking
(cf. Plate 69.1); while the arms are attached in such a way that they could be
moved in simulation of actual movement or gesture. This device is common
in Kwakiutl carvings. From the point of view of design, the movable arms
create a potentially open, as opposed to the more typically Salish closed design.
In the Comox figure there is no reserve, no restraint; but a characterization
which is made more life-like by the inclusion of such details as the navel,
fingernails, eyebrows and nostrils. Of the detail the shaping and linear handling
of the eyes are entirely Kwakiutl. The only Salish style elements found in this
carving are the rendering of simplified, sculptural shapes.

By comparison, the Comox house post on Plate 40.1 and the post figure
on Plate 39.1 have a reserve of pose, an enclosing outline, and a simple treatment
of the body that suggest a closer association with basic Salish style elements.
But in proportion and in the aggressive posture of the upper figure on Plate 40.1
a realism is again apparent. The shape of the head and the modelling of the
face in both carvings resemble that on Plate 39.2[66]. An obvious Kwakiutl
feature is seen in the way the eyes are shaped and carved, a treatment never
found among Salish works (cf. Plates 65, 67.1, 2).

Although highly stylized, the masked post figure on Plate 37 is, in its large
and simplified forms, similar to the examples on Plate 39.1, 2. In this carving
too analogies with Kwakiutl work are readily apparent. The mask with its
owl-like peg-eyes set within circular pits and its curiously shaped mouth bears
comparison with the Kwakiutl mask on Plate 71.2 and does not resemble any
Salish example. Von Sydow, however published[67]an example of a Comox carved

---

[65] Barnett states that the Comox were the "most aberrant group of Salish" and
"show a decided bias toward the kwakiutl" (1938, p. 120); and he later affirms
that the "Kwakiutl held all Salish except the Comox in contempt" (1942,
p. 383).

[66] There is a superficial suggestion here in the square shape of the head, the looped
arms, as though the hands were jammed in side pockets, and an indication of
trousered legs of the funerary figures from Area 3 (cf. Plate 30.1–5); but the calm,
contained expression of the latter is conspicuously missing.

[67] von Sysow, E. — Ahnenkult und Ahnenbild der Naturvölker, Zwicken, 1924,
Plate 18.

figure wearing a swaixwe mask. It has the heavy, naturalistic forms of Plate 39.2, an animated pose with slightly flexed knees and, as in Plate 28, one hand, in this case the left, supporting the mask. This mask has the typical design of the Salish type swaixwe (cf. Plate 42.1, 2). A curious feature, however, is the relief carving on the "tongue" which represents the tail and fins of a fish, giving the impression that the figure were swallowing a fish.

The Comox mask on Plate 38 also has a typical Salish design and constitutes the single example of Group 3 of Type A. It combines in an eclectic manner details from other swaixwe styles with a different set of proportions, suggesting a more human face. The animal-head nose and the flanking forearms, for instance, have some resemblance to like details on Plate 43, but here they function more completely as a nose. The animal heads on top also are similar to those on Plates 35 and 43, but are partly composite; while the treatment of the eyes and mouth compare with those on Plates 34, 48.2 and 49. Distinctive of this mask is the adaptation of swaixwe elements to represent more nearly human features. This implies a difference in concept, and is supported by the versions of the swaixwe appearing on Plate 37 and that illustrated by von Sydow. The Comox mask, however, does not bear any close similarities to the Kwakiutl swaixwe (cf. Plates 69.2, 70.2), and if, as Barnett states the Kwakiutl got this mask from the Comox, it must have been merely the general elements of the design, such as the peg-eyes, protruding tongue, and attached animal heads.

Comox sculpture in general is more closely related in style and content to that of the Kwakiutl than to the Salish. Perhaps, indeed, in some instances, as Barnett states with regard to the house post type of carving, they were "made by an inferior Kwakiutl artist"[68]; although few of the extant examples were carved by "inferior" sculptors.

Nanaimo

In contrast, Nanaimo carving has traits like those of other Salish sculpture on the Island and on the mainland. The two house posts on Plate 40.2, 3 differ in design from that on Plate 40.2 by following the Salish tradition of the single figure[69]. Not only do these carvings lack the aggressive vigor of the Comox specimen, but even in their descriptive approach to a specific event they employ an essentially static pose which is emphasized by the more restricting and angular outline. Salish style features are seen in the shape of the shoulders,

---

[68] Barnett, 1942, p. 384.

[69] In this respect it should be noted that the Comox carving stands in closer relationship to the northern totem pole tradition than does the single-figure composition of the Nanaimo. Where more than one figure appears in a Salish design, only one is a human being, the other or others are animals, as in Plates 29, 40.3.

the stylization of details, and in the use of parallel design motives. Strong undercutting around portions of the outline on Plate 40.3 implies a background of carving in the round with a fixed static pose; while in both carvings forms are treated as generalized shapes. The actual delineation of the eyes on Plate 40.3 represents a combination of like features found on Plates 33.1, 2 and 40.1; but the shape of the head, with the small, almost pointed chin, compares with that of such Sanetch carvings as Plate 50.1. Of the two Nanaimo posts, Plate 40.3 displays a more careful and proficient technique and a greater degree of articulation and modelling, as in the legs, arms and face; while Plate 40.2 has a flatter surface and a summary representation of parts.

The two Nanaimo loom-post carvings on Plate 41.1, 2, in contrast to the fundamentally descriptive character of the houseposts, have such typically Salish qualities as simplified forms and a vigorous, unrefined technique. The square shaped head of the small figure on Plate 41.1 somewhat resembles that of the funerary figures of Area 3, though the nearest stylistic parallel of this carving is that of the Skokomish comb on Plate 23.1. The small Nanaimo figure, however, shows a more concrete approach to nature. A similar style marks the carving of the animal on Plate 41.2, where the intention of the artist was to express and interpret, not, as in Kwakiutl and northern carvings, to represent nature. Few details are therefore described. The figure is a unified whole, the essential parts treated simply and broadly.

Of the three masks identified as Nanaimo (Plates 42.1, 2; 43), the one illustrated on Plate 42.2 is identical with the Cowichan example on Plate 48.1 and differs from the Lower Fraser mask on Plate 35 only in the use of bird in place of animal heads on the top. It is also similar to the Nanaimo version on Plate 42.1 where the only differences appear in the treatment of the surmounting bird heads and in the lack of a carved and painted groove above the eyes and bridge of the nose. Of this type of swaixwe mask that on Plate 43 is the most abstract and decorative in design. Its general shape and proportions agree with other swaixwe of this type, but in such design elements as tangent eye pits and flowing curves it is unique. Some similarity can be found between the "nose" and surmounting animal heads and those on Plate 37, and the circular motive on the forehead and that on Plate 34. But the decorative character of its elaborate surface pattern, dramatizing its plastic form, and the finished technique suggest northern influences.

Nanaimo style is largely Salish in character, but important non-Salish elements give it a heterogeneous quality. It is however one step nearer a more purely Salish style than that of the Comox.

Cowichan

Although linguistic ties link the Nanaimo with the Cowichan, the sculpture of the latter tribe is more closely allied stylistically with that of the Sanetch and the Songish to the south[70]. Here again, however, the treatment is so diversified that no localized tribal style can be distinguished. Four interrelated styles are nevertheless discernible in Cowichan work, each with similarities to that of other Salish areas, especially of Vancouver Island.

The four small drum figures on Plate 44.1 represent one of the styles. In the shape of the head of the two on Plates 44.2a and 44.2d there is a striking parallel with those on Plate 30, 1—5; while the arrangement of the arms and the animal are similar to those on Plate 29, with which the delineation of facial features also closely agrees. Two planes are used, however, in the modelling of the face in the Cowichan figures and the incisions at the sides of the mouth are missing. But it is nevertheless apparent that these three carvings belong to the same style tradition. Although similarities in design and style also relate Plates 44.2b and 44.2c with Plate 29, the treatment of the chin and upper chest suggest comparison with Plate 27 and with Puget Sound work; the headdress is somewhat like that of the Kwakiutl figure on Plate 67.1, and the flexed arms recall like features in Area 3 carvings (cf. Plate 30). The narrative content, rendered by simplified forms, firm outlines and a minimum of detail, is interpreted with Salish reserve. The compositional arrangement of the figures in almost identical pairs seems to be a Vancouver Island trait. In style they rank among the most important Salish sculptures.

The large house posts on Plates 46 and 55.1[71] are examples of a second Cowichan style. Though they are affiliated with the style tradition manifested by Plates 44.2a and 44.2d, they are far more realistic, including such details as ears, hands, genitalia and musculature of arms and chest. A realism is often, in fact, apparent in Salish carvings of Areas 4 and 5 and in that of their Kwakiutl neighbors. But the sculptural quality of these house posts indicates that this type developed from the adaptation of a three-dimensional tradition to fulfill new requirements. Certainly the carvings differ considerably from those of the more linear northern tradition, where design units are arranged as descriptive entities in a narrative sequence[72].

A third Cowichan style, represented on Plate 45, is comparable in many respects to that of the central Puget Sound area (cf. Plates 18.2, 20.1). The basic design, for example, consists of only four shapes: head, neck, torso and base. Like the Puget Sound power figures they are stylized; although, just the opposite of those of the spirit canoe carvings, the front surfaces of the semi-cylindrical shapes are rounded and those of the back are flat. The treat-

---

[70] Barnett states that linguistically the Nanaimo and the Cowichan are related, while the Sanetch are most closely connected with the Songish (and the Sooke); and that the Nanaimo, Cowichan and Sanetch are "in pronounced cultural agreement" (1939, p. 121).

[71] Plate 55.1 is not identified as Cowichan, but the figures it shows are almost identical in style with those of Plate 46.

[72] cf. Boas, 1897, p. 176; 1927, pp. 280—295.

ment in Plate 45, however, was dictated partly by the functional requirements of interior posts, the back surface of which had to be flat since the exterior planking of the house rested against it, and partly by the original shape of the half-log from which it was cut. A similar retention of a partly columnar shape is traditional to northern totem-pole carving.

The technique employed in Plate 45, of carving parts and details in depth, is Salish rather than northern, where the character of the rounded surface is retained. This Salish technique represents a concept of volume in depth and a free outline in the round, whether it appears in the more angular shaped Puget Sound carvings or in the rounded ones of the north Salish areas; whereas the northern non-Salish coastal technique shows a linear, relief concept in terms of adjustment in depth from the surface, in which the surface is always retained. In such style elements as the design of eyes and mouth, the treatment of the animal, and the use of descriptive detail the Cowichan post is entirely in the Vancouver Island Salish tradition. It is important to note that the arms are carved like those of the Puget Sound figure on Plate 15; while the breadth of surface handling and the slight curvature in the profile of the torso correspond to style elements from the same area. This figure has the sculptural vigor of Area 2 style and the characteristic content and detail of Area 5. A similar combination of style elements appears in the two Cowichan loom-post carvings, Plate 47.1, 2, where, however, the depression of the mouth area suggests some relationship with Sanetch and Songish carvings to the south.

The mask illustrated on Plate 48.1 is identical in style with the Nanaimo example on Plate 42.2 and that from the Fraser River on Plate 35. The other two Cowichan masks on Plates 48.2, 49 are similar in the essentials of their design to the Fraser River example on Plate 34. Two important differences, however, indicate that in concept these masks differ from the mainland specimen: the treatment of the mouth with tusks or teeth, and the high triangular nose give to this version of the swaixwe a more recognizable animal appearance, suggesting that these carvings were intended to represent beavers. In other respects, they are a rather severe and factual rendering of this type of mask.

The carvings by the two southern Vancouver Island peoples, the Sanetch and the Songish, have close stylistic resemblances one with the other; although they are also related to those of the peoples to the north[73]. In comparison with that of the more northern Vancouver Island Salish, their sculpture is generally simple in character and frequently modest, if not inferior in technique. No objects with the richness of form and style of the swaixwe masks come from these peoples. But the basic principles of Salish style nevertheless dominate their carvings.

---

[73] Barnett affirms that culturally the Nanaimo, Cowichan and the Sanetch are "in pronounced agreement"; while the Sanetch are most closely connected linguistically with the "Sooke and the Songish around Victoria and with the Klallam in Washington" (1938, p. 121).

Sanetch

Of the two southern Vancouver Island styles, Sanetch appears to be unequivocally Salish in its reliance upon simple shapes and directness of expression. No specific characterization can be made of a tribal style, since, as is common among Vancouver Island Salish peoples, Sanetch carvings show several related styles. An important one is represented by the grave-house figure on Plate 50.1, 2. Following the more dynamic open design of Areas 3 and 4 (cf. Plates 27, 30, 31), the pose of the figure and the rendering of parts of the body have that closer association with reality found in many carvings from this area. The strongest stylistic elements, such as the shaping of the head and the features of the face, indicate a kinship with those of Plate 29. The "collar" around the neck resembles somewhat similar forms in Puget Sound carvings (cf. Plate 13.1). Peculiar to this style are the small size of the head, the low relief design on the face, the rounded modelling of the eyes, and the large tab-like ears. The flexed arms and legs are full-volumed and the animal animated.

The figure on Plate 51 a, b has a rounded forehead, bulbous cheeks, depressed eye and mouth areas which recall the more abstract style of the Nanaimo masks. With the exception of the large flat ears, the design of the head, especially of the truncated lower portion of the face and the cylindrical neck below, not only resembles that on Plate 46, but also that of the Puget Sound figure on Plate 20.1. The cutting of the eyes and the treatment of a mouth zone correspond with like features on Plate 29; and the geometric shape of the base with those of Puget Sound carvings (cf. Plates 13.1, 19.1 a, 21.1). But the closest Sanetch parallels with the latter appear in the geometric post carvings, such as those on Plate 50.1, 2 and those of no tribal designation on Plate 56.1, 2.

Songish

Among Songish sculptures, although proportions and the treatment of facial features are similar, four styles can be distinguished. All of them are comparable to other Vancouver Island styles. The first is represented by the large house post on Plate 52. In design this is related to both the Cowichan carving on Plate 45 and the Sanetch post on Plate 51 a. But a strong angularity of outline and a geometric shaping of the plank-like base associate it with the geometric posts shown on Plates 53.1 and 55.2. The most important of its stylistic features are the convex rounding out of the surface of the neck and head from a flat background; the very slight modelling of facial features; the high forehead, large tab-like ears and painted mouth area; and the naturalistic rendering of the animals. The species and style of these animals are comparable to those on the house planks on Plate 57, the provenience of the latter merely given as "Vancouver Island, B. C.". Impressive and monumental in effect, the Songish post combines marked Puget Sound with obvious Vancouver Island style elements. The analogy with the latter is especially apparent in the use and placing of the animals and in the shaping of facial features; and similarities with Area 2 can be seen in the simple carving of surfaces and shapes, and in the painted designs of the face and neck.

The second Songish style Plate 53.2 is closely related in essentials to this post. It differs from it however in the flat surfacing of the base, upon which a design comparable to the carved geometric ornament on Plate 52 seems to have been painted. It also displays a lack of restraint in the treatment of narrative content, as seen by the design of the four figures and by the inclusion of the half-figure on the plinth. A degree of Vancouver Island realism is apparent in the descriptive handling of facial features and the rounded treatment of the surface of the face[74]. The third style, Plates 53.3, 54.3, represents an adaptation of the Cowichan type of house post (cf. 46, 55.1); but is has a close relationship of the above two Songish styles through its treatment of face and neck, and its feeling for flat surfaces, simple shapes and a minimum of carved detail. A fourth Songish style is illustrated by the geometric posts on Plates 53.1 and 56.1, 2[75]. These sculpturally consist of a flat, rectilinear base surmounted by two or more ovoid, half-barrel-like shapes separated by deep rings. The surfaces of these posts were frequently painted, as on Plate 53.1, with symbolic designs representing power. They should be compared with the geometric Sanetch posts on Plate 50.1, 2 and with the backs of the Snoqualmie figures on Plates 19.2 and 19.2a.

Two other carvings from Area 5, Plate 58.1, 2, suggest further developments of (1) the dynamic, momentary emotional style, and (2) the static, contained monumental Salish style, respectively. Their style relationships are not clear, although they are closer to those of Area 5 than to those of other areas. A third carving from this Area, shown on Plate 55.2, bears comparison in its general design with the Songish post on Plate 52 a, b, but the more realistic treatment of the head and the geometric rendering of the base set it apart. Curtis, who illustrates an example of this type of post[76], identifies it as Cowichan, and several similar carvings, recently acquired by the Provincial Museum in Victoria, B. C., have also been assigned the same provenience.

Vancouver Island sculpture contains therefore a number of varied and related styles. These are partly analogous with styles of Areas 3 and 4 and to a lesser degree with those of Area 2. The narrative content noted in the work of Areas 3 and 4 is often strongly apparent here; while the treatment varies from semi-geometric to naturalistic, from descriptive to expressive, from modelled

---

[74] The style of the mythical animals is comparable to that of the animals on Plates 52 and 57.

[75] cf. Ch. 3, pp. 80—81, above. Boas (1891, pp. 564, 570) states that this style of post and not those of Plates 52, 53.2, 3 was native to the Songish and that the others were importations.

[76] Curtis 1913, 9, opp. p. 108.

to broad surfaces. Inherent Salish features characterize all of the carvings to a greater or lesser degree.

The distribution of objects discloses that a large number are localized by tribe or by area, and that in a tribe or area a certain class is predominant. Thus, in Area 1, Western Washington, all of the objects are associated with or attributable to one tribe, and the most significant sculptures are a group of figurines; in Area 2, Puget Sound, the specimens are allied with five tribal groups, while the most important carvings here are a sizeable group of the large figure class; and in Area 3, Upper Fraser River, the few examples are assigned to two tribes, with funerary carvings of the large figure class dominating. The few carvings from Area 4, Straits of Georgia, however, are not attributable to any single tribe, nor are they characterized by any specific type or class; although as a group they bear fairly close relationship, as will be demonstrated below, with the distribution in Area 5, Vancouver Island. In the latter Area more than four-fifths of the objects are assigned to five tribes; and, although there is a far greater variety of classes and styles than in any other area, about one-half of the specimens are of the house post and post figure classes, thus indicating at least a degree of localization or specialization for this area as well.

Conversely, the distribution of the six classes of Salish sculpture shows to what extent the five areas are therein represented. As previously stated, not all classes of objects are found in all areas; only in Class 3 (house posts), where all of the carvings are from Area 5 (Vancouver Island), is there a restricted or local distribution. Class 1 (figurines), on the other hand, contains specimens from four of the five areas, Western Washington, Puget Sound, upper Fraser River and Vancouver Island; only in the Straits of Georgia region, Area 4, have no figurines been found. The thirty-seven sculptures of the large figures class 2, represent all of the five areas; while the six masks of Class 6 are limited to Areas 4 and 5.

To interpret fully the distribution of classes, however, it is necessary to differentiate between objects grouped within a class, since these show a variation in kind and degree. Thus in the figurines (Class 1) only those of Type A depict single full-length free-standing figures. The seven examples of this type, all but one of which come from the Quinault tribe of Area 1, show two distinct styles within the group and constitute the greatest number of homogeneously related objects in this type of carving. Of the remaining ten figures in this class the four of Type C most nearly approach these in size and in kind; but they differ considerably in style and in the fact that they were not conceived as single figures, that is as separate carvings in themselves, but rather as two pairs of interrelated figures. The four small carvings of Type B, although showing stylistic similarities to Type A figures, represent an even more marked variant than Type C, not only because of their diminutive size, but especially because of the way in which they combine with the shape of the comb below to form a decorative climax, thus constituting merely a part of a total object rather than the object itself. Related to this class only by their comparative smallness, the two heads of Type D show the most striking differences not only from those carvings of Type A, but also from all other figures within this class. It appears, therefore, that of the seventeen objects in the figurine class eleven show a definite relationship; that is, Types A and B. Eight of these come from Area 1, Western Washington, and the remaining three from Area 2, Puget Sound. This would tend to establish the provenience of the most characteristic specimens of this class in these two neighboring but not contiguous areas, with the greatest center in Area 1[77].

Of the thirty-seven large figure carvings (Class 2), eighteen, comprising Style 1 and 2 of Type A, are of the stake-figure kind. To these should be added the two examples of Type B, since they are so clearly related, thus increasing the total of this kind of figure to twenty. All of them are simplified figures of about the same size; and, although showing distinctive style differences, they belong to the same generic group of carvings. Nineteen of these figures come from Area 2 (Puget Sound), with the lone exception (Plate 6) deriving from Area 1[78]. In general, this large group consists of carvings representing three-quarter length figures in the round in which there is no indication of legs. In fact the representation of legs, coupled with a considerably more elaborate style, differentiates Type B from Type A. The remaining thirteen specimens   in Class 2 show a similar variation from those of Type A: they represent full-length figures which are less simple and more descriptive in character. Seven of them come from Area 3, Upper Fraser River, and three each from Area 4, Straits of Georgia, and Area 5, Vancouver Island. The large figure class of carvings, therefore, appears to consist of two very distinctive but rather tenuously related groups: one, the three-quarter stake-figures of Type A which entirely derive from Area 2, and the other, the more descriptive carvings of Types C and D. The two figures of Type B appear more related stylistically to those of Type A of Class 1 (figurines), of which they almost seem like enlarged versions. It should be noted that, within the two groups of Class 2, distribution is limited: in the case of the first, to Area 2, and in the second, to the inter-related if not contiguous Areas 3, 4 and 5.

The twenty-three examples of house posts (class 3) and post figures (class 4), with one exception, come from Area 5. But here too sufficient variation exists to establish three types in each class. The eighteen identifiable carvings of these two classes are distributed among six tribes. The examples of each type in

---

[77] Travellers and investigators support the relative important position of objects of the figurine class in this area, and likewise their comparative unimportance in other areas.

[78] To the nineteen from Area 2 should be added the four examples of style 5, Type A. Though these boards differ in kind from the stake-figures, yet they are clearly related stylistically as well as functionally.

the house post class, although they show a variation from the more descriptive to the more abstract, are not localized in one tribe. Thus of the three identified objects of Type A, two come from the Cowichan and one from the Songish; of the four of Type B, two are from the Songish and two from the Sanetch; and of the four Type C, two are from the Nanaimo and one each from the Sanetch and Songish. It appears, therefore, that the examples of house posts show within restricted areas a general distribution not limited by tribal lines. The same seems true for post figures (class 4), where four of the eight objects come from the Cowichan and the Nanaimo.

The eleven figure reliefs of Class 5 form a diverse group of objects with a wide distribution which includes four of the five areas, 1, 2, 4 and 5. The three type divisions, A, B and C, are here determined on the basis of stylistic similarities rather than on the kind of object; and, as a result, six of the seven carvings of Type A come from the related Areas 4, Straits of Georgia, and 5, Vancouver Island; the two of Type B, from Area 1, Western Washington; and the two of Type C, from Area 2, Puget Sound. It should be kept in mind that Class 5 is a restricted group and does not represent the extent of relief carving among the Salish, since, as has been frequently indicated, many other carvings show a relief technique and a partial relief handling.

The ten masks of Class 6, although they come from two areas, 4 and 5, are closely related, and appear to come from local regions or groups. Of the nine Type A examples two are from Area 4 and seven from Area 5; while the single example of Type B comes from Area 4. This class of carvings has the least variety and the most restricted distribution, not even excepting Classes 4 and 5, in which the objects themselves are more varied and are spread among a number of tribes.

Chapter Four

Characterization of Salish Sculpture

It is apparent that there were style centers in Salish sculpture and that influences spread from them. To establish these centers and the operation of their influences completely would require more accurate dating of existing specimens, as well as a greater number of objects, than are now available. But it is possible, on the basis of styles and relationships of surviving examples, to indicate what these centers probably were and to consider chronological hypotheses for the origins of styles and their dissemination.

STYLE CENTERS

The style center of an art is the region in which its features are less diluted by or intermingled with elements of other styles from outside sources. From an analysis of the objects themselves and from recorded ethnological material, it is now possible to determine where the centers of Salish sculpture were located and to specify their fundamental stylistic features.

Of the forty-odd styles distinguishable among extant specimens ten are indicative of style centers. These are: (1) Quinault; (2) Duwamish; (3) Lillooet; (4) Muskwium; (5) Lower Fraser; (6) Comox; (7) Nanaimo; (8) Cowichan; (9) Sanetch; and (10) Songish[1]. It should be noted that five of the centers are located on Vancouver Island, two on the Straits of Georgia, and only one in each of the remaining Salish areas.

Quinault

All of the fundamental features of content and style characteristic of the sculpture of Western Washington are found in such clarity in three carvings (Plates 1, 2, 3)[2] that it is evident that they represent a basic Salish style center. Small in size, static in design, dynamic in expression, these shamans' spirit wands reveal as essential elements four-sided shapes composed in the round; surfaces with broad, generally flat planes, each part rhythmically balanced and functionally integrated into an expressive whole; the figure reaching its climax in

---

[1] The names used to designate these various centers, as Quinault, Duwamish, Songish, etc., have been selected arbitrarily for convenience and should not be confused with the names used previously in the discussion of tribal styles.

[2] These carvings constitute that style previously denoted Style 1 of the Quinault tribe.

a large ovoid head where the three-zoned design of the face instantly commands attention. A sturdy articulation not only emphasizes the essential structural parts, but also enlists their aid towards the attainment of a tense but restrained expressiveness. Latent power and movement emanates from, but is kept contained within, these figures. Actual movement results from a projection and a recession in depth, the slight bevelling of the squarish forms creating a degree of shadow which produces a similar effect. The perforations within the quiet enclosing outline also reveal movement in depth through the contrast of solids and voids. As a consequence of the rich variation in the handling of surfaces, in the shaping of parts and in the total design, these carvings come within the category of a more elaborate sculptural tradition, although the breadth of treatment and the economy and directness of means would seem to indicate that a more simple tradition exerted enough influence to keep this in check. The use of extraneous materials and paint is also characteristic of this style.

The emphasis placed upon the outline and the way the planes defining the forms are cut disclose the important fact that the sculptor was working with a four-sided rather than a round piece of wood — i. e., he was carving from an essentially flat front and back surface[3]. It is therefore apparent that these figures were carved from thick planks. Hence these carvings are associated with a pronounced Northwest Coast culture trait, that of splitting cedar planks from logs[4]. This technique, it should be observed, appears in the manner in which the sculptor carves with the grain or at right angles to it. The association of essential parts of the human form, though summarily described, with actuality is also distinctive of this style.

Duwamish

The Duwamish style, as it appears on Plates 8, 9, 10, 11, 12 and 13.1[5], represents another important basic center. Marked by an abstract quality, it produced figures with essentially two-sided shapes in which a retention of the surface plane also related them to the tradition of carving from a split cedar plank, halved or quartered[6]. In these power figures of the larger figure class

---

[3] This approach would tend to result in two-sided figures; but the forms are given an actual depth by the treatment of front and back surface planes, rather than by carving the forms in the round.

[4] Goddard, 1934, pp. 35, 37–38; Underhill, 1945, pp. 74—77.

[5] These figures constitute Style 1, Type A, of Puget Sound, Area 2.

[6] Pl. 12, on the other hand, represents one of the few instances of a carving from this area with a rounded shape suggesting its origin from a log. But the figure is, in all other respects, characteristic of this area. The rounded back and flat front surface of these figures suggest a similarity with the technique of canoe carving and shaping. Even handles of nets, digging sticks, etc. were not made of simple poles but were split, leaving three-quarters of their total diameter to be rounded off. Thus the heart of the wood did not run down the center of the handle. This was done to achieve greater strength (Smith, verbally) .

CHART 5 — Style Centers, Marginal Styles, Similarities

Style Centers	Styles Marginal to those of Style Centers	Extra-Center Affiliations of Marginal Styles: Similarities
1. Quinault 1, 2, 3	1. 4, 5.1, 2 2. 6, 7.1	8, 17, 22 76.1, 2(Quileute and north)
2. Duwamish 8, 9, 10.1, 2, 11.1, 2, 12, 13.1	1. 13.2, 14, 15 2. 18, 19.1, 2, 19.1a, 2a, 20.1 3. 20.1, 2, 21.1, 2 4. 17 5. 22 6. 23.1, 2	27, 33.2 27 45, 52 13.2, 14, 5.1, 6 5.1, 6, 59.1, 60.2
3. Lillooet 27	1. 30.1–5 2. 31 3. 28	29, 44.1 weak Quinault, Duwamish; strong Kwakiutl: 65.1 27, 29, 50.1, 37, 65.1, 2
4. Muskwium 32	1. 29 2. 33.1, 2	27, 30.1–5, 44.2a, d, 28 strong Kwakiutl: 65.1, 70,2; weak 5.1, 28, 39.2, 29, 58.1, 69.1
5. Lower Fraser 34	1. 36 2. 35	69.2, 70.2, 71.2, 65.2 (weak) 42.1, 2, 43
6. Comox 40.1, 39.2	1. 37, 39.1 2. 38	strong: 65.2, 69.2, 70.2, 71.2; Weak: 28, 52a,72.2 34, 48.2, 43, 72.2
7. Nanaimo 42.1, 2, 43	1. 41.1, 2 2. 40.2, 3	23.2, 32, 29 40.1, 37, 48.2
8. Cowichan a) 46, 55.1 b) 45	1. 44.1 2. 48.1, 2, 49 3. 47.1, 2, 55.2	30.1–5, 31, 29 42.2, 42.1, 34 52, 51a, b
9. Sanetch 50.1a, b	1. 51 a, b,	45, 47.1, 2, 18.2, 20.1, 46, 67.2
10. Songish 53.1, 56	1. 52, 53.2 2. 53.3	50.1, 45, 51 a, b, 55.2, 57 46, 55.1

emphasis is placed on a few simple shapes. No voids break into the tight continuous outline, and the resulting closed forms, coupled with the enveloping surface treatment, produce an expression of constrained power. The only carved details, those of the face, project from a recessed area within the mass of the figure. Truncated curvilinear and angular shapes are arranged rhythmically, symmetrically; while the expressive force derives from the total character of the shapes. Any configuration or handling of surfaces is entirely in terms of total shapes. These carvings denote a center of sculpturing in the round. In general, the tradition is a simple and geometric one.

Lillooet

The Lillooet style center also shows a simple tradition of carving in the round (Plate 27). A continuous outline integrates the almost rigidly balanced and symmetrical parts. Characteristic of this style are the looped-arm pose, the carved relief rendering of the lower portion of the face, the particular manner of depicting facial features — curved overhanging brows, round eyes, creases flanking the mouth, downward pointing crescent-shaped mouth, and the reality of such carved descriptive details as the hands and the clavicle structure. A degree of modelling, although tenuously handled, is evident in the shaping of the face, arms and upper chest; while the flexed arms provide animation. Plate 27 is within the larger figure class and is presumably a commemorative grave figure. It remains as evidence of a fundamentally descriptive tradition, simple and restrained in character, broad and general in treatment, which had as its aim the concrete approximation of a human being.

Muskwium

The Muskwium style center is represented by the fine Salish animal sculpture shown on Plate 32. Although carved in a very high relief, the strength of the full-volumed forms indicates a tradition of three-dimensional carving[7]. Movement is expressed by a momentary and naturalistic pose. So convincing is his concept of animal form as an organic whole that the sculptor has created carved equivalents of nature. Structure, modelling, details combine to produce this effect. The carving is a surviving example of a strong naturalistic, although somewhat more elaborate and descriptive tradition, the intent being to present the animal as a living thing.

Lower Fraser

With much of the vigor of expression of these animals, the swaixwe mask, Plate 34, characterizes the Lower Fraser style center. Tradition and informants

---

[7] It should be noted that the fixed flat surface from which these figures project preserves a feeling of working horizontally into the material similar to that found in the other three centers discussed above.

alike indicate that this Salish type mask was of mainland origin, from whence it passed over to Vancouver Island to be appropriated and modified by both the Salish and the Kwakiutl. A prestige object, the most fundamental stylistic features of this mask are the boldly carved parts, notably the peg-eyes and the eye and mouth areas, and the amount of carved and painted descriptive detail. Of considerable importance is the convex curvature of the face within the side profiles, suggesting that the sculptor was cutting in from the curved surface of a segment of a log. Largeness of scale and treatment dominates the handling of parts; while the expression results from the organization of the separately carved elements into an active, dynamic design. All of these elements correspond to objects in nature, although the masks are not realistic. In general, the style is elaborate, emotional, dynamic.

Comox

The sixth style center, the Comox, is represented by Plates 39.2 and 40.1. In spite of such Kwakiutl elements as the realistic anatomical details and composite nature of Plate 39.2 and the treatment of facial features in both examples, the feeling for sculptural shapes, firm outlines and direct, simple statement marks this as an important northermost style. Compact designs closely relate the parts of the body, the surfaces of which are undisturbed by any pattern or linear detail. Although the pot belly and open mouth of Plate 39.2 and the hood over the head of Plate 40.1 are further Kwakiutl style elements, these are more than offset by the essentially Salish sculptural handling of form.

Nanaimo

The Nanaimo style center is best seen in the three masks on Plates 42.1, 2 and 43. They show the somewhat more abstract and decorative Vancouver Island design of the swaixwe. The surface patterns are richly carved and the animal heads are closely integrated as functional and expressive elements. Curvilinear shapes and lines dominate, with carved and painted detail now used to describe realistic elements such as the wing and feather designs on Plate 42.1. The rounded contour of the mask and the high projection of its forms likewise indicate a cutting back from a rounded log-like surface. This style is evidence of a richly elaborate, decorative tradition in which contrasts of light and shade play a leading role in the final effects.

Cowichan

Two distinctive but not entirely unrelated styles mark the Cowichan center. The first of these (a) is best seen in the three house posts on Plates 46 and 55.1. Narrative by implication, they combine a number of strikingly realistic details with figures of characteristic but non-realistic proportions. Forms are strongly three-dimensional and show a tradition of carving in the round; while an almost strict balance and symmetry are observed. In particular, the shaping of the heads and the rendering of facial features, as they appear on Plate 44.2, are fundamental to this style. Rounded surfaces here as elsewhere express the sense of an expanding volume.

The second Cowichan style, (b), is illustrated on Plate 45. In this post simplified forms are rendered by geometric, half-cylindrical shapes which suggest their origin from a half-log. All details, some in high and some in low relief, are carved on the rounded surfaces and a minimum of modelling appears in the animal, arms and face. Paint is used both to mark off parts and to render specific descriptive detail. A rigid, contained quality results from the organization of the shapes and their unbroken outline; although the position of the animal and the large alert eyes of the figures produce a dramatic tension and implied movement. Characteristic of this style are the sharply marked horizontals of the truncated parts and the fusion of relief carving tradition, evident in the rendering of surface parts, with a three-dimensional one, as indicated by the shaping of the basic parts.

Sanetch

An important Sanetch style center appears in the grave-house figures on Plate 50.1, 2. A simplified realism gives to the forms arranged in this dramatic pose a strong sculptural expression. A moderate realism exists in the treatment of joints and muscles; but the most distinctive style elements are the openness of the design, the shaping of the head, the schematic treatment of facial features. Forms are ample, almost large, and three-dimensional, and full attention is given to the rendering of expression by means of these forms, not by carved or painted detail. This is one of the most spectacular Salish styles.

Songish

The carvings of the Songish center, Plates 53.1 and 56, are fundamentally geometric in character. They consist of a series of segmented shapes, semi-circular in cross-section, truncated ovals in profile, surmounting and projecting beyond a rectilinear base. Considerable care was taken in the configuration of these shapes, their smooth surface planes defining a sense of inner volume comparable to the figures on Plates 19.2 and 19.2a of marginal Center 2 style. On the surfaces were painted designs (cf. Plate 53.1) that are non-descriptive and apparently independent of the meaning of the carved shapes themselves. This style also indicates an association with carving in the round by the retention of the original shape of the log.

MAJOR TRADITION

Seven major traditions may be discerned in Salish sculpture, four on the basis of style, three on technique.

CHART 6 — Traditions Manifested in Style Centers

I. Technique Traditions:

1. Plank Tradition: Centers 1, Quinault; 2, Duwamish; 3, Lillooet; 4, Muskwium; 9, Sanetch
2. Columnar Tradition: Centers 5, Lower Fraser; 6, Comox; 7, Nanaimo; 8, Cowichan; 10, Songish
3. Relief Tradition: Centers 4, Muskwium; 6, Comox; 8, Cowichan (b)

II. Style Traditions:

1. Simple: Centers 2, Duwamish; 3, Lillooet; 8, Cowichan; 9, Sanetch; 10, Songish
2. Elaborate: Centers 1, Quinault; 4, Muskwium; 5, Lower Fraser; 6, Comox; 7, Nanaimo
3. Geometric: Centers 2, Duwamish; 7, Nanaimo; 8, Cowichan (b); 10, Songish
4. Representational: Centers 1, Quinault; 3, Lillooet; 4, Muskwium; 5, Lower Fraser; 6, Comox; 8, Cowichan (a); 9, Sanetch

These combine as follows: – Elaborate and Rep. – 1, Duwamish; 4, Muskwium; 5, Lower Fr.; 6, Comox Simple and Geom. – 2, Duwamish; 8, Cowichan (b); 10, Songish: Elaborate and Geometric – 7, Nanaimo. Simple and Rep.– 3, Lillooet; 8, Cowichan (a); 9, Sanetch

A Correlation of I and II:

Technique Traditions	STYLE TRADITIONS			
	Elaborate and Representational	Simple and Geometric	Elaborate and Geometric	Simple and Representational
1. Plank	Center 1, Quinault Center 4, Muskwium	Center 2, Duwamish		Center 3, Lillooet Center 9, Sanetch
2. Columnar	Center 5, Lower Fraser Center 6, Comox	Center 8, Cowichan (b) Center 10, Songish	Center 7, Nanaimo	Center 8, Cowichan (a)
3. Relief	Center 4, Muskwium Center 6, Comox	Center 8, Cowichan(b)		

(A) *Style Traditions.* Five of the centers, Duwamish, Lillooet, Cowichan, Sanetch and Songish, have a tradition of simple carving; and five, Quinault, Muskwium, Lower Fraser, Comox and Nanaimo, a more elaborate tradition. Similarly, a geometric tradition appears in Duwamish, Cowichan (b), Nanaimo and Songish centers; and a representational one in Quinault, Lillooet, Muskwium, Lower Fraser, Comox, Cowichan (a) and Sanetch. A correlation of these traditions shows that the Quinault, Muskwium, Lower Fraser and Comox centers are elaborate and tend towards the representational; the Duwamish, Cowichan (b) and Songish, simple and geometric; the Nanaimo, elaborate and geometric; and the Lillooet Cowichan (a) and Sanetch, simple, tending toward the representational.

(B) *Technique Traditions.* It is apparent from the carvings themselves that the sculptors were dependent upon certain technique traditions. These may be of even greater importance than the style traditions for a further understanding of Salish sculpture. The carver worked from either (1) a four-sided plank, or (2) a columnar, log-like form; or, sometimes, (3) either of these combined with a surface or relief technique[8]. Five of the style centers, Quinault, Duwamish, Lillooet, Muskwium and Sanetch, belong to the plank tradition; five, Lower Fraser, Comox, Nanaimo, Cowichan and Songish, to the columnar; and three, Muskwium, Comox and Cowichan (b), to the composite or relief tradition.

An integration of the traditions thus defined (see Chart 6, opp. p. 171) furnishes a valuable clue to relationships between the ten centers. The five centers which fall within the plank tradition (Quinault, Duwamish, Lillooet, Muskwium and Sanetch) include the geographical nuclei of Coastal and Interior Salish. Common denominators relating the essential styles of the five centers in the plank tradition are flat surfaces, horizontal depth and tight constraining outlines. The Quinault of Center 1, for instance, shows in the depressed face, broad surface planes and long curves a relationship with Duwamish, style center 2; but its more representational character, as it appears in the treatment of the arms, not only indicates an association with Lillooet, Center 3 (Plate 27), but also suggests an analogy with Sanetch, Center 9 (Plate 50). The more elaborate elements in Quinault style refer to those of Comox, Center 6 (Plate 40.1), rather than to the geometric elaboration of Nanaimo, Center 7 (Plate 42.1). It would appear, therefore, that the technique tradition of the Quinault Center associates it with the Duwamish and Lillooet Centers. This is also indicated by style traditions, which further suggest an association with Comox, Center 6. Aside from relating it with Quinault, the stylistic features of the Duwamish Center, which appear in simple and geometric forms, also have an analogy with style elements found in Centers 8, Cowichan (b) (Plate 45) and 10, Songish (Plates 53.1, 56). But the nearest parallel to its strong, simple tradition is found in Lillooet, Center 3 (Plate 27). These comparisons show that the Duwamish Center is more closely related to that of Quinault and Lillooet than to any others. Apart from its affiliations with Duwamish and Quinault, Lillooet, Center 3 style, is also associated, through such stylistic features as the looped arms and treatment of the hands, with the more developed representational tradition of Center 9, Sanetch (cf. 50.1).

---

[8] For distributions and grouping of centers by these various traditions, cf. Chart 6, p. 109.

The Lillooet Center may be said therefore to be at the apex of a triangle, the sides of which lead to and relate it with such distant centers as the Quinault on the Coast of Washington and the Sanetch on Vancouver Island.

Two other centers manifest a plank tradition, the Muskwium, Center 4 (Plate 32) and the Sanetch, Center 9 (Plate 50.1). Through the dramatic realism of their styles, they are rather tenuously related; but the Muskwium shows certain analogies with Cowichan (a) style of Center 8 (Plates 46, 55.1). The Sanetch has its closest associations with Center 8 and with neighboring Vancouver Island marginal styles.

Technical features shared by the five centers of the columnar tradition, 5. Lower Fraser, 6. Comox, 7. Nanaimo, 8. Cowichan and 10. Songish, are evident in the retention of rounded surfaces, the development of vertical as well as horizontal depth, and the expression of an expanding inner volume. With the exception of 5 and 6, these centers lie within a relatively small area on the southeastern part of Vancouver Island. The closest similarities of their various styles are with others of that region; but numerous style elements indicate resemblances with mainland centers to the east and south. The mask representative of Center 5, Lower Fraser (Plate 34), for instance, not only shows some relationship in form and in the elaborateness of its design with those of Center 7, Nanaimo (Plates 42.1, 2, 43), but also reveals affinities in the character of its expressiveness with Quinault, Center 1 style. The nearest stylistic ties of the Comox, Center 6 (Plates 39.2, 40.1) are with Centers 7 Nanaimo (Plates 42.1, 43) and 8, Cowichan (a) (Plates 46, 55.1), and its most remote associations with Style Center 1, Quinault. An important relationship, on the basis of specific style elements and the traditional handling of geometric shapes, appears between Cowichan style (b) of Center 8 (Plate 45) and marginal Puget Sound styles. Further similarities relate the Cowichan with neighboring marginal Vancouver Island styles. The sixth Style Center within the columnar tradition is that of the Songish, Center 10 (Plates 53.1, 56). This is one of the simpler and certainly one of the most geometric of Salish styles, and in these respects it resembles the Duwamish.

The combination of the plank or the columnar traditions with a relief tradition appears most clearly in Centers 4, Muskwium (Plate 32), 6, Comox (Plates 39.2, 40.1), and 8, Cowichan (b) (Plate 45). It should be noted that strong suggestions of a relief tradition also exist in Duwamish, Center 2, and in Lillooet, Center 3. The associations between these various centers have already been indicated.

To recapitulate: a consideration of the style and technique traditions show that Duwamish, Center 2, occupies a central position and that, although relationships are suggested with centers on Vancouver Island to the north, the strongest affiliations seem to be with Quinault, Center 1, Lillooet, Center 3, and Songish, Center 10. To the west and south, Center 1 reveals correspondences not only with Center 2, but also with Lillooet, Center 3, to the north and east, and with the Vancouver Island Center 9, Sanetch. It receives influences, therefore, from two directions: (1) from the northeast, along the arc extending from the Lillooet through the Duwamish; and (2) from the north, presumably coming down along the coast. At the northeastern end of the arc passing through the Duwamish to the Quinault, the Lillooet evidences similarities with these two Centers and also, through intermediate styles, with Sanetch, Center 9. The clearest associations of the Muskwium and Lower Fraser Centers, 4 and 5, lie with Centers 7, Nanaimo, 8, Cowichan, and 9, Sanetch. Of the five Vancouver Island styles, those of Centers 6, Comox, 7, Nanaimo, and 8, Cowichan (a) are closely linked together; while Cowichan (b) shows resemblances not only with the Lillooet, Center 3, but also with marginal Puget Sound styles. The two other Vancouver Island style centers, 9 and 10, disclose relationships one with the other and present similarities with the Puget Sound area, Center 9, Sanetch, with marginal styles, and Center 10, Songish, with Duwamish itself. But no very clear idea of the strength of these associations can be had from a discussion of basic style centers alone. For this, the ties between them and marginal styles must be determined.

MARGINAL STYLES[9]

Center 2, Duwamish, in Area 2, Puget Sound. In the Puget Sound Area marginal style 1 (Plates 13.2, 14, 15) is so closely related to the Duwamish basic style center that it can scarcely be considered marginal. Other associations are suggested by the arrangement of the arms and the treatment of the neck with Lillooet, Center 3, (cf. Plate 27) and with marginal style 2 of Muskwium, Center 4, (Plate 33.2). On the other hand, Area 2 substyles 2 and 3 (Plates 18—21) are clearly marginal to Duwamish, Center 2, the tenuous and schematic handling of their essential elements indicating an origin from that source[10]. This marginal style 3 (Plates 20—21), moreover, shows in the handling of shapes, especially in the truncating of the head, resemblances with Plate 45 of Center 8, Cowichan (b), and Plate 52, a marginal Songish, Center 10 style. The treatment of the head and neck on Plate 18.2 of Center 2, marginal style 2, also shows some agreement with Plate 27 of Lillooet, Center 3. Area 2 marginal styles 2 and 3, therefore, reveal a close agreement with Center 2, Duwamish, style, a much weaker one with Center 3, Lillooet, and some similarities with Centers 8, Cowichan (b), and 10, Songish.

Of the other significant styles marginal to basic Center 2, the Nisqually figure on Plate 17, marginal style 4, shows a combination of design and style elements reminiscent of Plates 13.2 and 15 of Duwamish marginal style 2,

---

[9] cf. Chart 5 — "Style Centers, Marginal Styles and Similarities", opp. p. 104.
[10] Even without the data establishing a later chronology for these Snoqualmie figures (cf. Catalogue of Illustrations, pp. 131 — 132), the character of their style would affirm that fact.

and of Plates 5.1 and 6 of Center 1, Quinault marginal styles. The simple character of the style, however, brings this figure closer to that of Center 2. Its associations, it should be noted, all lie with those of Centers 1 and 2, there being no suggestions of any other basic style centers in this carving. The style relationships of the Skokomish figure on Plate 22, marginal style 5, on the other hand, although it too is marginal to Center 2, Duwamish, associate it primarily with the marginal Quinault figures on Plates 5.1 and 6, and secondarily with the non-Salish Wasco-Chinook style of the Columbia River figures on Plates 59.1 and 60.2. No specific features of style or content point to any other centers. The same is essentially true for the sixth Center 2 marginal style, Plate 23.1, 2. It is therefore apparent that styles marginal to Duwamish Center 2 reveal strong similarities to Marginal Center 1, Quinault, styles and a few comparatively weaker associations with Centers 3, Lillooet, 8, Cowichan (b), and 10, Songish, to the north.

Center 1, Quinault, in Area 1, Western Washington. Marginal style 1, of Center 1, Quinault, (Plates 4, 5.1) is most closely related to the style of that basic center. But it differs from it in the treatment of facial features, which lack the characteristic three-zoned arrangement, and in the more schematic rendering of form. The depressed faces of these figures resemble those on Plate 8 of Duwamish, Center 2, and Plate 17, marginal to Center 2; while the shape of the heads is similar to that on Plate 22, also marginal to Center 2. This marginal style of Area 1 serves as a link between basic Centers 1 and 2. Marginal style 2 of Center 1 (Plates 6, 7) displays an elaboration of the three-zoned facial design and an arrangement of the planes of the face to suggest the convex protrusion of cheeks. The latter feature is foreign to both basic and marginal styles of Centers 1 and 2, but is reminiscent of a convex handling of facial planes in styles to the north. Two Quilleute masks (Plates 76.1, 2) indicate that this feature, and the generally more elaborate character of this style, came down along the coast from the north. The relationships here appear therefore to be equally divided between Center 1, Quinault, and the north[11].

To determine the source of the most striking characteristic of basic Center 1 style, the three-zone facial design, it is important to note the strength of this design along the middle reaches of the Columbia River. Among the Wasco who live in that area it appears on such shamans' carvings as those on Plates 59.1, 60.2, 62.1, 2 and on decorative carvings, as on Plate 63.1, 2. This design was also used commonly on carved wooden and horn dishes throughout the region extending from the Columbia River as far north as Puget Sound. The design was not therefore restricted to one area. But it was used very extensively

---

[11] With regard to the convex handling of facial planes, it should be noted that the rounded modelling of the surface of the face to indicate cheek-bones is a common characteristic of Vancouver Island carving in general (cf. Plates 39.1, 45, 47, 51, 52, etc.).

in the Columbia River-Quinault region, especially in the middle Columbia River area. The appearance of this design on Plate 22 and on the Thompson carvings on Plate 26.1, 2 suggest moreover that its use was current along a geographic arc extending from the Quinault on the western coast of Washington to the upper reaches of the Columbia River and north to the Thompson Indians in the interior of British Columbia. This seems to have been a distinctly southern Salish trait, since the known northern occurrences of it are few in number and weak in character.

Center 3, Lillooet, in Area 3, Upper Fraser River. The styles marginal to that of Lillooet Center 3 show this center to be pivotal between influences from Centers 1, Quinault, and 2, Duwamish, and those from the west. For example, Plate 30.1—5, marginal style 1 of Center 3, continues the looped arm feature and the calm repose of Plate 27, the basic style of this center; but the more important style elements of Plate 30,1—5 relate these figures, perhaps through Plate 29, a marginal style of Muskwium, Center 4, with Plate 44.1, a style marginal to Cowichan, Center 8, on Vancouver Island. Only in the compact, closed designs of Plate 30,1—5 and in the contained character of expression are there suggestions of south Salish style. A second style marginal to that of Center 3 is shown on Plate 31. There are in this style slight parallels with those of Centers 1 and 2, but none at all with the style of Center 3, and only weak resemblances with Plate 30,1—5. Its strongest tie is with such Kwakiutl carvings as Plate 65.1. Of considerable importance as an indication of the direction of marginal influences is the third Center 3 marginal style (Plate 28). The dramatic pose and the treatment of form refer to Center 3 style (cf. Plate 27) and are associated with Plate 29, a marginal style of Muskwium, Center 4, and with Plate 50.1, Sanetch, Center 9 style. It is also related to Plate 37, a style marginal to Comox, Center 6, and to the Kwakiutl style of Plate 65.1, 2. Thus the direction of marginal influences felt most strongly in Area 3 is from the west.

Centers 4, Muskwium, and 5, Lower Fraser, in Area 4, Straits of Georgia. In many respects Plate 29, marginal style 1 of Center 4, shows closer relationships with Lillooet Center 3 style (Plate 27) than with that of Centers 4 or 5. The most important similarities are: the handling of facial features and planes, particularly those of the mouth zone, and the wide shoulders, looped arms and large hands. This figure is also closely suggestive in the shaping and treatment of the head and neck of like style elements on Plate 30,1—5, a marginal Lillooet Center 3 style, and Plates 44.2 a and 44.2 d, a marginal style of Cowichan, Center 8. It also agrees with the latter figures in the nature of the flexion of the arms, the carving of the animal, the constricted shaping of the torso and, especially, in the more narrative nature of its content. This style moreover has analogies in its expression and form with Plate 28, a marginal Lillooet Center 3 style. In consequences of these similarities, marginal style 1 of Center 4 appears to be a focal style in which elements of Center 3 style (Plate 27)

combine with those of marginal Center 3 styles (Plates 28, 30,1—5). Its influence is apparent to the west in Plate 44.1, a marginal style of Cowichan
Center 8. It seems therefore that the direction of these style relationships
was from east to west.

The second important marginal style of Center 4, as represented by Plate
33.1, 2, shows (1) strong Kwakiutl affiliations in the handling of facial features
and in its heavy forms (cf. Plates 65.1, 67.2); (2) a slight suggestion in the
geometric or schematic treatment of parts of marginal Quinault style (cf.
Plates 5.1 and 33.1); and (3) a reminiscence of Puget Sound style in its feeling
for compact forms or shapes. Moreover, the content and the momentary nature
of its expression relate both of these figures with Plate 28, a marginal Lillooet
Center 3 style, Plate 39.2 of Comox Center 6 style, and with Plate 58.1, a
Vancouver Island figure; while in the tension and strength of outline and in the
expressive use of shapes they agree with Plate 29. This style is therefore closely
associated with those of its own Area and with Kwakiutl style to the north
and west.

Two additional marginal styles in Area 4 are represented by the masks
on Plates 35 and 36. These are marginal to Lower Fraser, Center 5 style. The
closest analogies with Plate 36 appear in the Kwakiutl swaixwe masks on
Plates 70.2 and 71.2, and in the head of the figure on Plate 65.2. Although the
strongest relationships are therefore with Kwakiutl style, there is nevertheless
a suggestion of southern Salish Puget Sound influences in the carvings on
the attached side pieces and in the style of the bird heads. The second marginal
style to Center 5, Plate 35, is practically identical to that of Nanaimo, Center 7,
(Plate 42.1, 2).

It is apparent therefore that the marginal styles of Centers 4 and 5 establish
stronger ties between these centers and Vancouver Island styles than with
those to the south and east.

Marginal Styles to Centers in Area 5, Vancouver Island: Center 6, Comox.
Of the two styles marginal to Center 6, one is mainly Kwakiutl in its affinities
and the other Salish. Two examples, Plates 37 and 39.1, represent the first
of these. Both, in the extremely simplified, almost geometric handling of the
forms of the body, suggest a general similarity with such Salish examples as
Plate 41.1, a marginal Nanaimo Center 7 style, Plate 45 of Center 8, Cowichan
(b), and Plate 12 of Duwamish Center 2. The strongest resemblances, however,
are with Kwakiutl carvings. This is evident when the heads are compared
with the Kwakiutl examples on Plates 65.2, 69.2, 70.2 and 71.2. The second
marginal style to Center 6, Plate 38, although it too has associations with
Kwakiutl style (i. e., the attached parts and non-functional surface decoration),
these are relatively weak. Rather, very close relationships link it with Salish
style. The nose, for instance, compares with that of Plate 43 of Nanaimo,
Center 7 style; the shaping of the mouth, with Plate 34, Lower Fraser, style
Center 5; the surmounting animal heads, with Plate 35, a style marginal to

Center 5; and the treatment of the eyes, with Plates 48.2 and 49, a marginal style to Cowichan Center 8. The two styles marginal to Center 6, therefore, make clear its northerly location and the extent to which it has absorbed and adapted Kwakiutl influences.

Center 7, Nanaimo. Of the two marginal styles to Nanaimo, Center 7, the most important is that of the small decorative carvings on Plate 41.1, 2. The feeling for integrated and expressive form, for boldness of pattern and shapes, and for strong enclosing outlines suggest a comparison of Plate 41.1 with the marginal Duwamish Center 2 style of Plate 23.1, 2. The organic, unified handling of the small animal on Plate 41.2 resembles that of Plate 32 of Muskwium Center 4 style and Plate 29, a style marginal to that Center, and contrasts with the more elaborate and descriptive treatment of animal and bird heads on Plates 42.1 and 43 of Nanaimo, Center 7 style. In the narrative and descriptive nature of their content, the carvings of the second marginal Nanaimo, Center 7 style (Plate 40.2, 3), show strong non-Salish, probably Kwakiutl influences; while the nature of the high relief carving and the shaping of the background indicate the adaptation of a three-dimensional tradition to a relief technique and suggest Salish associations. A weak style relationship appears between these posts and the one on Plate 40.1, of Comox, Center 6 style; but the mask on the figure on Plate 40.2 is nearer in type to that represented on Plate 48.2 of marginal Cowichan Center 8 style, than to those worn by the masked figures on Plates 37 and 38. Since carved house posts did not constitute a traditional class of Salish sculpture, but were acquired from their Kwakiutl and Nootka neighbors, these carvings show a survival of weakened Salish characteristics used in combination with northern elements in a new, foreign type of carving. Hence this marginal style reveals dominant non-Salish and weak Salish associations.

It therefore appears that strong northern or non-Salish elements are mingled in the styles marginal to Nanaimo, Center 7, with equally strong Salish features, some of which indicate similarities with marginal Duwamish Center 2 style, some with Muskwium Center 4 style. These relationships contribute heavily to the formation of Nanaimo, Center 7, basic style.

Center 8, Cowichan. Three styles are marginal to Cowichan, Center 8. The first is represented by the four drum figures on Plates 44.1, 44.2a, b, c, d. They show in their simple rounded shapes, slight modelling of facial features and looped arms a similarity to the five figures on Plate 30.1—5, a marginal Lillooet Center 3 style. The strong, simplified forms of the body, Plate 44.2a, d, resemble those of Plate 31, another marginal Center 3 style; while the shape of the heads and treatment of facial features of Plate 44.2a, d compare with those of Plate 29, a marginal Muskwium Center 4 style, and those of Plate 44.2, b, c, with that of Plate 27, Lillooet, Center 3 basic style. In contrast to the carvings on Plates 39.2 and 40.1, Comox Center 6 basic style, these are traditional Salish style elements. This marginal style, in fact, establishes a relationship between marginal Lillooet Center 3 style and that of Cowichan (a), Center 8 (Plates 46, 55.1).

The second marginal Center 8 style, Plates 48.1, 2 and 49, is similar to that of Plate 35, a marginal Lower Fraser, Center 5 style, of Plate 42.1, 2, Nanaimo, Center 7, style and Plate 34, Lower Fraser, Center 5 style. This is a strong Salish style, in which only the realistic elements on Plates 48.2 and 49 have any ties with Kwakiutl or non-Salish work. The third marginal Cowichan Center 8 style is represented by Plates 47.1, 2 and 55.2. These are comparable in the treatment of the heads and facial features and in the geometric forms of the body or base to the house posts on Plate 51.a, b, a marginal Sanetch, Center 9 style, and Plate 52 a marginal Songish, Center 10 style. Cowichan marginal styles therefore reveal this Center as associated with styles to the east and south.

Center 9, Sanetch. The single style marginal to Center 9 is represented by Plate 51a, b. In the truncated treatment of the head and the shaping of the neck it refers to similar elements on Plate 45, Cowichan (b), Center 8 style and Plate 47.1, 2, a style marginal to that center. The design of the head also suggests a comparison with that of Plates 13.2 and 20.1, marginal Duwamish, Center 2 styles; while the schematic modelling of the face, emphasizing the flat mouth zone, is similar to that of Plate 46 of Cowichan (a) Center 8 style and Plate 67.2 of the Kwakiutl. This style therefore seems to be a local one with comparatively weak style influences from beyond its own general area.

Center 10, Songish. Of the two styles marginal to Songish, Center 10, the one figured on Plates 52 and 53.2 appears to be a combination of style elements from Cowichan and Sanetch centers. The architectural type of post, for instance, is the same as that illustrated on Plates 46 and 55.1 of Cowichan (a) Center 8 style; while the treatment of the head and neck is similar to that on Plates 45 of Cowichan (b) Center 8 and 51a, b, a style marginal to Sanetch, Center 9. The carving of facial features resembles most closely those on Plate 50.1 of Sanetch Center 9 style; but the animals agree in species with those on Plate 57 and in style with the Muskwium Center 4 example on Plate 32. The geometric character of the base of both posts refers to the geometric posts on Plates 53.1 and 56 of Songish, Center 10 basic style, and in design the base of Plate 52 resembles that of Plates 55.2 a style marginal to Cowichan Center 8.

The second marginal Songish style, Plate 53.3, is related to the first one and to Cowichan (a), Center 8 style (cf. Plates 46, 55.1). But evidences of Kwakiutl influence appear in such realistic details as the carved tunic and the round projections representing knees, the latter treatment being apparently a schematization of the Kwakiutl method of flattening the surface of the knee, thereby producing a circular plane (cf. Plates 65.1, 67.1). In general, the vitiated handling and expression of the figure show this marginal Songish style to be weak and derivative.

HISTORICAL DEVELOPMENT

Since specific chronological dating for individual specimens is lacking, it is necessary to reconstruct the historical development of Salish sculpture through its style relationships. Two alternate hypotheses must be considered. The first of these is that the center or point of origin of Salish sculptural art was along the coast, from whence influences developed inland, up the rivers. The second is the reverse of this and places the early centers up the rivers with the coastal art developing later under inland influences[12].

The evidence in support the first hypothesis is so remarkably weak as to be practically negligible. Any premise of a chronological arrangement of styles presupposes that later styles show a development elaboration or misunderstood handling of the essential features of an earlier one. When compared with up-river objects, the coastal Salish carvings show this development and elaboration. The following sequence, for example, testifies to this relationship: Plates 46—44.1—29—30.1—5—27. The up-river objects show the strongest handling of these style features, instead of a simplified, vague handling of them which would have resulted if this style had originated on the coast and had been taken inland up the rivers. New impulses and new contacts, on the contrary, seem to have modified these essential features as they appear in coastal carvings. For instance, the nature of house post carvings should be noted, as well as the general tendency of coastal art towards greater elaboration, description and representation[13]. But the similarities of coastal and interior styles suggest in some cases (cf. Plates 50.1, 29, 40.1, 45, 18.2, 20.1, 53.1, 19.2, 19.2a) a fairly strong retention of up-river features.

The only vestige of support for the first hypothesis would therefore appear to rest on the suppositions that the early basic objects which could have supported it have now all disappeared, that the surviving sculpture from the coastal areas represents a later development than once existed there, and that the up-river styles, being isolated from later influences, reveal the coastal art at the stage of its development when it moved up the rivers. Although this hypothesis cannot be completely ruled out, the opposing evidence derived from the relationships between styles and cultural data largely discredit it.

---

[12] In discussing the Salishan movements, Kroeber quotes Boas as saying that on archaeological and linguistic grounds he believed that the Salish had spread from the interior down the Fraser River to its mouth and had then expanded north and south along the coast. Concerning this statement Kroeber says "that primary coastward expansion does not seem altogether certain, and a flow up the Fraser not outside the bounds of possibility" (Kroeber, 1917, p. 391).

[13] Ethnological and anthropological data support this statement of the changes in the coastal regions of Vancouver Island and Western Washington of basic interior cultural patterns under new impulses coming down from the north (cf. Olson, 1936, pp. 11–13; Barnett, 1938, pp. 119—139).

On the other hand, the hypothesis for an inland or up-river origin is strongly supported by relationships and inter-relationships between basic style centers and marginal styles. The most significant affinities in this respect are those between Centers 2, 3, 4 and 5 and their marginal styles — i. e., those of Areas 2, Puget Sound; 3, Upper Fraser River; and 4, Straits of Georgia. Although style correspondences with adjacent and coastal objects can be discerned, the relative isolation or remoteness of the up-river points from the strong northern influences apparently made it possible for them to preserve more successfully the older character of their style. Since the Duwamish of the central Puget Sound area were the most isolated of the Salish, it would appear that the objects of basic style Center 2 reflect the older features of Salish style. The Quinault style of Center 1, through its connection both with the Duwamish center and with the old and important Columbia River center, may also be considered as retaining many of the older style characteristics; although these are somewhat modified by influences from the north[14]. An important fact favoring an earlier date for these up-river objects is the boldness and the surety of their approach to problems of design and expression: this shows that they were working within an old tradition and not within one that was losing sight of its strongest essentials through relatively new and foreign influences.

In conclusion, the oldest of the major styles appear to be, on the basis of style correspondences and relationships, those represented by Plates 2, 3, 8, 9, 12, 27, 29 and 32. The second oldest group would include Plates 4, 5.1, 17, 28, 34, 36, 37, 44.1 and 50.1; the third, Plates 6, 7, 18.2, 20.1, 30.1—5, 33.1, 35, 42.1, 43, 45 and 49; and the fourth, Plates 22, 31, 38, 39.1, 40.1, 3, 46, 51a, 53.2 and 56.2. Of these, the first group is entirely up-river, the second to a large extent, and the third and fourth dominantly coastal. If it were possible to specify a single center for the origin of Salish sculpture, the Duwamish would be the one. There should be noted, on the other hand, that two fundamental traditions, those of geometric and naturalistic form, appear mingled in Salish sculpture. Both of these traditions are ancient, and may in fact derive from separate centers of origin. It is tempting to place one of these near or in the Puget Sound area and the other up the Fraser. This, it is believed, further investigations will substantiate.

SUMMARY

Salish sculpture characteristically shows simplicity and clarity of carved shapes. These are defined by broad surface planes, that are concave, convex or flat, are contained within strong outlines and are integrated functionally and

---

[14] In spite of the fact that the Quinault have some of the cultural elements of a coastal culture, they were essentially a river people; while the deep reaches of Puget Sound, although salt-water, may be considered as creating an environment comparable to that of a river. The same applies to the peoples of the Straits of Georgia who lived up the inlets or deep indentations of the Straits.

rhythmically to express an organic whole. Parts are comparatively large in scale and their effectiveness derives to a great extent from their relationship to the total form and not from any small descriptive or decorative details. A vigor and directness of purpose pervades this sculpture. Elegance and refinement are of relatively little importance when compared with strength of expression through simple carved forms. Within these broad limits, two clearly differentiated strains in Salish sculpture are discernible, the southern and the northern[15]. These are divergent strains within the same tradition, the southern in all probability being the more basic.

In general the southern strain tends towards the abstract, relying upon stylized forms derived from, but not dependent upon nature. Content is highly personal, but it is presented in an objective, restrained manner. Balanced, static forms convey the idea of movement and power held in reserve, while horizontal depth, producing effects of light and shade, suggest action and movement. These carvings are expressive in terms of carved shapes and surfaces, although paint was used to cover them and to depict symbolic and a few real details. Single figures dominate and, even though they may have been used dramatically in company with other carvings, the original concept was in terms of the single figure.

The northern, when compared with examples of this strain, shows a greater reliance upon the actualities of human forms and emotions. Thus the carvings not only have a greater degree of lifelikeness, but also disclose a more specific, subjective and momentary content. A suggestion of the instantaneous emanates from these more individual dramatizations. The forms sometimes have strongly implied dynamic character; movement is expressed both horizontally and vertically. Generally the carvings are expressive by reason of the dramatic arrangement of their modelled and realistic detail, the latter often picked out or slightly embellished with paint. Although single figures are common, animals and figures are frequently combined in a meaningful composition; and where single figures are brought together in an object, they are carved with that relationship in mind. Both of these strains are important for a comprehension of this sculpture.

Salish sculpture is a distinctive art, thoroughly different in its salient elements from that of the more northern peoples of the Northwest Coast. The latter is basically representational and decorative; the carvings are frequently large immovable objects of impressive size, such as house fronts, heraldic crests and posts, totem poles and huge post figures. Many masks and smaller carvings were also made, but these essentially agree in style with the larger objects (cf. Plates 69.2, 71). Emphasis is placed on an elaborate surface carving by

---

[15] The southern strain centers in Area 2, Puget Sound, and also appears in Areas 1, Western Washington, and 3, Upper Fraser River; while the northern extends westward from Area 3 and embraces Areas 4, Straits of Georgia, and 5, Vancouver Island.

means of which a primarily linear style depicts in high or low relief the descriptive and decorative details[16]. Conventionalized in many cases, these details break up the surfaces into a number of comparatively small units. Whether narrative or heraldic in meaning, the fundamental purpose of the majority of the carvings is to impress by displaying the antecedents of power and wealth of individuals or restricted groups within the society. Towards this end many figures are interrelated in complex designs, not only on totem poles, but also frequently on masks. The single figure, when it occurs, is usually considered not as an expression of an idea through form, but as the statement of the melodramatic peak in a series of actions which refer back and forward to the beginning and conclusion of the drama. This dramatic quality is quite frequently developed to the point of aggressiveness (cf. Plates 67.1, 2, 68.1). In practically every respect this art differs from that of the Salish.

The southern Kwakiutl and Nootka, constituting the more important of the immediate neighbors of the northern Salish[17], agree culturally and temperamentally with the more northern peoples. Their sculpture confirms this affinity. But it also reveals important features found in Salish art. These features, in fact, indicate that their sculpture should be considered as transitional between that of the northern or typical Northwest Coast and that of the Salish. The association of Kwakiutl and Nootka potlatch and other figures with carvings of the northern Salish strain (cf. Plates 65.1, 2, 28, 29, 50.1) indicate that, if they were not at one time influenced by the older Salish tradition, they at least shared with them their basic sculptural elements[18]. A like relationship appears in certain types of masks of the Kwakiutl when compared with the Salish swaixwe masks (cf. Plates 34, 36, 42.1, 43, 69.2, 70.2, 71.2). It seems likely, therefore, that in these respects the Kwakiutl especially, who were a northern people, appropriated an art form with which they came into contact in the southern part of the Northwest Coast, and, with the acquisition of metal tools, developed it and imprinted upon it certain northern elements[19]. That Salish carving did not enjoy a florescence after the acquisition of metal suggests that (1) it represented an old tradition which had previously reached its peak and had

---

[16] It should be noted that, in general, this relief carving follows the surface of the plane, i. e. the sculptor carves in from the surface, retaining in his finished work the original character of the surface. Thus a totem pole retains the original columnar shape of its surface.

[17] That is, precisely, those of southern and western British Columbia and of Vancouver Island. It should be noted that the northern art strain is common to these Salish.

[18] For instance, the breadth of surfaces, the feeling for shapes and their integration, and the expression of a full or contained volume. In other words, a similar fundamental feeling for carved forms as expression. The details and the content of these figures, however, are northern.

[19] This runs counter to the theory that the Kwakiutl, with their more complex culture, influenced the Salish but received little from them.

become by that time vitiated, or that (2) the conservatism of the people and their disdain of innovation and elaboration worked against a development of virtuosity. The latter reason would explain why northern contacts, and in fact those with all marginal non-Salish peoples, led to comparatively few borrowings. The art of the marginal peoples of the Columbia River valley and of western Washington stands in a relationship to that of the Salish similar to the art of the Kwakiutl.

It appears, therefore, that Salish sculpture represents an older southern tradition on the Northwest Coast which differs from the northern later and more richly elaborate style of wood carving; while the peoples immediately adjoining the Salish on the north and southwest produced an art transitional between the two, but with more pronouncedly northern stylistic affiliations. Salish carving consequently must be considered in its proper light as an art differing in content, in concept, and in formal aspects from that of the north, yet manifesting a very important tradition which is as much a part of the Northwest Coast as that of the better known northern peoples.

The true character of the Salish, or southern, and of the northern art traditions, can perhaps be more clearly understood and differentiated when it is considered to what extent each art reflects or represents two fundamentally different peoples and cultures. The Salish are proud and reserved, temperamentally self-contained and conservative; while the northerners are haughty, aggressive and acquisitive. Their society is dominated by a number of individually powerful units within a group of strong larger units, all of a restrictive nature, in which aristocratic lineage, personal prestige and evidences of power are asserted. Although power and prestige also count for much among the Salish, their society is more democratic or communal; that is, it is basically organic rather than parasitical, interdependent rather than interrelated.

In ceremonial patterns and concepts, moreover, an equally marked difference appears. The Salish dramatic performances, although conducted by a group of shamans, are held for the therapeutic or general welfare, not only of an individual but of the community at large. Relatively simple paraphernalia are used, the meaning and symbolic interpretation of which is understood by all spectators who are, properly speaking, participants rather than spectators, since they frequently assist in the pantomime of the dramatic performances. On the other hand, the more important of the northern ceremonials revolve around complexly organized restricted groups. Their fundamental purpose appears to have been of a repressive nature, to increase personal prestige, or to display personal power or wealth. Employing elaborate paraphernalia, with tricks and illusions to impress the assembled spectators, the performances could not be shared by anyone outside of the restricted group. Secrecy was in many instances all important. Since any art must remain in the final analysis an expression of a people and their culture, it is understandable why the northern tradition, when considered in terms of the above features, is profuse, mundane, assertive and descriptive, and why the Salish is relatively calm, imaginative and expressive.

As an art, the sculpture of the Salish peoples is a strong, direct and simple expression in terms of the most satisfying aspects of carving. With certainty and assurance of purpose, the sculptor achieves an integration of form. The breadth of surfaces and the vigor of shapes retain or convey their nature as carvings in wood; while the reduction of parts to simple essentials and their strong articulation into a structural, firmly interdependent unity gives immediate expression to the form as a whole. This unity tends to make the formal sculptural relationships within the figure instantly apparent, and, since these are so closely connected with the purpose in the mind of the sculptor, the expression of content is also easily and quickly grasped.

Repeated contacts with these apparently simple carvings disclose most graphically the rhythms, the balancing of masses, the unity of line, and the importance of light and shade resulting from variations of surface and from receding and projecting planes. Thus, although their carvings are easily read and as easily comprehended sculpturally, they must be seen often to be fully appreciated. Only then is it discovered that their summary shapes have captured the permanent, the tangible, the universal aspect of form, and that the calm, contained quality of their static poses manifests a restraint, a vigor, a latent energy constituting what may properly be called a classic art of an early phase as yet undisturbed by or showing no signs of the grandiose perfectionism which destroys this quality in developed classic arts.

BIBLIOGRAPHY

BANCROFT, H. H.
    1884.   History of the Northwest Coast. San Francisco, 2 vols.

BARBEAU, MARIUS
    1929.   Totem Poles of Gitksan, Upper Skeena River, British Columbia. *National Museuuu of Canada, Bulletin 61, Anthropological Series No. 12.* Ottawa.

BARNETT, H. G.
    1938.   The Coast Salish of Canada. *American Anthropologist, Vol. 40,* pp. 118—141.
    1939.   The Gulf of Georgia Salish. *Anthropological Records, Vol. 1,* pp. 221—295. Berkeley.
    1942.   The Southern Extent of Totem Pole Carving. *Pacific Northwest Quarterly, October,* pp. 379—389.

BOAS, FRANZ
    1888.   The Houses of the Kwakiutl Indians, British Columbia. *Proceedings of the U. S. National Museum, Vol. 11,* pp. 197—213.
    1889.   Notes on the Snanaimuq, *American Anthropologist, Vol. 2,* pp. 321—328.
    1891.   The Indians of British Columbia: Lku'ngen, Nootka, Kwakiutl, Shuswap. *Report of the British Association for the Advancement of Science, 1890,* pp. 553—715.
    1894.   The Indian Tribes of the Lower Fraser River, *British Association for the Advancement of Science, Sixty-fourth meeting,* pp. 453—463.
    1897a. The Social Organization and the Secret Societies of the Kwakiutl Indians. *Report of the U. S. National Museum for 1895,* pp. 313—738.
    1897b. The Decorative Art of the Indians of the North Pacific Coast. *American Museum of Natural History, Bulletin 9,* pp. 123—176.
    1900.   Chapter on Art; and Conclusions. In Teit, The Thompson Indians of British Columbia. *Publications of the Jesup North Pacific Expedition, Vol. 1,* pp. 376—390.
    1903.   The Decorative Art of the North American Indians. *Popular Science Monthly, Vol. 63,* pp. 481—498.
    1904.   Primitive Art. *A Guide Leaflet to Collections in the American Museum of Natural History No. 15.*
    1908.   Notes on the Lillooet Indians. *Publications of the Jesup North Pacific Expedition, Vol. 2,* pp. 292—300.
    1909.   The Kwakiutl of Vancouver Island. *Publications of the Jesup North Pacific Expedition, Vol. 5, Pt. 2,* pp. 301—522.
    1910.   Methods in Indian Woodwork. *The Red Man, Vol. 2, No. 8.* pp. 3—10.
    1921.   Ethnology of the Kwakiutl. *Bureau of American Ethnology, Annual Report 35, Pts. 1 and 2.*
    1927.   Primitive Art. Oslo and Cambridge.

BOIT, JOHN
    1920.   Boit's Leg of the Columbia, 1790—1792. *Proceedings, Massachusetts Historical Society, Vol. 53*, pp. 217—275.

CODERE, HELEN
    1947.   The Swaixwe Myth, *Journal of American Folklore* in press.

COOK, CAPT. JAMES
    1785.   A Voyage to the Pacific Ocean, Vol. 2, London, 3 vols.

COUES, ELLIOTT
    1897.   New Light on the Early History of the Greater Northwest. The manuscript journals of Alexander Henry . . . and David Thompson. 1799—1814. New York.

CURTIS, EDWARD S.
    1913.   The North American Indian, vol. 9. Cambridge.

DALL, W. H.
    1885.   On Masks, Labrets and certain Aboriginal Customs. *Smithsonian Institution, 3rd Annual Report*, pp. 67—202.

DIXON, CAPT. GEORGE
    1789.   A Voyage Round the World but more particularly to the Northwest Coast of America. London.

DORSEY, GEORGE A.
    1902.   The Dwamish Indian Spirit Boat and its Use. *Free Museum of Science and Art of the University of Pennsylvania, Bulletin 3*, pp. 227—238.

DOUGLAS, F. H., and RENE D'HARNONCOURT
    1941.   Indian Art of the United States. New York.

EELLS, MYRON
    1887.   The Indians of Puget Sound. *American Antiquarian and Oriental Journal, Vol. 9*, pp. 1—9, 97—104, 211—219, 219—276.
    1889.   The Twana, Chemakum, and Clallum Indians of Washington Territory. *Report, Smithsonian Institution for 1887, Pt. 1*, pp. 605—681.

EMMONS, G. T.
    1930.   The Art of the Northwest Coast Indians. *Natural History, Vol. 30*, pp. 282—292.

FARRAND, LIVINGSTON
    1902.   Traditions of the Quinault Indians. *American Museum of Natural History, Memoir 4, Pt. 3*, pp. 77—132.

FRACHTENBERG, LEO J.
    1920a. Eschatology of the Quileute Indians. *American Anthropologist, Vol. 22*, pp. 330—340.
    1920b. The Ceremonial Societies of the Quileute Indians. *American Anthropologist, Vol. 23*, pp. 320—352.

GIBBS, GEORGE
    1855.   Report on the Indian Tribes of the Territory of Washington. *Pacific Railroad Report, Vol. 1*, pp. 402—436. Washington.
    1877.   Tribes of Western Washington and Northwestern Oregon. *Contributions to North American Ethnology, Vol. 1*, pp. 157—241. Washington.

GODDARD, PLINY E.
  1934. Indians of the Northwest Coast. *American Museum of Natural History, Handbook 10.*

GUNTHER, ERNA
  1927. Klallam Ethnography. *University of Washington Publications in Anthropology, Vol. 1.*

HAEBERLIN, HERMAN K.
  1918a. SBetetda'q, A Shamanistic performance of the Coast Salish. *American Anthropologist, Vol. 20,* pp. 249—257.
  1918b. Principles of Esthetic Form in the Art of the North Pacific Coast. *American Anthropologist, Vol. 20,* pp. 258—264.

HAEBERLIN, H. K. and ERNA GUNTHER
  1930. The Indians of Puget Sound. *University of Washington Publications in Anthropology, Vol. 4.*

HALE, HORATIO
  1846. Ethnology and Philology. United States Exploring Expedition, 1838—42, under the command of Charles Wilkes, Vol. 6. Philadelphia.

HILL-TOUT, CHARLES
  1905. The Salish Tribes of the Coast and Lower Fraser River Delta. *Annual Archaeological Report, 1905, Appendix to Report of Minister of Education,* pp. 225—235. Ontario.
  1907. British North America, Vol. 1. London.

HODGE, F. W., editor
  1907—10. Handbook of the American Indian north of Mexico. *Bureau of American Ethnology, Bulletin 30,* 2 vols. Washington.

HOSMER, JAMES K.
  1902. History of the Expedition of Captain Lewis and Clark, 2 vols. Chicago.

HOWAY, F. W.
  1924. The Early Literature of the Northwest Coast. *Proceedings and Transactions of the Royal Society of Canada, series 3, Vol. 18,* pp. 1—18. Ottawa.

IRVING, WASHINGTON
  1868. Astoria. New York.

JENNESS, DIAMOND
  1934. The Indians of Canada. *National Museum of Canada, Bulletin 65.* Ottawa.

JEWITT, JOHN R.
  1815. A Narrative of the Adventures and Sufferings of ... Three Years among the Natives of Nootka Sound. Middletown.

KROEBER, A. L.
  1917. The Tribes of the Pacific Coast of North America. *Proceedings of the 19th International Congress of Americanists,* pp. 385—410. Washinton.
  1923. American Culture and the Northwest Coast. *American Anthropologist, Vol. 25,* pp. 1—20.
  1939. Cultural and Natural Areas of Native North America. *University of California Publications in American Archaeology and Ethnology,* Vol. 38.

LA PEROUSE, J. F. DE G. DE
    1797. Journals of ... Paris.
    1798. Journals of ... London.

LEVI-STRAUSS, CLAUDE
    1943. The Art of the Northwest Coast at the American Museum of Natural
          History. *Gazette des Beaux-Arts, Vol. 24*, pp. 175—182.

LEWIS, A. B.
    1906. Tribes of the Columbia Valley and the Coast of Washington and
          Oregon. *American Anthropological Association, Memoir 1.*

LEWIS, M., and W. CLARK
    1904—4. Original Journals of the Lewis and Clark Expedition, 1804—6,
          R. G. Thwaites, editor. New York.

MEARES, J.
    1791. Voyages made in the Years 1788 and 1789 from China to the North-
          west Coast of America, 2 vols. London.

NEWCOMBE, C. F.
    1909. Guide to the Anthropological Collection in the Provincial Museum.
          Victoria.
    1923. Menzies' Journal of Vancouver's Voyage. *Archives of British Co-
          lumbia, Memoir 5*, pp. 1—171.

NIBLACK, A. P.
    1888. Coast Indians of Southern Alaska and Northern British Columbia.
          United States National Museum, Report, pp. 275—386.

OLSON, RONALD L.
    1927. Adze, Canoe and House Types of the Northwest Coast. *University
          of Washington Publications in Anthropology, Vol. 2.*
    1935. The Indians of the Northwest Coast. *Natural History, Vol. 35*,
          pp. 183—197.
    1936. The Quinault Indians. *University of Washington Publications in
          Anthropology, Vol. 6.*

PORTLOCK, N.
    1789. A Voyage Round the World. London.

RAY, VERNE F.
    1938. Lower Chinook Ethnographic Notes. *University of Washington
          Publications in Anthropology, Vol. 7.*

ROSS, ALEXANDER
    1904. Adventures of the First Settlers on the Oregon or Columbia River...
          Early Western Travels, Thwaites, editor, Vol. 7.

SAPIR, EDWARD
    1922. Vancouver Island Indians. *Encyclopedia of Religion and Ethics,
          Hastings editor, Vol. 12*, pp. 591—595.

SCHOOLCRAFT, HENRY R.
    1853. Information Respecting the History, Condition and Prospects of
          the Indian Tribes of the United States. Philadelphia.

SMITH, HARLAN I.
    1911. Totem Poles of the North Pacific. *Natural History, Vol. 11*, pp.
          77—82.
    1923. An Album of Prehistoric Canadian Art. *National Museum of Canada,
          Bulletin 37.* Ottawa.

SMITH, MARIAN W.
    1939.   Review of R. L. Olson, The Quinault Indians. *Journal of American Folklore, Vol. 52, No. 204*, pp. 220—221.
    1940a. The Puyallup Nisqually. New York.
    1940b. The Puyallup of Washington. In Acculturation in Seven American Indian Tribes, Linton editor, pp. 3—36. New York.
    1941.   The Coast Salish of Puget Sound. *American Anthropologist, Vol. 43*, pp. 197—211.
    1946.   Petroglyph Complexes in the History of the Columbia-Fraser Region. *Southwestern Journal of Anthropology, Vol. 2*, pp. 306—322.

SPIER, L., and E. SAPIR
    1930.   Wishram Ethnography. *University of Washington Publications in Anthropology, Vol. 3*.

SPIER, LESLIE
    1936.   Tribal Distribution in Washington. *General Series in Anthropology, Vol. 3*.

SPROAT, G. M.
    1868.   Scenes and Studies of Savage Life. London.

STERN, BERNARD
    1934.   The Lummi Indians of Northwest Washington. New York.

STEWARD, JULIAN H.
    1937.   Petroglyphs of the United States. *Smithsonian Institution, Annual Report 1936*, pp. 405—425.

STRONG, WM. DUNCAN
    1945.   The Occurrence and Wider Implications of a "Ghost Cult" in the Columbia River, Suggested by Carvings in Wood, Bone, and Stone.*American Anthropologist, Vol. 47*, pp. 244—251.

SWAN, JAMES G.
    1857.   The Northwest Coast: or Three Year's Residence in Washington Territory. New York.
    1869.   The Indians of Cape Flattery. *Smithsonian Institution,Contributions to Knowledge, No. 220*.

SWANTON, JOHN R.
    1921.   The Salish. *Encyclopedia of Religion and Ethics, Vol. 11*, pp. 97—100.

TEIT, JAMES
    1900.   The Thompson Indians of British Columbia. *Publications of the Jesup North Pacific Expedition, Vol. 1*, pp. 163—375.
    1906.   The Lillooet Indians. *Publications of the Jesup North Pacific Expedition, Vol. 2*, pp. 193—200.
    1928.   The Middle Columbia Salish. *University of Washington Publications in Anthropology, Vol. 2*.

TYRRELL, J. B., editor
    1916.   David Thompson's Narrative of his Explorations in Western America, 1784—1812. *Publications of the Champlain Society, Vol. 12*, Toronto.

UNDERHILL, RUTH
    1945.   Indians of the Pacific Northwest. *United States Office of Indian Affairs, Indian Life and Customs Pamphlets, Vol. 5*.

VAILLANT, GEORGE
    1939.   Indian Arts in North America. New York.

VANCOUVER, GEORGE
    1798.   A Voyage of Discovery to the North Pacific Ocean... 1790—1795.
           London.

WATERMAN, T. T.
    1923.   Some Conundrums in Northwest Coast Art. *American Anthropologist, Vol. 25*, pp. 435—451.
    1930.   The Paraphernalia of the Duwamish "Spirit-Canoe" Ceremony. *Indian Notes, Museum of the American Indian, Heye Foundation, Vol. 7*, Nos. 2—4.

WATERMAN, T. T. and RUTH GRIENER
    1921.   Indian Homes of Puget Sound. *Indian Notes and Monographs, Museum of the American Indian, Heye Foundation, Miscellaneous Series 9.*

WATERMAN, T. T. and collaborators
    1921.   Native Houses of Western North America. *Indian Notes and Monographs, Museum of the American Indian, Heye Foundation, Miscellaneous Series 11.*

WILKES, CHARLES
    1845.   Narrative of the United States Exploring Expedition, 1838—1842. Philadelphia.

WILLOUGHBY, CHARLES
    1889.   Indians of the Quinaielt Agency, Washington Territory. *Smithsonian Institution, Annual Report 1886, Pt. 1*, pp. 267—282.

CATALOGUE OF ILLUSTRATIONS

Pl. 1 . . . . . . Shaman's Wand, Quinault, Washington
American Museum of Natural History, N. Y., 16/4953 cedar; ca.
19½" H. overall; figure ca. 10" H; traces of black and red
paint; attached deer-hoof rattles; black beads for eyes.
From catalogue: — Shaman guardian spirit wand; collected by
James Terry, 1882; Quinault Indians, Washington.

Pl. 2 . . . . . . Shaman's Wand, Quinault, Washington
American Museum of Natural History, N. Y., 16A/4921 cedar;
ca. 20" H. overall; figure ca. 12" H.; painted black; horsehair
for hair.
From catalogue: — Representation of a shaman guardian spirit:
shaman's seqwa'nc; collected by Livingston Farrand, 1898;
Quinault Indians, Washington.

Pl. 3a, b . . . Shaman's Wand, Quinault, Washington
Chicago Natural History Museum, 19789 cedar; 18¾" H.;
painted red, face to either side of nose unpainted; attached
deer-hoof rattles.
From catalogue: — Wooden ceremonial image, painted red, rattle
around neck; collected by Rev. Myron Eells, Nov.-Dec., 1892;
Quinault Tribe, Washington.

Pl. 4a, b . . . Shaman's Wand, Quinault, Washington
Museum of the American Indian, Heye Foundation, N. Y.,
5/9519 cedar; 10⅝" H. overall; figure ca. 4½" H.; unpainted.
From catalogue: — Represents spirit controlled by shaman;
collected by Leo J. Frachtenberg; acquired in 1917; Quinault
Tribe, Taholah, Washington.

Pl. 5.1 . . . . . Shaman's Wand, Quinault, Washington
Museum of the American Indian, Heye Foundation, N. Y.,
5/9521 cedar; 19¼" H. overall; figure ca. 13" H.; painted
red; deer-hoof rattles attached; shell inlay eyes.
From catalogue: — Represents spirit controlled by shaman;
collected by Leo J. Frachtenberg; acquired in 1917; Quinault
Tribe, Taholah, Washington.

Pl. 5.2 . . . . . Shaman's Wand, Quinault, Washington
Museum of the American Indian, Heye Foundation, N. Y.,
5/9520 cedar; 21½" H. overall; figure ca. 14" H.; painted
brownish-red; deer-hoof rattles attached; shell inlay eyes.
From catalogue: — Represents spirit controlled by shaman;
collected by Leo J. Frachtenberg; aqcuired in 1917; Quinault
Tribe, Taholah, Washington.

Pl. 6a, b . . . Shaman's Figure, Quinault, Washington
American Museum of Natural History, N. Y., 16/4946 cedar; 36″
H.; painted red and white; shell inlay eyes; bone inlay teeth.
From catalogue: — Represents spirits controlled by shamans: set
up around his home during his rites, or used as grave marker;
collected by Livingston Farrand, 1898; Quinault Tribe, Bay
Center, Washington.

Pl. 7.1 . . . . . Shaman's Board, Washington
American Museum of Natural History, N. Y., 16/6946 cedar; ca.
6′ H. × 3′ W. × 1½″ thick; painted dark maroon and black;
shell inlay eyes.
From catalogue: — Large Tamanous board; collected by Harlan
I. Smith, 1899; Bay Center, Washington.

Pl. 7.2 . . . . . Carved and Painted Planks (drawing), Washington
Drawn by Mr. Eld; published in "Wilkes Exploring Expedition",
vol. 5, Philadelphia, 1849, p. 128; Source: south of the
"Chickeeles" River; Description: "These planks were placed
upright, and nothing could be learned of their origin. The
colors were exceedingly bright, of a kind of red pigment"
(op. cit., p. 129).

Pl. 8 . . . . . . Spirit Canoe Figure, Duwamish, Washington
Chicago Natural History Museum, 55949 red cedar; 35″ H.;
painted uniformly a brownish-orange;
From catalogue: — Carved and painted red cedar human figure
with peg extremities; cedarbark band around neck; used in
ceremonies at long house; collected by G. A. Dorsey, Field
Museum Exped., Sept. 1899; S-quak-So (Salish stock), shore
of Washington Lake near Seattle, Washington.

Pl. 9 . . . . . . Spirit Canoe Figure, Duwamish, Washington
Chicago Natural History Museum, 55953 cedar; 41″ H.; painted
darkish brown, arms black, and some traces of black on other
parts of figure.
From catalogue: — Carved cedar human figure, painted features,
arms painted across on chest; bark band on neck and head;
used in ceremonies at long house; collected by G. A. Dorsey,
Field Museum Expedition, Sept. 1899; S-quak-So (Salish
stock), Shore of Washington Lake near Seattle, Washington.

Pl. 10.1 . . . . . Spirit Canoe Figure, Duwamish, Washington
University Museum, Univ. of Penna., Philadelphia, 37683 cedar;
ca. 32″ H.; painted allover white, traces of black and red.
From catalogue: — Carved wooden image for spirit boat; collected
by G. A. Dorsey, John Wanamaker Expedition of 1900;
Duwamish, Cedar River, Washington.

Pl. 10.2 . . . . . Spirit Canoe Figure, Duwamish, Washington
University Museum, Univ. of Penna., Philadelphia, 37683 cedar;
ca. 45″ H.; painted allover dark red, features of face painted
in heavy faint black lines.
From catalogue: — Carved wooden image for spirit boat; collected
by G. A. Dorsey, John Wanamaker Exped. of 1900; Duwamish, Cedar River, Washington.

Pl. 11.1 . . . . . Spirit Canoe Figure, Duwamish, Washington. Back of 10.1.

Pl. 11.2 . . . . Spirit Canoe Figure, Duwamish, Washington. Back of 10.2.

Pl. 12a, b . . . Shaman's Power Figure, Washington
American Museum of Natural History, N. Y., 16/7649 cedar; ca. 50" H.; traces of red and white paint.
From catalogue: — Wooden figure from West Seattle, Washington; purchased of M. R. Harrington, 1900.

Pl. 13.1 . . . . . Spirit Canoe Figure, Duwamish, Washington
Chicago Natural History Museum, 55952 red cedar; 41" H.; front painted allover white, with details in black, back painted allover black.
From catalogue: — Carved and painted red cedar human figure with peg extremities; bark band about neck; used in ceremonies at long house; collected by G. A. Dorsey, Field Museum Exped., Sept. 1899; S-quak-So (Salish stock), shore of Washington Lake near Seattle, Washington.

Pl. 13.2 . . . . . Spirit Canoe Figure, Duwamish, Washington
Chicago Natural History Museum, 55951 cedar; 36½" H.; painted red, black and white.
From catalogue: — Carved and painted cedar human figure, arms crossed on chest; peg extremities; used in ceremonies at long house; collected by G. A. Dorsey, Field Museum Exped., Sept. 1899; S-quak-So (Salish stock), shore of Washington Lake near Seattle, Washington.

Pl. 14a, b . . . Spirit Canoe Figure, Duwamish, Washington
Chicago Natural History Museum, 55954 cedar; 46" H.; painted white, pinkish-red, red and black; originally cedarbark band around top of head.
From catalogue: — Carved cedar human figure, painted face, striped body, bark band on head; used in ceremonies at long house; collected by G. A. Dorsey, Field Museum Exped., Sept. 1899; S-quak-So (Salish stock), shore of Washington Lake near Seattle, Washington.

Pl. 15 . . . . . . Spirit Canoe Figure, Duwamish, Washington
Chicago Natural History Museum, 55948 red cedar; 28" H.; painted yellowish-red, black and white; originally cedarbark band around neck.
From catalogue: — Carved and painted red cedar human figure with peg extremities; cedarbark band around neck; used in ceremonies at long house; collected by G. A. Dorsey, Field Museum Exped., Sept. 1899; S-quak-So (Salisk stock), shore of Washington Lake near Seattle, Washington.

Pl. 16.1—4 . . Spirit Canoe Boards, Duwamish, Washington
University Museum, Univ. of Penna., Philadelphia, 37683 cedar; ca. 72" H.; painted red, black and white.
From catalogue: — Carved cedarwood planks for spirit boat; collected by G. A. Dorsay, John Wanamaker Expedition of 1900; Duwamish, Cedar River, Washington.

Pl. 17 . . . . . . Spirit Canoe Figure, Washington
University of Washington Museum, Seattle, Wash., 3547 cedar;
50″ H.
From catalogue: — Collected from White River Indians, Puget
Sound region, Washington; received from old University
Museum, through Mrs. H. A. Boner, 1890.

Pl. 18.1 . . . . Spirit Canoe Figure, Snoqualmie, Washington
Museum of the American Indian, Heye Foundation, N. Y., 10/161
cedar; 40½″ H.; design in pinkish-red painted on unpainted
surface.
From catalogue: — Wooden figure used in spirit canoe ceremony;
represents a female earth spirit that gives shaman power to go to
the underworld; collected by T. T. Waterman, 1920, from the
Snoqualmie Tribe, Puget Sound, Tolt, Washington.

Pl. 18.2 . . . . . Spirit Canoe Figure, Snoqualmie, Washington
Museum of the American Indian, Heye Foundation, N. Y., 10/163
cedar; 40¼″ H.; design in pinkish-red against dark ground.
From catalogue: — Wooden figure used in spirit canoe ceremony,
representing a female earth spirit that gives shaman power to
go to underworld; coll. by T. T. Waterman, 1920, Snoqualmie Tribe, Puget Sound, Tolt, Washington.

Pl. 19.1 . . . . . Spirit Canoe Figure, Snoqualmie, Washington
Museum of the American Indian, Heye Foundation, N. Y., 10/162
cedar; 39″ H.; design painted pimkish-white on unpainted
surface, back of figure dull greenish-black.
From catalogue: — Wooden figure used in spirit canoe ceremony,
representing an earth being with one eye; collected by T. T.
Waterman, 1920, from the Snoqualmie Tribe, Puget Sound,
Tolt, Washington.

Pl. 19.2 . . . . . Spirit Canoe Figure, Snoqualmie, Washington
Museum of the American Indian, Heye Foundation, N. Y., 10/164
cedar; 39½″ H.; head and torso painted overall white, neck
light reddish-white, sides and back of head and torso dark
greenish-black.
From catalogue: — Wooden figure used in spirit canoe ceremony,
representing an earth spirit whose name is "Stump" and
represents a tree stump; collected by T. T. Waterman, 1920,
from the Snoqualmie Tribe, Puget Sound, Tolt, Washington.

Pl. 19.1a . . . . Spirit Canoe Figure, Snoqualmie, Washington
Back view of Plate 19.1.

Pl. 19.2a . . . . Spirit Canoe Figure, Snoqualmie, Washington
Back view of Plate 19.2.

Pl. 20.1 . . . . . Spirit Canoe Figure, Snoqualmie, Washington
University of Washington Museum, Seattle, Wash., 1/105 cedar;
38″ H.: painted black, red and white.
From catalogue: — Collected by Mr. Harry Steeve; received from
Jerry Kanin, 1937; Snuqualmi Tribe, Tolt, Washington.

Pl. 20.2 . . . . . Spirit Canoe Figure, Snoqualmie, Washington
University of Washington Museum, Seattle, Washington, 1/106
cedar; 43½″ H.; painted black, red and white.

From catalogue: — Collected by Mr. Harry Steeve; received from
Jerry Kanin, 1937, Snuqualmi Tribe, Tolt, Washington.

Pl. 21.1 . . . . . Spirit Canoe Figure, Snoqualmie, Washington
University of Washington Museum, Seattle, Wash., 1/107 cedar;
44″ H.; painted white, red and black.
From catalogue: — Collected by Mr. Harry Steeve; received from
Jerry Kanin, 1937, Snuqualmi Tribe, Tolt, Washington.

Pl. 21.2 . . . . . Spirit Canoe Figure, Snoqualmie, Washington
University of Washington Museum, Seattle, Wash., 1/108 cedar;
38 ½″ H.; painted white, red and black.
From catalogue: — Collected by Mr. Harry Steeve; received from
Jerry Kanin, 1937; Snuqualmi Tribe, Tolt, Washington.

Pl. 22.a, b . . Shaman's Power Figure, Skokomish, Washington
Chicago Natural History Museum, 19812 cedar; 31 ½″ H.; traces
of red and black paint.
From catalogue: — Carving representing human figure, legs off
at knees; collected by Rev. Myron Eells, Nov.— Dec. 1892;
gift from Dept. of Ethnology, World's Columbian Exposition;
Skokomish Reserve (Skokomish Tribe), Washington.

Pl. 23.1 . . . . . Comb, Skokomish, Washington
Chicago Natural History Museum, 19651 maple; 7 ¾″ H. × 2 ½″
W.; figure 4⁷/₈″ H.; traces of black paint.
From catalogue: — Carved wooden comb, human figure; collected
by Rev. Myron Eells, Nov.— Dec. 1892; gift from Dept. of
Ethnology, World's Columbian Exposition; Puget Sound
(Skokomish Tribe), Washington.

Pl. 23.2 . . . . . Comb, Skokomish, Washington
Chicago Natural History Museum, 19652 maple; 6⁷/₈″ H. × 2 ½″
W.; figure ca. 4″ H.; traces of black coloration.
From catalogue: — Carved wooden comb, human figure with high
hat; collected by Rev. Myron Eells, Nov.— Dec. 1892; gift
from Dept. of Ethnology, World's Columbian Exposition;
Puget Sound (Skokomish Tribe), Washington.

Pl. 24.1 . . . . . Horn Dish, Skokomish, Washington
Chicago Natural History Museum, 19877
Mountain sheep horn; 6″ diameter.
From catalogue: — Carved horn dish from mountain sheep, in-
cised chevrons and figure of man; collected by Myron Eells,
Nov.— Dec. 1892; gift from Dept. of Ethnology, World's
Columbian Exposition; Twana (Skokomish) Tribe, Washing-
ton.

Pl. 24.2 . . . . . Horn Dish, Chehalis, Washington
Museum of the American Indian, Heye Foundation, N. Y., 15/4647
mountain sheep horn; 8″ diameter.
From catalogue: — Chehalis Tribe of Salish, Washington.

Pl. 25 . . . . . . Shaman's Wand, Western Montana
Denver Art Museum, Denver, Colo., QS 1—1—B.
From catalogue: — skin clothing over wood; unevenly smeared
with red; deer-hoofs pendant on right shoulder; black glass-

bead eyes; 25 ¾″ H. Salish doctor's figure; said to have been made about 1870—1880; bought from private collection in Western Montana, fall of 1940.

Pl. 26.1 . . . . . Carved Wooden Head, Thompson, British Columbia
American Museum of Natural History, N. Y., 16/8009 maple; ca. 7″ H.; painted red in part; shredded cedarbark and horsehair for hair.
From catalogue: — Carved head showing hair dress; collected by James Teit, Museum Expedition, 1900; Thompson Indians.

Pl. 26.2a, b. . Carved Wooden Head, Thompson, British Columbia
American Museum of Natural History, N. Y., 16/8014 maple; ca. 7″ H.; painted red in part; horsehair for hair.
From catalogue: — Carved head showing style of hair dress; collected by James Teit, Museum Expedition, 1900; Thompson Indians.

Pl. 27 . . . . . . Grave Figure, Lillooet, British Columbia
Museum of the American Indian, Heye Foundation, N. Y., 18/7392 cedar; 68″ H.; traces of dark color.
From catalogue: — Lillooet grave figure; collected by G. G. Heye; portage between Anderson and Seton Lakes, British Columbia.

Pl. 28 . . . . . . Grave Figure, Lillooet, British Columbia
American Museum of Natural History, N. Y., 16/7075 cedar; ca. 52″ H.; no traces of color.
From catalogue: — From west side of Lillooet River about 4 miles above delta or ¾ of a mile below bridge, near Douglas, Brit. Columbia. Collected 1899 by Harlan I. Smith. Several duplicates were not purchased of the Indians; all were in row faced east; one large different (from rest) not secured.

Pl. 29 . . . . . . Grave Figure, British Columbia
National Museum of Canada, Ottawa, VII— G—357 cedar; ca. 4′ H.; much weathered, but some traces of black and red paint.
From catalogue: — Salish grave figure; collected by Harlan I. Smith in 1929 at Patricia Bay, British Columbia.

Pl. 30.1—5. . Grave Figures, Fraser River, British Columbia
Photograph from Chicago Natural History Museum.

Pl. 31 . . . . . . Carved Figure, Thompson, British Columbia
Chicago Natural History Museum, 19136 cedar; 38″ H.; traces of red and black paint.
From catalogue: — Collected by Carl Hagenbeck; received by purchase from Carl Hagenbeck, March 20, 1918, Fraser River Canyon, Spuzzum, British Columbia.

Pl. 32 . . . . . . Grave Monument, British Columbia
National Museum of Canada, Ottawa, VII— G—359 cedar; ca. 6′ along base; some traces of original red, black and white paint.
From catalogue: — Chief's coffin: this coffin was discovered in an old Indian cemetery near Vancouver. The animal figures in

full relief represent mythological creatures believed to have
played a part in the dead man's ancestral history. Collected
by Dr. Duncan C. Scott in 1930 at Musquiam, British Columbia.

Pl. 33.1 . . . . . Carved Figure, British Columbia
Photograph from National Museum of Canada, Ottawa cedar;
ca. 5′6″ H.; red, white and black paint.

Pl. 33.2 . . . . . Carved Figure, British Columbia
Photograph, from National Museum of Canada, Ottawa cedar;
ca. 5′6″ H.; red, white and black paint.

Pl. 34 . . . . . . Mask, Katsey, Fraser River, British Columbia
American Museum of Natural History, N. Y., 16/4662 cedar; ca.
21″ H. × 9″ W.; painted light blue, red and white.
From catalogue: — Xoaexoe mask, Katsey Reserve, Port Ham-
mond, British Columbia; collected by Harlan I. Smith,
Museum Expedition, 1898.

Pl. 35 . . . . . . Mask, Lower Fraser River, British Columbia
American Museum of Natural History, N. Y., 16/9222A cedar;
ca. 20″ H. × 10″W.; painted dark blue, white and red; red
feathers and down on sticks above head.
From catalogue: — Xoaexoe mask, Lower Fraser River; collected
by James Teit, Museum Expedition, 1903.

Pl. 36.a, b . . . Mask, Fraser River, British Columbia
Museum of the American Indian, Heye Foundation, N. Y.,
6/9935 cedar; 11 ¼″ H.; painted in part white, green, black.
From catalogue: — Xwai-Xwai mask. Has flat carvings in form
of men at sides. Two bird-head projections from forehead and
projections from cheeks. Mouth part broken. Only half of
face painted. D. F. Tozier collection; Fraser River, British
Columbia.

Pl. 37 . . . . . . Grave Post, Comox, British Columbia
American Museum of Natural History, N. Y., 16/4694 cedar;
5′2″ H.; no traces of paint remaining.
From catalogue: — Grave post, Xoaexoe face; Comox, British
Columbia; collected by Harlan I. Smith, Aug. 1898.

Pl. 38 . . . . . . Mask, Comox, British Columbia
American Museum of Natural History, N. Y., 16/4724A cedar;
ca. 21″ H. × 9″ W.; painted red, black, white.
From catalogue: — Mask Xoaexoe, Comox, British Columbia;
collected by Harlan I. Smith, Museum Expedition, 1898.

Pl. 39.1 . . . . Figure, Comox, Vancouver Island, British Columbia
American Museum of Natural History, N. Y., 16/4711 cedar.

Pl. 39.2a, b . . Funerary Figure, Comox, Vancouver Island, B. C.
Provincial Museum, Victoria, B. C., 2359 cedar; 4′ H.; painted
allover red; copper eyes.
From catalogue: — Collected by Dr. C. F. Newcombe at Comox,
Vancouver Island, B. C., 1911.

Pl. 40.1 . . . . . House post, Comox, Vancouver Island, B. C.
Chicago Natural History Museum, 85482 cedar; 11' H.; faint
traces of color.
From catalogue: — Totem pole of cedar — two human figures;
collected by Dr. C. F. Newcombe, Field Museum Expedition,
1903; Comox, Vancouver Island, B. C. (Kanitchin-Salish
stock).

Pl. 40.2 . . . . . House post, Nanaimo, Vancouver Island, B. C.
Chicago Natural History Museum, 18982 red cedar; 12' H.; faint
traces of color.
From catalogue: — Carved house post of red-cedar, representing
a chief wearing a feathered mask and tunic, with a rattle in
his left hand — belonging to the Sqacqoc dance; base squared;
gift from Dept. of Ethnology, World's Columbian Exposition,
received Oct. 31, 1893; Nanaimo (Salishan stock), Vancouver
Island, B. C.

Pl. 40.3 . . . . . House post, Nanaimo, Vancouver Island, B. C.
Chicago Natural History Museum, 18981 red cedar; 11'6" H.;
faint traces of color.
From catalogue: — Carved house post of red cedar; representing
a man holding a bird; base squared; gift from Dept. of Ethnology, World's Columbian Exposition, received Oct. 31, 1893;
Nanaimo (Cowichan-Salishan stock), Vancouver Island, B. C.

Pl. 41.1 . . . . . Loom-post, Nanaimo, Vancouver Island, B. C.
Chicago Natural History Museum, 85378—E cedar; 65" H.
overall; top 17" H.; figure 12" H.; faint traces of black only
on figure and post end.
From catalogue: — Loom post, collected by Dr. C. F. Newcombe,
Field Museum Expedition, 1903—4; Nanaimo (Cowichan-
Salishan stock), Vancouver Island, B. C.

Pl. 41.2 . . . . . Loom-post, Nanaimo, Vancouver Island, B. C.
Chicago Natural History Museum, 85378—E cedar; 63½" H.
overall; top 17" H.; animal figure 8¾" H.; animal painted
pinkish-red, white and black.
From catalogue: — Loom-post; collected by Dr. C. F. Newcombe,
Field Museum Expedition, 1903—4; Nanaimo (Cowichan-
Salishan stock), Vancouver Island, B. C.

Pl. 42.1 . . . . . Mask, Nanaimo, Vancouver Island, B. C.
Museum of the American Indian, Heye Foundation, N. Y.,
18/1063 cedar; 17½" H.; painted red, black and white.
From catalogue: — Mask represents Skway-whay, a mythical
being that came from above; collected by G. T. Emmons;
Nanaimo, Vancouver Island, B. C.

Pl. 42.2 . . . . . Mask, and Costumed Dancer, Nanaimo, Vancouver Island, B. C.
Photograph from National Museum of Canada, Ottawa.

Pl. 43 . . . . . . Mask, Nanaimo, Vancouver Island, B. C.
National Museum of Canada, Ottawa, VII—G—335 cedar; ca.
18" H.; painted red, black, white.
From catalogue: — Dance mask; collected by Harlan I. Smith,
1929; Nanaimo, British Columbia.

Pl. 44.1 . . . . . Drum, Cowichan, Vancouver Island, B. C.
> Chicago Natural History Museum, 85491 cedar; 11' long; each of four figures ca. 19" H.; figures painted red, black and white.
> From catalogue: — Plank drum: two rough boards nailed alongside one another with slats; at each end and in center small figures; collected by Dr. C. F. Newcombe, Field Museum Expedition, 1903—4; Nanaimo (Cowichan-Salish stock), Vancouver Island, B. C.

Pl. 44.2a, b . . . . Drum, Vancouver Island, B. C.
> Detail, left half of Plate 44.1

Pl. 44.2c, d. . Drum, Cowichan, Vancouver Island, B. C.
> Detail, right half of Plate 44.1

Pl. 45 . . . . . . House post, Cowichan, Vancouver Island, B. C.
> Museum of the American Indian, Heye Foundation, N. Y., 15/8961 cedar; 78" H.; painted white, black, red, green.
> From catalogue: — House-carving, representing a man holding a sea otter; collected by G. T. Emmons; Duncan (Cowichan Salish), Vancouver Island, B. C.

Pl. 46 . . . . . . House posts, in situ, Cowichan, Vancouver Island, B. C.
> Photograph from Museum of the American Indian, Heye Foundation, N. Y.

Pl. 47.1, 2. . . Loom-parts, Cowichan, Vancouver Island, B. C.
> Museum of the American Indian, Heye Foundation, N. Y., 16/2071 cedar; 6'9½" H.; unpainted.
> From catalogue: — Loom-posts; collected by G. T. Emmons, Duncan, Vancouver Island, B. C.

Pl. 48.1 . . . . . Mask, Cowichan, Vancouver Island, B. C.
> American Museum of Natural History, N. Y., 16.1/1871 cedar; ca. 20" H. × 10" W.; painted black, white, red.
> From catalogue: — Mask known as Skhway-whay, used in whirlwind dance, Cowichan; exchange with G. T. Emmons, 1929.

Pl. 48.2 . . . . . Mask, Cowichan, Vancouver Island, B. C.
> Royal Ontario Museum of Archaeology, Toronto, 2796 cedar; 17¼" H.; painted red, black, white.
> From catalogue: — Mask, Cowichan, Vancouver Island, B. C.

Pl. 49a, b . . . Mask, Cowichan, Vancouver Island, B. C.
> Museum of the American Indian, Heye Foundation, N. Y., 16/2080 cedar; 19³/₈" H.; painted red, black, white.
> From catalogue: — Mask with protruding eyes rep. a beaver, and two eagle heads on top for ears; collected G. T. Emmons; Duncan, Vancouver Island-Cowichan Tribe of Salish.

Pl. 50.1a, b . . Grave House, Sanetch, Vancouver Island, B. C.
> Museum of the American Indian, Heye Foundation, N. Y., 18/7911 cedar; carved figure 4'8" H.; no traces of color remaining.
> From catalogue: — Grave house of two chiefs, Sq-a-tichten and Nisjeem, buried about 1853. Carved figure in front called Moq-moquiten and the mythical minks called squa-mit-chen.

Obtained from Jimmy Jim, great grandson of Nisjeem; collected by George G. Heye; West Saanich Reservation, Vancouver Island, B. C.

Pl. 50.2 ..... Portions of Grave House, in situ, Sanetch, Vancouver Island, B. C.
Photo. from National Museum of Canada, Ottawa; boards with animal figures at right in Museum in Ottawa, VII-G-355, 356 cedar; 5'6" × ca. 4'; faint traces of white and red paint.
From catalogue: — Salish boards with quadrupeds; collected by Harlan I. Smith in 1929; Brentwood, Brit. Columbia.
(for carved figure and boards at left, see Pl. 50,1 above)

Pl. 51a, b ... House post, Sanetch, Vancouver Island, B. C.
Museum of the American Indian, Heye Foundation, N. Y., 18/6854 cedar; 10'5" H.; no traces of color remaining.
From catalogue: — Exterior house post; collected by G. G. Heye, presented by Mrs. Thea Heye; East Saanich Reservation, Vancouver Island, B. C.

Pl. 52a, b ... House post, Songish, Vancouver Island, B. C.
Museum of the American Indian, Heye Foundation, N. Y., 2/5904 cedar; ca. 7' H.; color, red, white, black.
From catalogue: — House post bearing a carved face rep. the owner's guardian spirit, and two carvings representing skawichens; received in exchange from Univ. of Penna. Museum; Songish Tribe, Vancouver Island, B. C.

Pl. 53.1 ..... House post, Songish, Vancouver Island, B. C.
Museum of the American Indian, Heye Foundation, N. Y., 18/6853 cedar; 11'6" H.; red, white and black paint.
From catalogue: — Interior house post; red, white and black painted decoration representing spirits of the house; collected by G. G. Heye; East Saanich Reservation, Vancouver Island, B. C.

Pl. 53.2 ..... House post, Songish, Vancouver Island, B. C.
Chicago natural History Museum, 79788 cedar; ca. 6'2" H.; color red, white, black.
From catalogue: — House post, four quadrupeds on body of man-like figure: minks; human figure: spirit seen by owner in woods when preparing for secret society, Tiyi'-wan; collected by G. A. Dorsey (Dr. C. F. Newcombe), Field Museum Expedition, July 1900; Victoria, B. C. (Songish-Salishan stock).

Pl. 53.3 ..... House-post, Songish, Vancouver Island, B. C.
Chicago Natural History Museum, 79787 cedar; ca. 7'4" H.; color, red, white, black.
From catalogue: — House post; a carving representing human figure holding a mink diagonally in front of him (probably spirit seen by owner when preparing for a secret society); collected by G. A. Dorsey (Dr. C. F. Newcombe), Field Museum Expedition, July 1900; Victoria, B. C. (Songish-Salishan stock).

Pl. 54.1—4 .. House posts, Vancouver Island, B. C.
Chicago Natural History Museum (cf. Plates 40, 53.3, above).

Pl. 55.1 . . . . . House posts, in situ, Vancouver Island, B. C.
                    Photograph from Chicago Natural History Museum (photo. no.
                        16326).

Pl. 55.2 . . . . . House post, in situ, Vancouver Island, B. C.
                    Photograph from National Museum of Canada, Ottawa (photo no.
                        72855).

Pl. 56.1 . . . . . House posts, in situ, Vancouver, Island, B. C.
                    Photograph from National Museum of Canada, Ottawa (photo
                        no. 17048).

Pl. 56.2 . . . . . House post, in situ, Thunderbird Park, Victoria, B. C.
                    Provincial Museum, Victoria, B. C., 5041 cedar. . .
                    From catalogue: — Inside house posts; received by museum 1940
                        from Thunderbird Park, Victoria, B. C.; provenience: from
                        building on Discovery Island.

Pl. 57 . . . . . . House-frame with carved house posts, in situ, Vancouver Island,
                        B. C.
                    Photograph from National Museum of Canada, Ottawa (photo
                        no. 72867).

Pl. 58.1 . . . . . Carved Figure, British Columbia
                    Museum of the American Indian, Heye Foundation, N. Y.,
                        20/5639 cedar; 38 ¼″ H.; dark coloration, traces black, red.
                    From catalogue: — Large wooden human figure, traces of red
                        and black painted decoration; exchange with Julius Carle-
                        bach; British Columbia Salish.

Pl. 58.2 . . . . . Carved Figure, Vancouver Island, B. C.
                    Provincial Museum, Victoria, B. C., 2839 cedar; ca. 6′6″ H.; no
                        traces of color remaining.
                    From catalogue: — Totem-pole figure; Departure Bay, Vancouver
                        Island, B. C.

Pl. 59.1 . . . . . Shaman Figure, Columbia River, Oregon
                    American Museum of Natural History, N. Y., T—22125 cedar;
                        15 ½″ H.; faint traces of red, white, black paint; haliotis
                        shell eyes.
                    From catalogue: — Carved human figure; collected by James
                        Terry, 1882; from Tum-wa-ta, Memaluse Rock, Columbia
                        River, Oregon.

Pl. 59.2 . . . . . Shaman Figure, Columbia River, Oregon
                    American Museum of Natural History, N. Y., T—22124 cedar;
                        13 ¾″ H.; faint traces of red, white, black paint.
                    From catalogue: — Dancing stick with carved human figure;
                        collected by James Terry, 1882; from Tum-wa-ta, Memaluse
                        Rock, Columbia River, Oregon.

Pl. 60.1 . . . . . Shaman Figure, Columbia River, Oregon
                    American Museum of Natural History, N. Y., T—22126 maple;
                        8 ¼″ H.; traces of black paint; haliotis shell eyes.
                    From catalogue: — Carved human figure. . . with shield; collected
                        by James Terry, 1882; from Memaluse Rock, Columbia
                        River, Oregon.

Pl. 60.2 . . . . . Carved Figure, Wasco, Columbia River, Oregon
Chicago Natural History Museum, 87603 cedar; 12″ H.; no traces
of paint.
From catalogue: — Ancient carved human figure, hollow head;
collected by Fred Harvey, purchased Aug. 10, 1905; Upper
Memallose Island (Wasco-Chinook stock).

Pl. 61.1 . . . . . Horn Dish, Chinook, Washington
Chicago Natural History Museum, 19693 mountain sheep horn;
7 ¾″ diameter.
From catalogue: — Carved dish made of mountain sheep's horn,
incised chevrons and figure of man on body; collected by
L. L. Bush, received as gift from Dept. of Ethnology, World's
Columbian Exposition, Oct. 31, 1893; Shoalwater Bay
(Chinook), Washington.

Pl. 61.2 . . . . . Wooden Mortar, Wasco, Washington
Chicago Natural History Museum, 87705 hard wood; 11½″
diameter × 9″ H.; stained very dark, reddish black.
From catalogue; — Wooden mortar, handles deeply carved,
representing human figure, mended on one side with tin,
perforated bottom; collected by Fred Harvey; by purchase
Aug. 10, 1905; The Dalles, Washington (Wasco-Chinook
stock).

Pl. 62.1 . . . . . Shaman's Stick, Wasco, Washington
Chicago Natural History Museum, 87630.2 hard wood, probably
ash; 28″ H. overall; upper part 4 ¼″ H.; carved head 2 ¼″
H.; some traces of red paint on upper part.
From catalogue: — Shaman's tamnous stick, carved with human
head; collected by Fred Harvey; by purchase Aug. 10, 1905;
The Dalles, Washington (Wasco-Chinook stock).

Pl. 62.2 . . . . . Shaman's Stick, Wasco, Washington
Chicago Natural History Museum, 87630.4 hard wood, probably
ash; ca. 28″ H. overall; upper part 9″ H.; carved figure 5 ¼″
H.; traces of red paint on entire upper part.
From catalogue: — Shaman's tamnous stick, carved with human
figure; collected by Fred Harvey; by purchase Aug. 10, 1905;
The Dalles, Washington (Wasco-Chinook stock).

Pl. 63.1 . . . . . Carved Spoon, Wasco, Washington
Chicago Natural History Museum, 69083 hard wood; 6″ L.
overall; animal and figure 1 ¾″ × 2″; no real traces of color.
From catalogue: — Spoon of wood, broad, shallow, thick bowl,
short carved (in relief) handle: bear and man on handle;
collected by M. L. Miller, May-Oct. 1901; Field Museum
Expedition; near The Dalles, Washington (Wasco).

Pl. 63.2 . . . . . Carved Spoon, Wasco, Washington
Chicago Natural History Museum, 69089 hard wood; 9½″ L.
overall; handle 4 ¾″ L.; figure ca. 3 ¼″ L. × 1 ¼″ W.; some
traces of black paint on arms and head of figure.
From catalogue: — Spoon of wood, broad bowl, human figure in
relief on handle (said to have been made from 60 to 70 years
ago); collected by M. L. Miller, May-Oct. 1901; Field Museum
Expedition; near The Dalles, Washington (Wasco).

Pl. 64.1 . . . . Shaman's Wand, Quileute, Washington
Museum of the American Indian, Heye Foundation, N. Y.,
5/7575 cedar; 15½'' H.; dark red and white.
From catalogue: — Represents spirit controlled by shaman;
collected by Leo J. Frachtenberg, acquired in 1913; Quileute
Tribe, Washington.

Pl. 64.2 . . . . . Hand Mask and Rattle, Kwakiutl (Nootka ?), Vancouver Island,
B. C.
Museum of the American Indian, Heye Foundation, N. Y., 5/615
cedar; 13'' H.; red, black, white; deer-hoof rattles attached;
loop wrapped with shredded cedarbark, with feathers in-
serted at back.
From catalogue: Shaman's guardian spirit wand; collected from
Kwakiutl, B. C. (Nootka origin ?).

Pl. 65.1a, b, c Carved Figure, Kwakiutl, Vancouver Island, B. C.
Milwaukee Public Museum, 17384 cedar; 54'' H.; no traces of
color remaining.
From catalogue: — Large wooden image, female, Kwakiutl; col-
lected by S. A. Barrett; acquired June 15, 1915; Vancouver
Island, B. C.

Pl. 65.2a, b . Carved Figure, Kwakiutl, Vancouver Island, B. C.
Milwaukee Public Museum, 17618 cedar; 11½'' H.; no traces of
color remaining.
From catalogue: — Carved wooden figure; collected by S. A.
Barrett; acquired June 15, 1915; Vancouver Island, B. C. —
Kwakiutl.

Pl. 66.1 . . . . . Carved Figure, Kwakiutl, Vancouver Island, B. C.
Museum of the American Indian, Heye Foundation, N. Y., cedar;
ca. 5'7'' H.: dark reddish stain.

Pl. 66.2 . . . . . Carved Figure, Kwakiutl, Vancouver Island, B. C.
Museum of the American Indian, Heye Foundation, N. Y.,
6/8754 cedar; 5'7'' H.; dark coloration, head greenish.
From catalogue: — Totem carving representing standing human
figure. . .
D. F. Tozier collection; Vancouver Island, B. C. — Kwakiutl.

Pl. 67.1 . . . . . Potlatch Figure, Kwakiutl, Vancouver Island, B. C.
Museum of the American Indian, Heye Foundation, N. Y.,
6/8791 cedar; 4'2'' H.; painted allover red; design in red and
black painted on copper and face.
From catalogue: — Wood carving representing standing human
figure holding copper against breast with left hand; right arm
extended, hand pointing upward; headdress of flat, circular
form; painted design in red and black on copper and face;
body painted red; D. F. Tozier collection; exchange with Mr.
W. R. Paalen May 1941; Vancouver Island, B. C.

Pl. 67.2 . . . . . Potlatch Figure, Kwakiutl, Vancouver Island, B. C.
Museum of the American Indian, Heye Foundation, N. Y.,
6/8794 cedar; 4'2'' H.; painted red and black.
From catalogue: — Wood carving representing standing human

male figure; legs resting on crude base; right arm pointed outward, one finger extended; left hand over groin; figure has flat topped hat; representation of copper across right side, top under left arm, decorated in lines of red and black paint. D. F. Tozier Collection; Vancouver Island, B. C.

Pl. 68.1 . . . . . Carved Figure, Haida, British Columbia
Museum of the American Indian, Heye Foundation, N. Y., 2/600 maple; dark reddish-black; $17^1/_8''$ H.
From catalogue: — Figure, Haida; by purchase; Haida, British Columbia.

Pl. 68.2, 3 . . . House posts, Haida, British Columbia
Museum of the American Indian, Heye Foundation, N. Y., 15/9198, 15/9199 maple; both $11'6\frac{1}{2}''$ H.; red, white, black.
From catalogue: — House post carved to represent an animal with a face underneath; on the animal's ears are carved frog figures; made about 1850 in a neighboring village and presented to chief Frog-ears of the abandoned village located at the north end of Sukkwan (this repeated for both figures); 68.2: acquired by purchase; 68.3: exchange with Kansas City Art Museum, Dec. 14, 1931; from north end of Sukkwan Island, off the west coast of Prince of Wales Island, Alaska.

Pl. 69.1 . . . . . Mask, Kwakiutl, Vancouver Island, B. C.
Chicago Natural History Museum, 19 305 cedar; $22\frac{3}{4}''$ H.; painted white an black with red lips. cedarbark hair.
From catalogue: — Wooden mask, human form. . . Vancouver Island, Northwest Coast (Kwakiutl).

Pl. 69.2 . . . . . Mask, Kwakiutl, Vancouver Island, B. C.
American Museum of Natural History, N. Y., 16/8382 cedar; ca. 22'' H.; painted red, white, green, black.
From catalogue: — Mask, Kwakiutl, Vancouver Island, B. C.

Pl. 70.1 . . . . . Mask, Kwakiutl, Vancouver Island, B. C.
Museum of the American Indian, Heye Foundation, N. Y., 8/1658 cedar; 18'' H.; painted red and black.
From catalogue: — Mask representing bear's head; purchased from Fred Harvey; Vancouver Island, B. C. — Kwakiutl.

Pl. 70.2 . . . . . Mask, Kwakiutl, Vancouver Island, B. C.
Museum of the American Indian, Heye Foundation, N. Y., 6/9153 cedar; ca. 20'' H.; painted red, black, white, green.
From catalogue: — Large mask representing human face; eyes, nostrils and mouth cut through; tongue protruding; has two small masks attached to flaring piece on each side and raven head in round on forehead; D. F. Tozier Collection; Vancouver Island, B. C., Kwakiutl.

Pl. 71.1 . . . . . Mask, Kwakiutl, Vancouver Island, B. C.
Chicago Natural History Museum, 19 266 cedar; ca. 20'' H.; red, black, green.
From catalogue: — Wooden mask of Xoa'exoe, the earthquake dancer (see 1895 Report for U. S. National Museum, p. 497 and p. 516); Kwakiutl.

Pl. 71.2 . . . . . Mask, Kwakiutl, Vancouver Island, B. C.
Chicago Natural History Museum, 19 269 cedar; 11¾" H.; mica
on eyes cheeks and eyebrows.
From catalogue: — Wooden mask of Xoa'exoe; beak-like nose,
mica on eyes, cheeks and eyebrows; Vancouver Island (Fort
Rupert), Kwakiutl.

Pl. 72.1 . . . . . Mask, Quileute, Washington
Museum of the American Indian, Heye Foundation, N. Y.,
5/9729 cedar; 14" long; black and red.
From catalogue: — Dancing mask used during whaling ceremony;
collected by Leo J. Frachtenberg; Quileute, Washington.

Pl. 72,2 . . . . . Mask, Nootka, Washington (Vancouver Island, B. C.)
Chicago Natural History Museum, 19 852 cedar; ca. 16" long; red,
white, black, green.
From catalogue: — Mask rep. the Hapektoak-belt of the thunder-
bird; coll. J. G. Swan; received as gift from Dept. of Eth.
Col. Exp. 1893.

Pl. 73a, b . . . "Ancient" Mask, Bella Coola, British Columbia
Museum of the American Indian, Heye Foundation, N. Y.,
20/1791 maple (?), 11" H.; charred black, decorated with gum
in which had been an inlay.
From catalogue: — Ancient mask; Bellacoola Tribe, British
Columbia.

Pl. 74.1a, b. . "Ancient" Mask, Bella Coola, British Columbia.
Museum of the American Indian, Heye Foundation, N. Y.,
20/1792 maple (?); 13¹/₈" H.; charred black, decorated with
gum in which had been an inlay.
From catalogue: — Ancient mask; Bellacoola Tribe (?), British
Columbia.

Pl. 74.2 . . . . "Ancient" Mask, Bella Coola, British Columbia.
Museum of the American Indian, Heye Foundation, N. Y.,
20/1793 maple (?); 14³/₈" H.; charred black, with incised
decoration.
From catalogue: — Ancient mask; Bellacoola Tribe (?), British
Columbia.

Pl. 75a, b . . . Mask, Makah, Washington.
Chicago Natural Historal Museum, 61 903 cedar; 14" H.; painted
black, red, white.
From catalogue: — Tlokwally dance (Qualu bo quth), plain
wooden mask, cylindrical shaped mouth; collected by G. A.
Dorsey, Field Museum Exped., June, 1900; Neah Bay
(Makah), Washington.

Pl. 76.1 . . . . Mask, Quileute, Washington
Museum of the American Indian, Heye Foundation, N. Y.,
19/8753 cedar; 10" H.; painted red and black.
From catalogue: — By purchase; Quileute Tribe, Washington.

Pl. 76.2 . . . . . Mask, Quileute, Washington.
Museum of the American Indian, Heye Foundation, N. Y.,
10/6883 cedar; 11" H.; painted very dark red and black.
From catalogue: — By purchase; Quileute Tribe, Washington.

PLATES

PLATE 1

SHAMAN'S WAND, Washington, Quinault
American Museum of Natural History, N.Y., 16/4953

PLATE 2

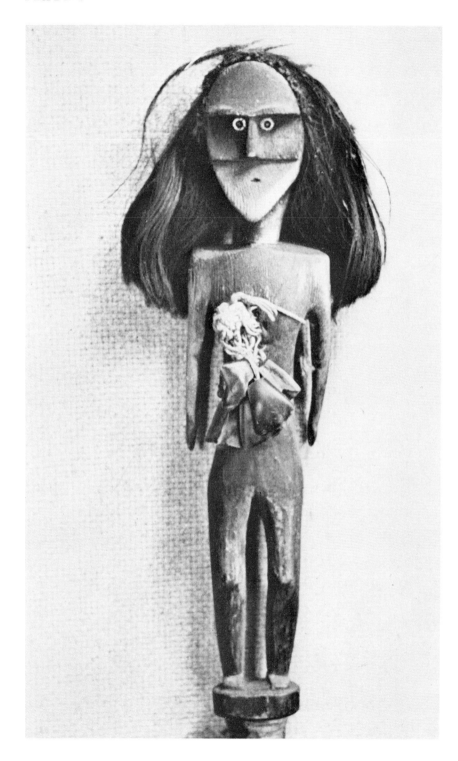

SHAMAN'S WAND, Washington, Quinault
American Museum of Natural History, N.Y., 16A/4921

PLATE 3

a

b

a, b SHAMAN'S WAND, Washington, Quinault
Chicago Natural History Museum, 19789

PLATE 4

a

b

SHAMAN'S WAND, Washington, Quinault
Museum of the American Indian, Heye Foundation, N.Y., 5/9519

PLATE 5

1   2

1 SHAMAN'S WAND, Washington, Quinault
Museum of the American Indian, Heye Foundation, N. Y., 5/9521

2 SHAMAN'S WAND, Washington, Quinault
Museum of the American Indian, Heye Foundation, N. Y., 5/9520

PLATE 6

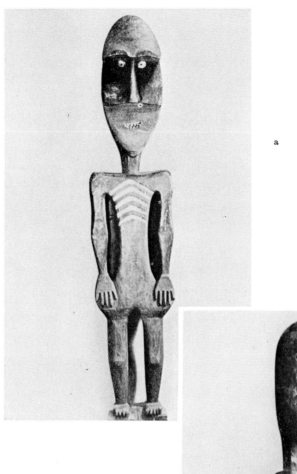

a

b

a, b SHAMAN'S FIGURE, Washington, Quinault
American Museum of Natural History, N.Y., 16/4946

PLATE 7

1

  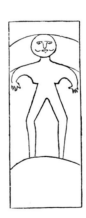  

2

1 SHAMAN'S BOARD, Washington
American Museum of Natural History, N.Y., 16/6946

2 CARVED AND PAINTED PLANKS (DRAWING), Washington
From "Wilkes Exploring Expedition", vol. 5, Phila., 1849, p. 128

PLATE 8

SPIRIT CANOE FIGURE, Washington, Duwamish
Chicago Natural History Museum, 55949

PLATE 9

SPIRIT CANOE FIGURE, Washington, Duwamish
Chicago Natural History Museum, 55953

PLATE 10

1   2

1 SPIRIT CANOE FIGURE, Washington, Duwamish
   University Museum, Univ. of Penna., Phila., 37683

2 SPIRIT CANOE FIGURE, Washington, Duwamish
   University Museum, Univ. of Penna., Phila., 37683

PLATE 11

1   2

1 SPIRIT CANOE FIGURE, Washington, Duwamish
Back view of Pl. 10.1

2 SPIRIT CANOE FIGURE, Washington, Duwamish
Back view of Pl. 10.2

PLATE 12

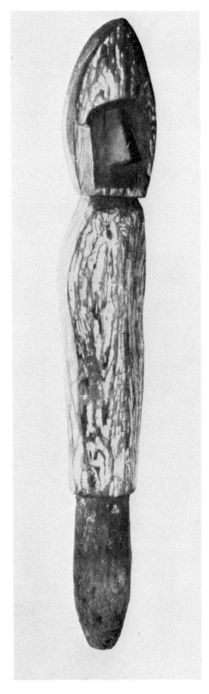
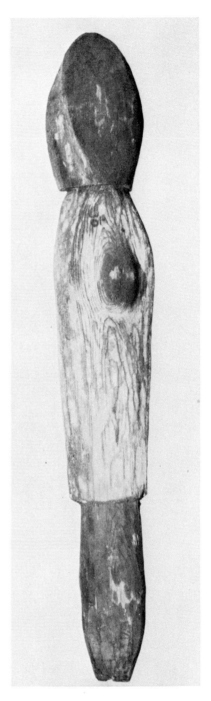

a   b

a, b SHAMAN'S POWER FIGURE, Washington
American Museum of Natural History, N.Y., 16/7649

PLATE 13

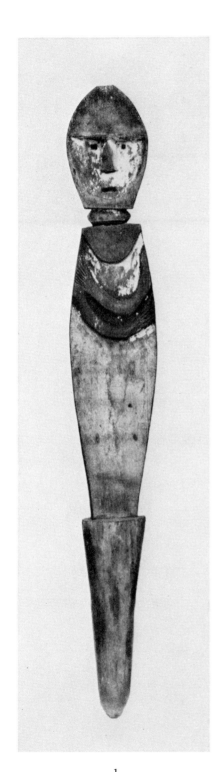
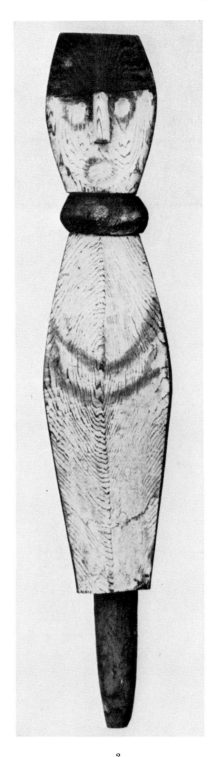

1   2

1   SPIRIT CANOE FIGURE, Washington, Duwamish
Chicago Natural History Museum, 55952
2   SPIRIT CANOE FIGURE, Washington, Duwamish
Chicago Natural History Museum, 55951

PLATE 14

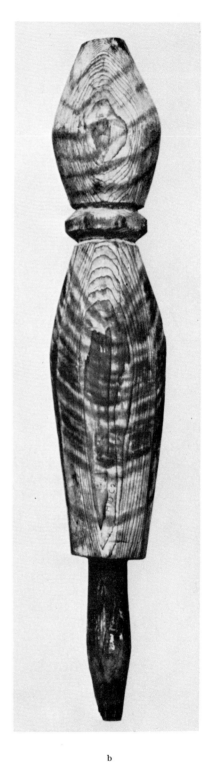

a

b

a, b SPIRIT CANOE FIGURE, Washington, Duwamish
Chicago Natural History Museum, 55954

PLATE 15

SPIRIT CANOE FIGURE, Washington, Duwamish
Chicago Natural History Museum, 55948

PLATE 16

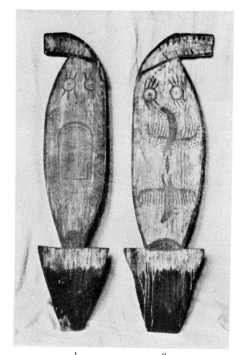

1   2

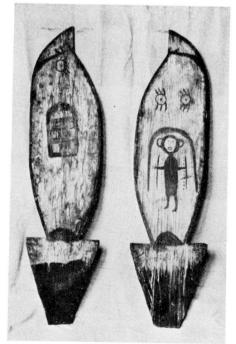

3   4

1,2 SPIRIT CANOE BOARDS, Washington, Duwamish
University Museum, Univ. of Penna., Phila., 37683

3,4 SPIRIT CANOE BOARDS, Washington, Duwamish
University Museum, Univ. of Penna., Phila., 37683

PLATE 17

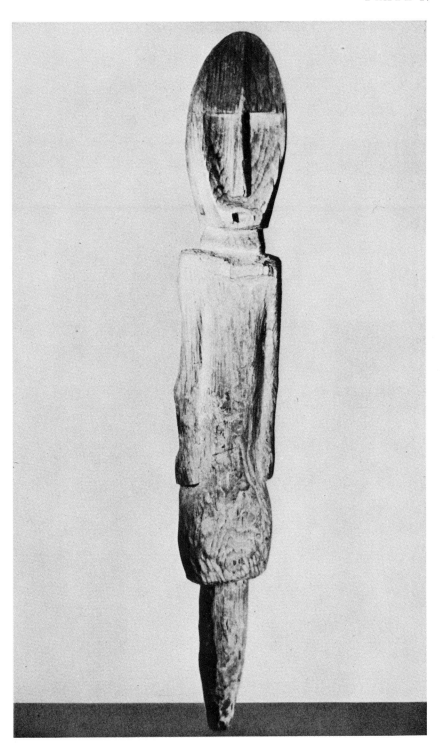

SPIRIT CANOE FIGURE, Washington
Univ. of Washington, Museum, Seattle, Wash., 3547

PLATE 18

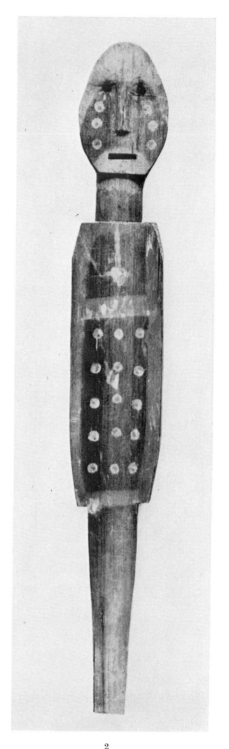

1   2

1 SPIRIT CANOE FIGURE, Washington, Snoqualmie
Museum of the American Indian, Heye Foundation, N.Y., 10/161

2 SPIRIT CANOE FIGURE, Washington, Snoqualmie
Museum of the American Indian, Heye Foundation, N.Y., 10/163

PLATE 19

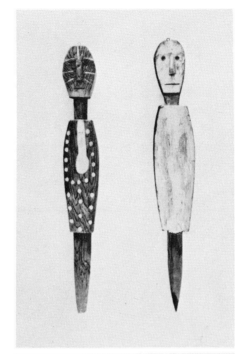

1   2

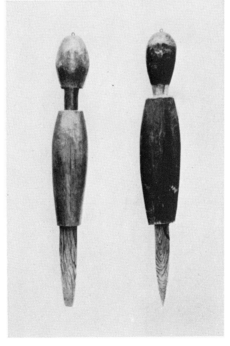

1a   2a

1 SPIRIT CANOE FIGURE, Washington, Snoqualmie
Museum of the American Indian, Heye Foundation, N.Y., 10/162

2 SPIRIT CANOE FIGURE, Washington, Snoqualmie
Museum of the American Indian, Heye Foundation, N.Y., 10/164

1a SPIRIT CANOE FIGURE, Washington, Snoqualmie
Back view of Pl. 19.1

2a SPIRIT CANOE FIGURE, Washington, Snoqualmie
Back view of Pl. 19.2

PLATE 20

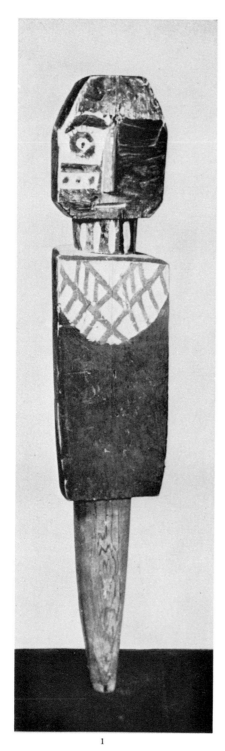

1

2

1 SPIRIT CANOE FIGURE ,Washington, Snoqualmie
   Univ. of Washington Museum, Seattle, Wash., 1/105

2 SPIRIT CANOE FIGURE, Washington, Snoqualmie
   Univ. of Washington Museum, Seattle, Wash., 1/106

PLATE 21

 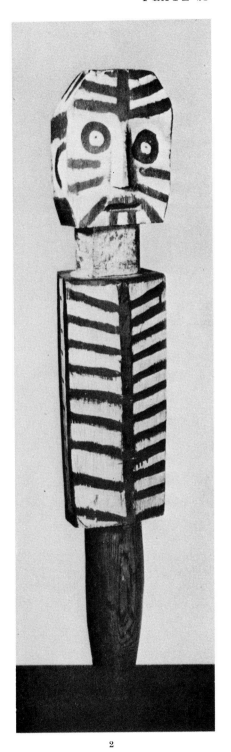

1   2

1   SPIRIT CANOE FIGURE, Washington, Snoqualmie
Univ. of Washington Museum, Seattle, Wash., 1/107

2   SPIRIT CANOE FIGURE, Washington, Snoqualmie
Univ. of Washington Museum, Seattle, Wash., 1/108

PLATE 22

a   b

a, b   SHAMAN'S POWER FIGURE, Washington, Skokomish

Chicago Natural History Museum, 19812

PLATE 23

1

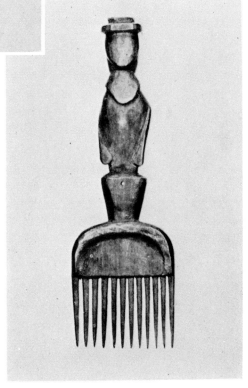

2

1 COMB, Washington, Skokomish
Chicago Natural History Museum, 19651

2 COMB, Washington, Skokomish
Chicago Natural History Museum, 19652

PLATE 24

1

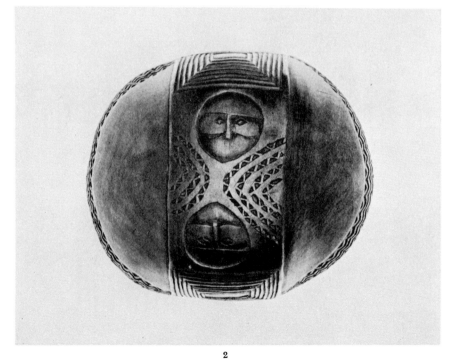

2

1 HORN DISH, Washington, Skokomish
Chicago Natural History Museum, 19877

2 HORN DISH, Washington, Chehalis
Museum of the American Indian, Heye Foundation, N.Y., 15/4647

PLATE 25

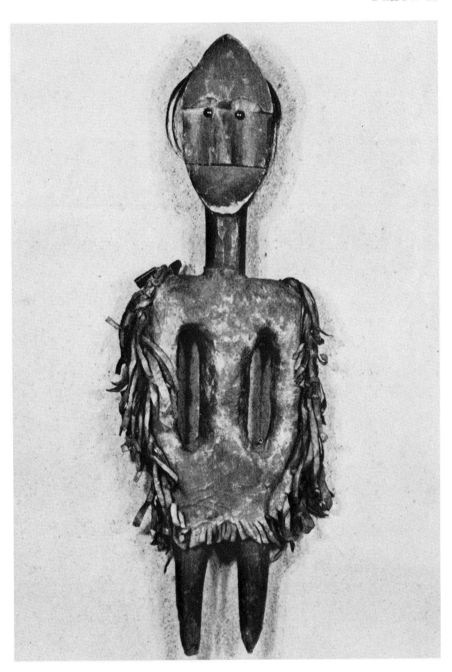

SHAMAN'S WAND, Western Montana
Denver Art Museum, Denver, Colo., Qs 1—1—P

PLATE 26

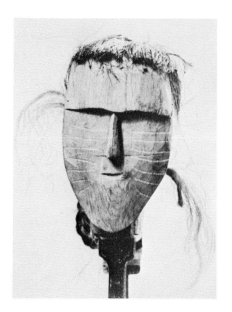

1

2 a   2 b

1 CARVED WOODEN HEAD, British Columbia, Thompson
American Museum of Natural History, N.Y., 16/8009

2 a, b CARVED WOODEN HEAD, British Columbia, Thompson
American Museum of Natural History, N.Y., 16/8014

PLATE 27

GRAVE FIGURE, British Columbia, Lillooet
Museum of the American Indian, Heye Foundation, N.Y., 18/7392

PLATE 28

GRAVE FIGURE, British Columbia, Lillooet
American Museum of Natural History, N.Y., 16/7075

PLATE 29

GRAVE FIGURE, British Columbia
National Museum of Canada, Ottawa, VII—G—357

PLATE 30

1–5 RAVE FIGURES, British Columbia, Fraser River
Photo. from Chicago Natural History Museum

PLATE 31

CARVED FIGURE, British Columbia, Thompson
Chicago Natural History Museum, 19136

PLATE 32

GRAVE MONUMENT, British Columbia
National Museum of Canada, Ottawa, VII—G—359

PLATE 33

1

2

1,2 CARVED FIGURES, British Columbia
Photos. from National Museum of Canada, Ottawa

PLATE 34

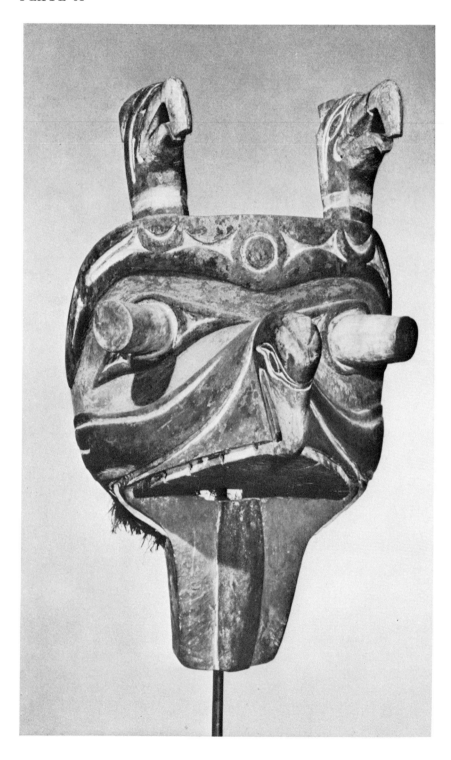

MASK, British Columbia, Katsey, Fraser River
American Museum of Natural History, N.Y., 16/4662

PLATE 35

MASK, British Columbia, Lower Fraser River
American Museum of Natural History, N.Y., 16/9222 A

PLATE 36

a

b

a, b MASK, British Columbia, Fraser River
Museum of the American Indian, Heye Foundation, N.Y., 6/9935

PLATE 37

GRAVE POST, British Columbia, Comox
American Museum of Natural History, N.Y., 16/4694

PLATE 38

MASK, British Columbia, Comox
American Museum of Natural History, N.Y., 16/4724 A

PLATE 39

1

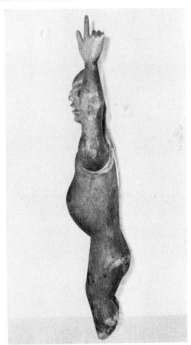

2 a   2 b

1 FIGURE, British Columbia, Comox, Vancouver Island
American Museum of Natural History, N.Y., 16/4711

2 a, 2 b FUNERARY FIGURE, Vancouver Island, B. C., Comox
Provincial Museum, Victoria, B. C., 2359

PLATE 40

1   2   3

1 HOUSE-POST, Vancouver Island, B. C., Comox
Chicago Natural History Museum, 85482

2 HOUSE-POST, Vancouver Island, B. C., Nanaimo
Chicago National History Museum, 18982

3 HOUSE-POST, Vancouver Island, B. C., Nanaimo
Chicago Natural History Museum, 18981

PLATE 41

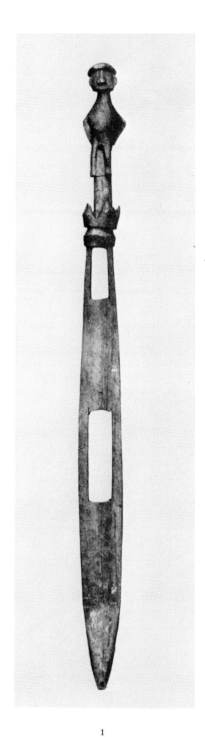
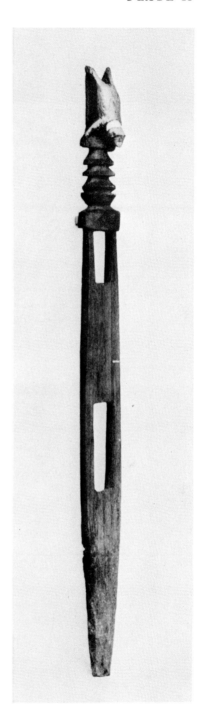

1   2

1,2 LOOM-POSTS, Vancouver Island, B. C., Nanaimo
Chicago Natural History Museum, 85378—E

PLATE 42

1

2

1 MASK, Vancouver Island, B. C., Nanaimo
Museum of the American Indian, Heye Foundation, N. Y., 18/1063

2 MASKED AND COSTUMED DANCER, Vancouver Island, B. C., Nanaimo
Photo. from National Museum of Canada, Ottawa

PLATE 43

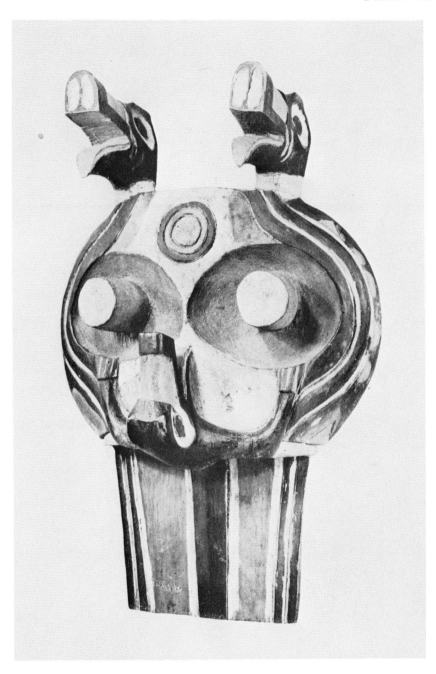

MASK, Vancouver Island, B. C., Nanaimo
National Museum of Canada, Ottawa, VII—G—335

PLATE 44

1

2 a

2 b

2 c

2 d

1 DRUM, Vancouver Island, B. C., Cowichan
Chicago Natural History Museum, 85491

2 a, b, c, d DRUM, Vancouver Island, B. C., Cowichan
Details, left and right half of Pl. 44,1

PLATE 45

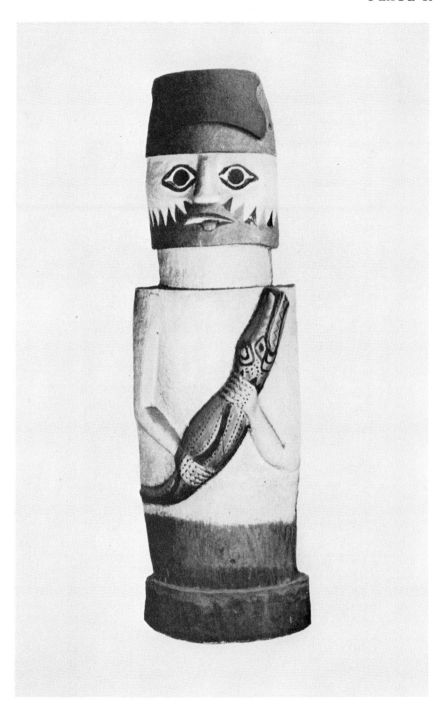

HOUSE-POST, Vancouver Island, B. C., Cowichan
Museum of the American Indian, Heye Foundation, N.Y., 15/8961

PLATE 46

HOUSE-POSTS, Vancouver Island, B. C., In Situ, Cowichan
Photo. from Museum of the American Indian, Heye Foundation, N.Y.

PLATE 47

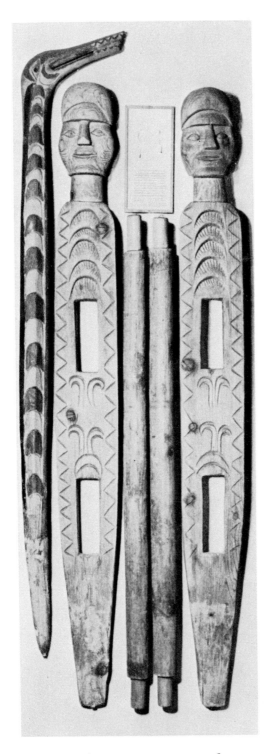

1   2

1, 2 LOOM-POSTS, Vancouver Island, B. C., Cowichan
Museum of the American Indian, Heye Foundation, N. Y., 16/2071

PLATE 48

1

2

1 MASK, Vancouver Island, B. C. Cowichan
American Museum of Natural History, N. Y., 16.1/1871

2 MASK, Vancouver Island, B. C., Cowichan
Royal Ontario Museum of Archaeology, Toronto, 2796

PLATE 49

a

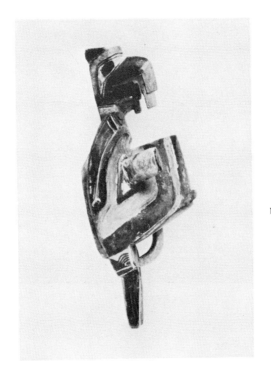

b

a, b MASK, Vancouver Island, B. C., Cowichan
Museum of the American Indian, Heye Foundation, N. Y., 16/2080

PLATE 50

1 a   1 b

2

1, a b GRAVE HOUSE, Vancouver Island, B. C., Sanetch
Museum of the American Indian, Heye Foundation, N.Y., 18/7911

2 PORTIONS OF GRAVE HOUSE, Vancouver Island, B. C., In Situ, Sanetch
Photo. from National Museum of Canada, Ottawa

PLATE 51

a

b

a, b HOUSE-POST, Vancouver Island, B. C., Sanetch
Museum of the American Indian, Heye Foundation, N.Y., 18/6854

PLATE 52

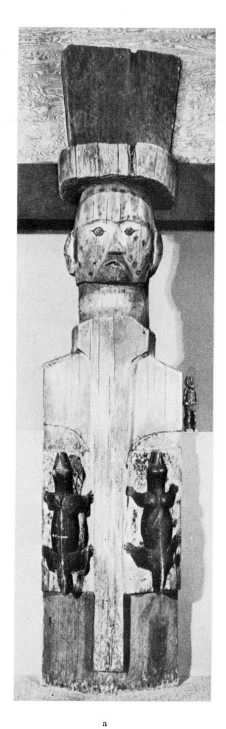

a   b

a, b HOUSE-POST, Vancouver Island, B. C., Songish
Museum of the American Indian, Heye Foundation, N. Y., 2/5904

PLATE 53

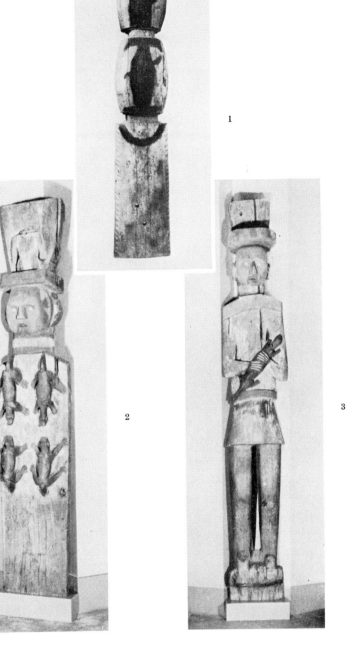

1

2

3

1 HOUSE-POST, Vancouver Island, B. C., Songish
Museum of the American Indian, Heye Foundation, N.Y., 18/6853

2 HOUSE-POST, Vancouver Island, B. C., Songish
Chicago Natural History Museum, 79788

3 HOUSE-POST, Vancouver Island, B. C., Songish
Chicago Natural History Museum, 79787

PLATE 54

1   2   3   4

1–4 HOUSE-POSTS, Vancouver Island, B. C.
Chicago Natural History Museum (cf. Pls. 40, 53, above)

PLATE 55

1

2

1 HOUSE-POSTS, Vancouver Island, B. C., In Situ
Photo. from Chicago Natural History Museum

2 HOUSE-POST, Vancouver Island, B. C., In Situ
Photo from National Museum of Canada, Ottawa

PLATE 56

1

2

1 HOUSE-POSTS, Vancouver Island, B. C., In Situ
Photo. from National Museum of Canada, Ottawa

2 HOUSE-POST, Thunderbird Park, Victoria, B. C., In Situ
Now in Provincial Museum, Victoria, B. C., 5041

PLATE 57

HOUSE-FRAME WITH CARVED HOUSE-POSTS, Vancouver Island, B. C., In Situ
Photo. from National Museum of Canada, Ottawa

PLATE 58

1

2

1   CARVED FIGURE, British Columbia
Museum of the American Indian, Heye Foundation, N.Y., 20/5639

2   CARVED FIGURE, Vancouver Island, B. C.
Provincial Museum, Victoria, B. C., 2839

PLATE 59

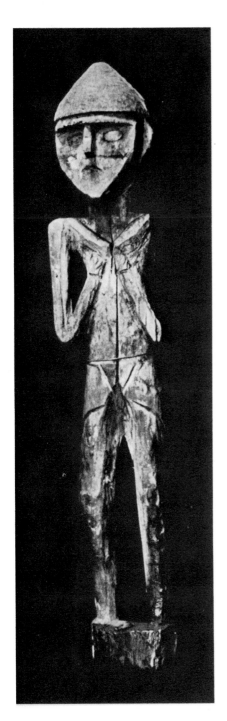

1   2

1 SHAMAN FIGURE, Oregon, Columbia River
American Museum of Natural History, N. Y., T—22125

2 SHAMAN FIGURE, Oregon, Columbia River
American Museum of Natural History, N. Y., T—22124

PLATE 60

1

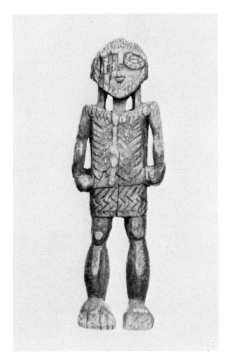

2

1 SHAMAN FIGURE, Oregon, Columbia River
American Museum of Natural History, N.Y., T—22126

2 CARVED FIGURE, Oregon, Wasco, Columbia River
Chicago Natural History Museum, 87603

PLATE 61

1

2

1 HORN DISH, Washington, Chinook
Chicago Natural History Museum, 19693

2 WOODEN MORTAR, Washington, Wasco
Chicago Natural History Museum, 87705

PLATE 62

1 SHAMAN'S STICK, Washington, Wasco
Chicago Natural History Museum, 87630.2

2 SHAMAN'S STICK, Washington, Wasco
Chicago Natural History Museum, 87630.4

PLATE 63

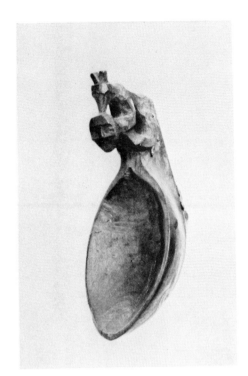

1

2

1, 2 CARVED SPOONS, Washington, Wasco
Chicago Natural History Museum, 69083, 69089

PLATE 64

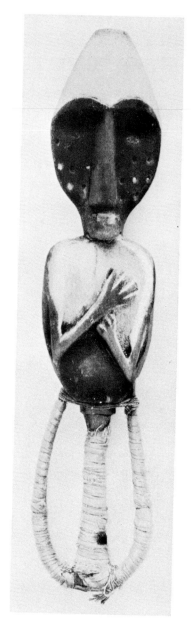

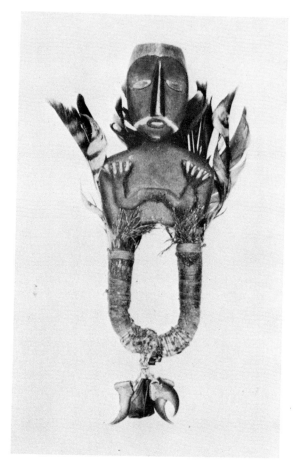

1

2

1 SHAMAN'S WAND, Washington, Quileute
Museum of the American Indian, Heye Foundation, N.Y., 5/7575

2 HAND MASK AND RATTLE, Vancouver Island, B. C., Kwakiutl (Nootka?)
Museum of the American Indian, Heye Foundation, N.Y., 5/615

PLATE 65

1a   1b   1c

2a   2b

1a, b, c   CARVED FIGURE, Vancouver Island, B. C., Kwakiutl
Milwaukee Public Museum, 17384

2a, b   CARVED FIGURE, Vancouver Island, B. C., Kwakiutl
Milwaukee Public Museum, 17618

PLATE 66

1

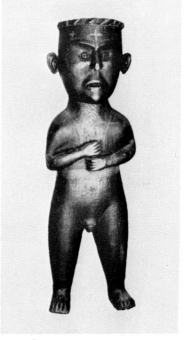

2

1 CARVED FIGURE, Vancouver Island, B. C., Kwakiutl
Museum of the American Indian, Heye Foundation, N.Y.

2 CARVED FIGURE, Vancouver Island, B. C., Kwakiutl
Museum of the American Indian, Heye Foundation, N.Y., 6/8754

PLATE 67

1   2

1, 2 POTLATCH FIGURES, Vancouver Island, B. C., Kwakiutl
Museum of the American Indian, Heye Foundation, N.Y., 6/8791, 6/8794

PLATE 68

1

2   3

1 CARVED FIGURE, British Columbia, Haida
Museum of the American Indian, Heye Foundation, N.Y., 2/600

2, 3 HOUSE-POSTS, British Columbia, Haida
Museum of the American Indian, Heye Foundation, N.Y., 15/9198; 15/9199

PLATE 69

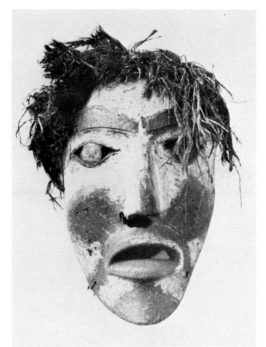

1

2

1 MASK, Vancouver Island, B. C., Kwakiutl
Chicago Natural History Museum, 19305

2 MASK, Vancouver Island, B. C., Kwakiutl
American Museum of Natural History, N. Y., 16/8382

PLATE 70

1

2

1 MASK, Vancouver Island, B. C., Kwakiutl
Museum of the American Indian, Heye Foundation, N.Y., 8/1658

2 MASK, Vancouver Island, B. C., Kwakiutl
Museum of the American Indian, Heye Foundation, N.Y., 6/9153

PLATE 71

1

2

1   MASK, Vancouver Island, B. C., Kwakiutl
    Chicago Natural History Museum, 19266

2   MASK, Vancouver Island, B. C., Kwakiutl
    Chicago Natural History Museum, 19269

PLATE 72

1

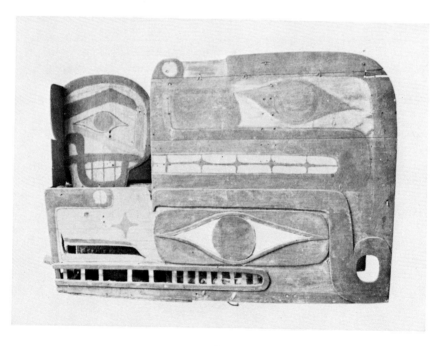

2

1 MASK, Washington, Quileute
Museum of the American Indian, Heye Foundation, N.Y., 5/9729

2 MASK, Vancouver Island, B. C., Nootka
Chicago Natural History Museum, 19852

PLATE 73

a

b

a, b "ANCIENT" MASK, British Columbia, Bella Coola
Museum of the American Indian, Heye Foundation, N.Y., 20/1791

PLATE 74

1 a

1 b

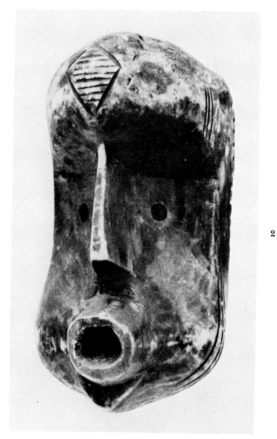

2

1 a, b "ANCIENT" MASK, British Columbia, Bella Coola
Museum of the American Indian, Heye Foundation, N.Y., 20/1792

2 "ANCIENT" MASK, British Columbia, Bella Coola
Museum of the American Indian, Heye Foundation, N.Y., 20/1793

PLATE 75

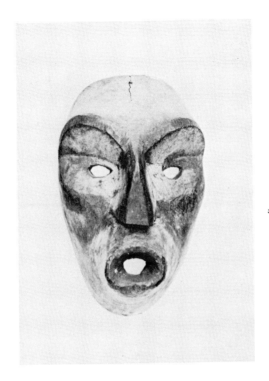

a

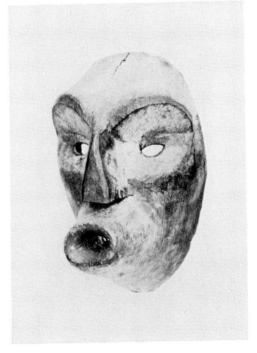

b

a, b MASK, Washington, Makah
Chicago Natural History Museum, 61903

PLATE 76

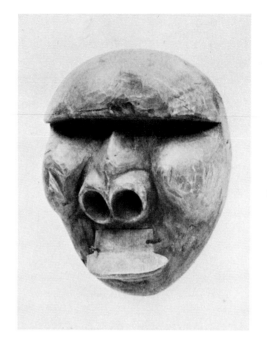

1

2

1 MASK, Washington, Quileute
Museum of the American Indian, Heye Foundation, N.Y., 19/8753

2 MASK, Washington, Quileute
Museum of the American Indian, Heye Foundation, N.Y., 10/6883